M. R. JAMES

MICHAEL COX

M. R. JAMES

An Informal Portrait

Oxford New York

OXFORD UNIVERSITY PRESS

1983

Oxford University Press, Walton Street, Oxford OX2 6DP

London Glasgow New York Toronto
Delhi Bombay Calcutta Madras Karachi
Kuala Lumpur Singapore Hong Kong Tokyo
Nairobi Dar es Salaam Cape Town
Melbourne Auckland
and associates in
Beirut Berlin Ibadan Mexico City Nicosia

British Library Cataloguing in Publication Data

Cox, Michael
M. R. James.
1. James, Montague Rhodes
2. Scholars—Great Britain—Biography
3. Authors, English—20th century—Biography
I. Title
001.2'092'4 CT788.J/
ISBN 0–19–211765–3

Set by Promenade Graphics Limited, Cheltenham.
and printed in Great Britain by
Butler and Tanner Ltd.,
Frome, Somerset

TO DIZZY

PREFACE

WHEN I began this book, a biography of M. R. James was long overdue. The principal published source of information for anyone who wished to know more about the creator of *Ghost Stories of an Antiquary*, as I did, was S. G. Lubbock's brief 1939 *Memoir*. The limitations of Lubbock's book (charming though it is) were frankly acknowledged by the author in a prefatory disclaimer, which contained the hope that the volume's inadequacy would 'spur some abler portrait-painter to achieve a full-length portrait'.

That hope was, one assumes, an unintentional challenge to the modesty of future biographers; but, that apart, there is no doubt that M. R. James deserved a more substantial biographical memorial than Lubbock felt able to give him. In a life of quiet distinction he was Provost of King's College, Cambridge, and of Eton; Vice-Chancellor of Cambridge University at the outbreak of the First World War; a scholar of international repute; a mimic of brilliance; an early and adventurous cyclist; a man of great good humour and kindness; a friend and inspiration to many Cambridge undergraduates and Etonians; and the author of arguably the finest ghost stories in the English language.

'He hoped to escape a musty biography and bibliography,' wrote Oliffe Richmond, a friend of Monty, 'knowing that his monumental labours would live after him and needed no advertisement.' Beneath his sociable and unassuming exterior, M. R. James was a formidably accomplished scholar and his phenomenal labours do indeed live after him. His academic interests (extensive, like his memory) ranged over Apocrypha (his *Apocryphal New Testament*, published in 1924, is still widely read), hagiology, classical archaeology and literature, biblical studies, medieval art and iconography and Western manuscripts. His great series of manuscript catalogues, published between 1895 and 1932, set new standards and still underpin modern codicological studies. Amongst the manuscript collections he catalogued were those of Eton, Lambeth, Westminster Abbey, the John Rylands Library, every Cambridge college and the Fitzwilliam Museum. It was, as A. F. Scholfield said in the *Dictionary of National Biography*, a 'prodigious achievement', involving the development of pioneering techniques of description besides countless hours of painstaking work. In his work on Apocrypha, too, he broke new ground. To quote Scholfield again: 'He was the first scholar in England to cultivate this field, and he did for Apocrypha much what the Bollandists have done for hagiography: he brought it out of the category of literary lumber into being a comprehensible documentation of human thought and life for the modern educated reader.'

Compared with the immense amount of time and labour this level of scholarship demanded, the ghost stories, with which the name of M. R. James is now perhaps generally associated, were the work of a moment. Nevertheless, they are by common consent in the front rank of the English ghost story tradition and are all deservedly still in print.

As well as his outstanding achievements as a scholar and a writer of supernatural fiction, Monty James's personal qualities made him a much respected and revered figure at Cambridge and later at Eton. If he was not an educator in a narrow pedagogic sense, he inspired friendship, devotion, and emulation as few are able to do and he lives on in the affectionate and grateful memories of many still living.

With all this in mind, and having by then examined the unpublished and not altogether successful attempt at a biographical study of James by Sir Shane Leslie, I began on some serious research into this quintessentially English life, unaware that the Revd Dr R. W. Pfaff of the University of North Carolina had already spent some time working on the material. His *Montague Rhodes James* appeared in 1980, by which time my book was in draft. Dr Pfaff's aim had been to provide a comprehensive description and assessment of James's scholarship within a carefully researched biographical framework. In respect of its presentation of James's scholarly achievements it is unlikely to be superseded and should be consulted by any reader who wishes to be accurately informed about the work of one of England's greatest scholars.

My own more limited aim has been to produce an informal biographical portrait of M. R. James for the general reader that still tries to observe a proper balance between the various strands of his life, but without dwelling at too great a length on any one of them. It would have served no useful purpose, even if I had been capable of the task, to duplicate Dr Pfaff's more scholarly approach, though I hope I have conveyed a sense of Monty's academic interests flowing on purposefully and continually throughout his life. On the other hand, I have not attempted a detailed critical analysis of the ghost stories (though a properly informed study of them is certainly needed): that would have weighted the narrative too much in their favour. So I have restricted myself to generalities, indicating only the most immediately relevant relationships between Monty's fiction and his life and concentrating more on the first collection of tales, *Ghost Stories of an Antiquary*, than on subsequent volumes.

One final, but fundamental, point needs to be made. M. R. James was a man whose knowledge was perhaps only equalled by his disinclination to talk openly about himself. He seemed constitutionally opposed to intimate self-revelation—certainly in public, but also to a large degree in private. His published recollections, *Eton and King's*, may seem curiously impersonal for this reason, though it apparently shows how he wished to appear to posterity.

One result of this reserve is to encourage the belief that he lived at a superficial level, even that he was somehow emotionally deficient. Though this was far from the case, it remains true that there are very few moments of real introspection amongst a collection of private papers that is extensive by any standards. (The situation might conceivably have been different in some degree if important sequences of letters—for instance, from Monty to his Eton tutor H. E. Luxmoore or to his close friend Sir Walter Morley Fletcher—had not been, apparently, lost.)

It follows that several questions must remain unanswered, or at best lightly touched upon, in the absence of firm documentary evidence, and as a rule I have avoided speculation for its own sake (a most M. R. Jamesian trait). Many modern readers may be puzzled, for instance, by the lack of what we now call 'normal' heterosexual relationships in James's life. Whilst admitting that this is something to be explained, it needs to be emphasized that the material simply does not exist that would illuminate the emotional and psychological causes for this apparent passivity. I may as well state here, as a personal opinion only, that I do not believe Monty's sexuality (whatever its precise characteristics were) ever became problematic in his life in the way that it did for his friend Arthur Benson. Unlike Benson, Monty could live on easy and affectionate terms with young men, even handsome young men, without agonizing over them—except, as the First World War showed, when they were in danger, or when they died. Even then he exposed his feelings reluctantly. Undoubtedly there were homosexual

For permission to consult manuscript material in their possession I gratefully tender thanks to the Provost and Fellows, Eton College, Windsor; the British Library; the Syndics of Cambridge University Library; the Syndics of the Fitzwilliam Museum, Cambridge; the Provost and Fellows, King's College, Cambridge; the Master and Fellows, Magdalene College, Cambridge; the Master and Fellows, Trinity College, Cambridge.

For permission to quote from unpublished material I am indebted to Mr Bernard Babington Smith and Mrs E. Lloyd-Jones; Mr Hugh Carey; Professor Charles Fletcher; Mrs Anne Hopkinson; Mr Nicholas Rhodes James; the Master and Fellows, Magdalene College, Cambridge; Mrs Jean Wrangham.

I apologize in advance to those concerned if I have failed to seek permission to quote from unpublished or published sources when I should have done so.

A few individuals from the preceding list must be singled out for more extended mention. I am particularly grateful to Nicholas Rhodes James, M. R. James's great-nephew and present literary heir, for reading an early draft of part of this book and giving me his support and approval.

It is a very great sadness to me that Bernard Fergusson, Lord Ballantrae, did not live to see this book published. He gave me warm and generous encouragement at a difficult time in its writing, for which I am deeply grateful.

Hugh Carey has read and commented on every chapter, supplied me with unpublished material, photographs and hospitality, and helped me in countless other ways. His knowledge of and sensitivity to Monty James's milieu have been of immense help to me and the book would be a great deal more imperfect than it is if I had not had the benefit of his generous guidance.

I should also like to record my especial appreciation to Patrick Wilkinson for reading those portions of the book that relate to King's, to Patrick Strong and Paul Quarrie at Eton for their help and kindness and for making a non-Etonian feel at home at that unique institution, and to Peter Croft and Michael Halls of King's for their enthusiastic help and hospitality.

Mrs Anne Hopkinson kindly supplied me with transcriptions of family letters relating to M. R. James and her brother Professor Charles Fletcher went to the trouble of sending me some anecdotes of him. I am grateful for the kindness and interest shown by the late

C. E. Wrangham, who generously typed out his recollections of Monty James as Provost of Eton and who sadly died before having a chance to read the typescript of this book.

Finally, I must thank my wife and family for putting up with so much.

Though several people have been good enough to read and comment on the book prior to publication, it is necessary to emphasize that I alone am responsible for any errors or omissions that may remain.

CONTENTS

ILLUSTRATIONS

NOTE

'I HOPE you don't think it a cheek calling you Monty,' wrote an acquaintance to M. R. James in 1899, 'but I believe you prefer it.'

Throughout the main text of this book I refer to M. R. James as Monty, through no presumption of familiarity, but because he was so addressed by many of his close friends, and even by those who were not particularly close to him. He nearly always signed himself 'MRJ', by which initials he was also widely known (I so refer to him in the Notes). His father often addressed him in letters as 'Toby' or 'Tobe'.

Herbert James, M. R. James's father, is always so called. Herbert Ellison Rhodes James, Monty's elder brother, is referred to as 'Ber', one of the names by which he was known in the family, to avoid confusion with his father.

Monty often addressed letters to 'My dear people' when writing home. I have assumed this primarily meant his parents, although the letters were probably also read by his sister Grace.

In quoted matter from manuscript material, contractions such as '&', 'yr', and 'shd' have been expanded, and occasionally punctuation has been added or amended in the interests of clarity.

How many have there been, how many are there now, who look back upon Eton or King's, or both, with a love which no other spot on earth can inspire, and who say with the Eton poet, My brothers and my home are there? About these places have been woven cords of affection which bind together the most diverse natures and stretch over the whole world: cords which run through a man's whole life and do not part at the supreme moment of death.

M. R. James

We need examples of people who, leaving heaven to decide whether they are to rise in the world, decide for themselves that they will be happy in it and have resolved to seek, not greater wealth but simpler pleasure, not higher fortune but deeper felicity, making the first of possessions self-possession.

John Ruskin, *The Stones of Venice*

FIRST BEGINNING
1862–1873

To my father and to my mother ... we, their children owe everything.

Sydney Rhodes James, *Seventy Years*

From quiet homes and first beginning,
Out to the undiscovered ends ...

Hilaire Belloc, 'Dedicatory Ode'

FAMILIAL ties were not things M. R. James ever cared to discuss at any length. He designedly, almost perversely, kept them out of his volume of recollections, *Eton and King's*, together with 'the expression of emotions with which I may be reasonably believed to be familiar'. This reticence was absolutely typical and fundamental to his character, even though there was nothing to hide from public scrutiny—no loveless childhood to be thrust out of mind; no parental iniquities to be kept secret: nothing, in fact, but an exceptionally secure and happy home and affectionate parents who put their duty towards their children second only to their duty towards God.

As for 'family' in the wider sense, Monty James was never one to be obsessively preoccupied with his ancestry. He noted with what seemed only mild interest that the family had once owned something over 3,000 slaves in Jamaica. By the time his father was born, in 1822, the family's former prominence as plantation magnates was fast becoming a memory.[1] The knell had been sounded by the abolition of the slave trade in 1807, and when William Rhodes James, Monty's grandfather, finally left Jamaica for England in 1818 he was by no means a wealthy man. William was a widower, but soon after returning to England he married again. His second wife, Caroline, bore him eight children, the second of whom, Herbert, was Monty's father. The family settled at Wyndham House in Aldeburgh, Suffolk, some time before William's death in 1842, after which Caroline remained in Aldeburgh and

devoted herself to good works. These earned her a memorial window
in the church, which Monty—by then well qualified to judge—later
called 'the worst painted window (perhaps) in the country'.

Herbert James was sent to a well-known preparatory school at East
Sheen, Temple Grove, and then to Eton, with which the family already
had some connection. Herbert entered Eton as an Oppidan (a
fee-paying boarder lodging in a house). Later he was awarded a
scholarship and moved into College, the ancient nucleus of Eton. The
move suggests the need to conserve the family's financial resources,
for life in College at this period, though it was slowly improving, was
hard, sometimes brutal, and was not often embraced out of choice.
Herbert, however, seemed happy enough as a Colleger, complaining
only of the food ('Mutton always, sometimes hot, sometimes cold') and
intimating that it was rather hard to keep clean.

A close friend of Herbert's at Eton was William Johnson (later
Cory), that extraordinary and charismatic personality who was to
exercise a considerable influence at Eton as a master. Herbert followed
Johnson to King's College, Cambridge, then a closed corporation
existing for the sole use of Etonian Collegers. But reform was in the air
and Herbert's Head Master, E. C. Hawtrey, pointed out to him that it
was now a privilege to be a member of King's. 'There was a time',
wrote Hawtrey, 'when it was a great sacrifice both morally and
intellectually'.[2] Monty was to follow his father to Temple Grove, Eton
and King's and he shared with him an abiding attachment to his public
school and college; indeed, in Monty the attachment was intensified to
an extraordinary degree and shaped the course of his whole life.

What he was not to share was his father's absolute certainty about
his vocation. As a boy at Eton, Herbert had told his mother that he
wished to excel in divinity above everything else, and once at
Cambridge his religious views—firmly evangelical in nature—were
confirmed and strengthened by the spiritual legacy of Charles Simeon,
a former Kingsman and the leading Cambridge evangelical of the
previous decade. Herbert was to remain closely associated with the
evangelical wing of the Church of England all his long life, and in him,
as his obituary in *The Times* said, 'the Simeon spirit worked strongly'.

Herbert proceeded to the degree of BA in 1847 and was ordained
deacon the following year. He first took up a curacy in Aldeburgh,
where his mother still lived. In 1852, having taken priest's orders three
years previously, he left Aldeburgh for Dover, as one of two curates to
the Revd John Ellison Bates at Christ Church, Hougham. It was in

Dover that he met his future wife, Mary Emily Horton, the daughter of a distinguished naval man. They were married in 1854 at Helmingham in Suffolk and soon afterwards Herbert, whose marriage had terminated his King's Fellowship, was appointed Perpetual Curate of Goodnestone next Wingham in Kent.*

Though Goodnestone was a rural parish it was not to be despised by Herbert James on that account. As he wrote of the rural ministry in his only published work, *The Country Clergyman and His Work* (1890): 'I am bold to say of this Field that it stands second to none in interest and importance.' Shunem, he said, required its prophets as well as Jericho.

Herbert and Mary Emily had four children. The eldest, Sydney, was born at Aldeburgh in 1855, the year of the move to Goodnestone; in 1857 there was a second son, Herbert Ellison, known as 'Ber' or 'Bertie'; a daughter, Grace Caroline, was born in 1860; and finally, the youngest child, Montague, was born at Goodnestone on 1 August 1862.

Three years after Monty's birth the family left Goodnestone for Suffolk. In 1855 Jane Anne Broke, a relative of Herbert James's by marriage,† had inherited Livermere Hall, a seventeenth-century house near Bury St Edmunds, from her uncle; with it had gone the patronage of the Livermere living, which became vacant in 1865 and was offered to Herbert by Jane's trustees (she was then twelve years old). Herbert's acceptance brought him a gross income of just over £400 a year, a parish of about as many souls, and a rectory standing on the edge of Livermere Park. S. G. Lubbock described the rectory in his *Memoir*:

The little village is on the edge of Livermere Park, scattered about a crossing of roads. A long grove of trees—plane, chestnut, oak and lime—shadows a cart track leading to the great East Anglian church with its Decorated nave and chancel, and squat tower with wooden belfry. Between village and church a short drive leads to the Rectory with grass on the right and shrubberies on the left as you enter. Beyond the white-walled, slate-roofed house is the croquet lawn with shrubberies all about it, and a winding path cunningly following its gentle slopes; it had all been planned, you were told, by Capability Brown.

---

* There are two villages called Goodnestone (pronounced Gŏŏneston) in Kent: this one, between Sandwich and Canterbury, and another near Faversham.

† Mary Emily's brother, William Horton, married twice. His second wife was Anna Maria Broke, whose first husband had died in 1855, leaving her with two daughters: Jane and Frederica. Jane (known to Monty as 'Janie' or 'Cousin Jane') married James St Vincent de Saumarez; 4th Baron de Saumarez, in 1882; Frederica ('Freda') married Sir Lambton Loraine in 1878.

Monty was deeply attached to Livermere. Though village and park have changed much since he first knew them the rectory still stands and would be recognized by him, and the mere (from which the village takes its name) and adjoining Ampton Water still dominate what is left of the park. His parents are buried in the churchyard; their shared grave is marked by a tall stone cross, erected by Monty and engraved with the word 'PAX'.

The countryside immediately surrounding Livermere Rectory made a lasting impression on Monty. He celebrated his home landscape in an undated poem called 'Sounds of the Wood':

> Let me lie here beneath the waving fern,
>   Each eve above me shall the beetle hum,
> From off the mere, above the oaks, the hern
>   Come sailing, and the rook fly cawing home.
>
> Hither shall come no harsh discordant sound,
>   Only by day the spotted thrush sing clear,
> At night the owl hoot, and the distant hound
>   Barks and the ducks cry faint along the mere.
>
> And while the moon silvers the glade with light
>   And shines where underneath the moss I lie
> The far Church clock toll booming through the night
>   And on the wind the gusty echoes die.
>
> And when the moon wanes, and the breeze blows chill;
>   There, where the farm looms up against the grey,
> The cock shall crow far off upon the hill,
>   Waking from many a barn the answering lay.
>
> Thus, with such sounds, both night and day shall pass,
>   So shall the seasons, so the years shall fly.
> They shall not break my sleep beneath the grass
>   Till time hath passed into eternity.[3]

Another undated piece, in prose, describes childhood scenes in fond and delicately drawn detail: 'You know where the Ampton water tracks round rather suddenly, on one side fringed by broad reed beds—a sea of whispering green under a summer breeze and of rustling gold in autumn; while the flat shore behind them is covered thickly, first with underwood of alders and currant and raspberry bushes run wild, and then, as it slopes slightly upward, with a larger growth of beech and oak and fir, while the park fence in the ditch bounds these in turn.'[4]

In an entirely different mood is the following, written for his sister Grace and sent home from Cyprus in 1888:

> All through the rushes, and in the bushes,
> Odd creatures slip in the dark,
> And sulky owls with feathery cowls
> Go sweeping about the park.
>
> You hear on the breeze from behind the trees
> The Ampton clock begin,
> And when it is still, how thin and shrill
> The bell of the Hall chimes in.
>
> Then the horses stir and the sleepy cats purr
> And something moves in the fern.
> And did you not see in the hollow oak tree
> Two eyes begin to burn?
>
> You heard a foot pass, it trailed over the grass,
> You shivered, it came so near.
> And was it the head of a man long dead
> That raised itself out of the mere?[5]

As a child, judging from this, Monty perhaps invented terrors for his sister's pleasure; it is clear, at any rate, that he was keenly alive to the sinister side of the Suffolk countryside, and no doubt he peopled it suitably. The rectory and the park at Livermere are described in his last published ghost story, 'A Vignette', which was written in 1935 and appeared posthumously in the *London Mercury* in 1936:

You are asked to think of the spacious garden of a country rectory, adjacent to a park of many acres, and separated therefrom by a belt of trees of some age which we knew as the Plantation. It is but about thirty or forty yards broad. A close gate of split oak leads to it from the path encircling the garden, and when you enter it from that side you put your hand through a square hole cut in it and lift the hook to pass along to the iron gate which admits to the park from the Plantation . . . To be sure, it is difficult, in anything like a grove, to be quite certain that nobody is making a screen out of a tree and keeping it between you and him as he moves round it and you walk on. All I can say is if such an one was there he was no neighbour or acquaintance of mine, and there was some indication about him of being cloaked or hooded.

'A Vignette' seems to embody some of the imaginative experiences of Monty's boyhood at Livermere—if not, as I have sometimes thought, the memory of something that seemed real to him at the time and that shaped his subsequent attitude towards the supernatural.

Though this was the only time he made direct use of Livermere in a ghost story, there are others, like 'Lost Hearts', in which the images of his childhood surroundings emerge with renewed potency:

The wind had fallen, and there was a still night and a full moon. At about ten o'clock Stephen was standing at the open window of his bedroom, looking out over the country. Still as the night was, the mysterious population of the distant moonlit woods was not yet lulled to rest. From time to time strange cries as of lost and despairing wanderers sounded from across the mere. They might be the notes of owls or water-birds, yet they did not quite resemble either.[6]

In spite of his later dedication to the scientific amassment of facts, Monty James was essentially a creature of imagination. His appreciation of the supernatural was stimulated early and never left him; with this went a dim apprehension of unknown forces at work behind the façade of everyday life, forces that could break through the thin fabric of what we call 'reality' at any moment in what his favourite writer of supernatural fiction, J. S. Le Fanu, called an 'intrusion of the spirit-world upon the proper domain of matter'.* This view of the world had much in common with the immemorial beliefs still current in a village like Livermere in the nineteenth century: the Rector spoke disapprovingly of 'the quasi-religious belief of some who have an esoteric confidence in witchcraft' and of those who still betook themselves to the village wise man or woman. 'I can personally testify', he wrote, 'that the progress of the XIXth Century with all its boasted advancement has failed to explode this and kindred superstition.'[7] They were, besides, superstitions that the youngest son of Livermere Rectory could never quite rid himself of.

*   *   *

Both Herbert and Mary Emily James openly confessed their love for the four children, seeing them as God's gifts and counting the health and prosperity of each one as further indications of the Creator's goodness. 'Our mercies are many, darling,' Monty's mother told him in 1874, when he was twelve, 'and our children among the greatest, to us parents.' With the concept of the radical and inherent sinfulness of

* 'Mr Justice Harbottle', *In a Glass Darkly* (1886).

man at the heart of the evangelical outlook, it was natural for both Mary Emily and Herbert to lay great stress on God's mercy, and they were deeply and sincerely grateful when, as they saw it, such mercy was dispensed. But their logic of grace and salvation had no harshness in it. The evangelical tradition, with its emphasis on personal responsibility and rectitude, the awful literalness of Scripture, philanthropy and the continual, undeviating sense of God's presence, is often associated with a distinctively repressive form of family life—a classic expression of which is Samuel Butler's *The Way of All Flesh*. But for every example of misguided zeal, there were many evangelical homes in which a gentler piety ruled. The James household was one such, in which both parents exercised a firm but loving discipline.

All the children were encouraged to develop their individual interests. Those of Ber, the middle brother, led him to a career in the Royal Army Medical Corps; Sydney was a keen sportsman, spent a good deal of his life schoolmastering, and ended it as Archdeacon of Dudley. The fact that Monty never made Sydney's formal commitment to the Church caused his father some disappointment, and possibly real sadness; yet one feels that it was Monty, of all his sons, who was closest to the Rector's heart. As for Grace, she remained at home, dutifully and apparently willingly looking after her parents well into middle age when, against all expectation, she married her father's former curate.

Mary Emily's vigilance for the well-being of her 'chicks' became something of a family joke. The wonder is that in doting so completely on her children she did not smother them with maternal solicitude and jeopardize their independence of mind. Gurney Lubbock's estimation of her seems just: 'She had the deep, far-reaching unselfishness of a character which, for all her gentleness, was strong and incisive. With her quiet but rich sense of humour, she enjoyed her sons' affectionate chaff, and for all her unselfishness and devotion she never fussed them.'[8]

Even though Monty was the youngest child, and therefore particularly likely to suffer from over-zealous parental concern, his sturdy individuality was never threatened and he was free—within the limits of his deeply conventional nature—to fashion his own life. He developed an indulgent attitude towards his parents, never worshipping them blindly, but always respectful, affectionate, and attentive to their needs.

The parents both served as models of simple Christian piety for the children, both of them living out daily a faith that was deep but unobsessive. Although the Rector's dogmatism was happily tempered by a large fund of natural affection, religious commitment was expected of the children and encouraged in every way by parental example. 'He, of all men whom I have ever met,' wrote Sydney of his father, 'walked most closely with God.' The children's lives had a regular devotional pattern. Even when Gurney Lubbock visited Livermere years later there were still prayers before breakfast and in the evening, as well as a daily Psalm, which was read and 'tersely expounded' by the Rector. Sydney, writing of the home life of his contemporary H. E. Ryle,* remarked that 'The atmosphere of the house was, like that of my own home, devotional . . . '[9] Religious instruction at Livermere was of course mainly given by the Rector; but as he was often away on Church business his wife saw to it that the routine continued. 'The children come to me for hymns and text at 4,' she writes to her husband in 1870, when Monty was eight. 'Montie has an idle fit upon him just now.'

Dogma was central to Herbert James's religious thinking. He traced what he called the 'anarchy of belief' to an antagonism towards dogma and claimed that people were hampered by misbeliefs 'because they are not taught fully what to believe'. Theology, he maintained, remained a necessity:

There is a plan of salvation, a symmetry as well as a substance about God's truth which cannot be dispensed with. Its lines are defined for our guidance. They suggest inquiry, they repress ill-regulated speculation. Badly will that teacher fare who thinks it possible to be free from their environment and wholesome restraint. He would be like a kite cut loose from its string. He might have a certain liberty, and soar to a certain height. But he soars only to fall, and the higher the height, the more damaging the descent.[10]

This emphatic trust in doctrine and precept must have had an effect on Monty. It showed itself, perhaps, in the way he tended to distrust intellectual inquiry that was not rooted in a sensitive respect for tradition and orthodoxy; and part, at least, of his lifelong disinclination to pass much beyond what his upbringing and education had taught

---

* Herbert Edward Ryle (1856–1925) was Herbert James's godson. After College at Eton he went up to King's and was elected to a Fellowship in 1881. In a long and distinguished career he was President of Queens', Cambridge, and Bishop of Winchester. His father, J. C. Ryle, Bishop of Liverpool, was Sydney James's godfather.

him to believe must be attributable to his father's condemnation and avoidance of 'ill-regulated speculation'.

Interesting light is shed on Monty's religious upbringing by his father's method of correcting the unsatisfactory theological views of Stewart Headlam, then a young man just down from Cambridge whose father was a friend of Herbert's. Headlam, who was deeply under the influence of F. D. Maurice (Professor of Moral Philosophy at Cambridge and a prominent Christian Socialist), came to Livermere in 1869, when Monty was seven, and stayed for a year. 'Mr James', he wrote, 'was very kind to me . . . But it is a fact that he tried to overpower me with Bible texts and his own interpretation of them. He would take out his Greek Testament and argue about the relative significance of περί and ὑπερ, and I, with my batch of Maurice sermons in my trunk, was proof against his persuasions.'[11]

As always 'James of Livermere', as he was known amongst the evangelical party, fell back on what he called the 'Book of Books'. Though he achieved nothing with Stewart Headlam he undoubtedly inculcated a thorough knowledge of Scripture—if not an unshakable trust in the infallibility of Scriptural authority—in his youngest son. The Rector similarly laid great emphasis on 'the public ministry of the Word' and was himself a celebrated preacher, both locally and nationally. This, too, had an effect on Monty, who also had a gift for oratory, though again he lacked his father's didactic instincts.

Inevitably, the devotional atmosphere of Livermere Rectory stimulated Monty's imagination as a child. As he later recalled:

There was a time in my childhood when I thought that some night as I lay in bed I should be suddenly roused by a great sound of a trumpet, that I should run to the window and look out and see the whole sky split across and lit up with glaring flame: and next moment I and everybody else in the house would be caught up into the air and made to stand with countless other people before a judge seated on a throne with great books open before him: and he would ask me questions out of what was written in those books—whether I had done this or that: and then I should be told to take my place either on the right hand or the left.[12]

At the age of nine he was writing in a notebook labelled 'Sermon Notes' such things as: 'THE RICH FOOL. One thing we must all always remember, namely "that we may die at any moment". But what succeeds death? Heaven or Hell? And what besides? We shall be called to account for what we do.' Elsewhere are copied out pious maxims: 'God is love'; 'Duty comes first, whatever you may say'; 'Thou God seest me'; 'To the righteous death is life, to the wicked it is not so. We see here that God's threats are not mere words.'[13] These concepts took hold and never left him. 'I am as clear as ever I was', he proclaimed in 1933, obliquely acknowledging his evangelical upbringing, 'that I shall be judged for what I have done and what I have been ... And that thought is every bit as serious if it is not so sensational as the picture of it that I used to have.'[14]

But it would be wrong to think of him as being habitually serious and pious as a child, or to picture the rectory as a home without freedom and laughter. Monty was far from being a sombre child: photographs of him at the ages of three and six, said Gurney Lubbock, show 'the calm humorous expression that is seen in every portrait of him, young or old'. He passed his childhood at Livermere, as far as is known, at peace with himself, his family, and his surroundings, a clever, sensitive boy with a rich sense of humour, a lively imagination (he wrote stories with titles like 'The boy and the birds' or 'Ye Guinea pig His Story'), and an ear for language—sociable, affectionate and dutiful, but also marvellously self-contained.

His preliminary schooling was done at home: Latin and Greek were taught by his father (and taught well), French and probably some Italian by his mother. Sydney naturally preceded him to school—first to an establishment at Aldeburgh and then to Haileyburgh, with a scholarship, in 1867. Monty was often at Aldeburgh (where Ber also went to school) until his grandmother died in 1870. 'The first painted window ever I saw is in the church here,' he wrote from Aldeburgh fifty years later. 'The first organ I heard is likewise here and the first anthem performed I know not on what occasion caused me to burst into tears of apprehension and be led from the sacred edifice.'[15]

When he was eleven it was Monty's turn to begin his formal education. The place chosen was his father's old preparatory school, Temple Grove.

CHAPTER 2

TEMPLE GROVE
1873–1876

Probably most sensitive and perceptive boys, when first translated
from home amenities and amiable domestic discipline, regard with
dejection and dismay the bareness and publicity of the barrack life
of school.

A. C. Benson, 'O. C. Waterfield' in *Memories and Friends*

THERE were about 130 boys at Temple Grove when Monty entered
the school. It seemed in retrospect 'an alarmingly big community for a
small boy to be pitchforked into, and the rainy day in September 1873
on which my father left me there is one of the most lachrymose in my
remembrance'. A fragment of a story, written probably in 1885, seems
to draw on these memories:

People who do not know much about it—who never were boys of twelve or
were such stupid ones that they have forgotten it on purpose—such people will
not believe how excruciatingly sentimental boys of that age are apt to become
on certain occasions—notably when leaving home: but so it is, and it is not by
any means a bad trait in their characters.[1]

He hungered for home throughout his first term and into 1874,
writing on 26 January: 'Dear Mama, You can't think how I hate being
here. I cry every night in bed, and if some one does not come to see me
soon, I don't know what I shall do . . . I have only about two whom I
can call my friends.' His mother wrote back immediately to reassure
her 'darling old Mons':

Cheer up, and look up! I felt very sad when I read your note, and wished I
could give you a hug and a tickling! But, my darling, I trust the soreness of
leaving home has already a little diminished and that it will yet do so. Every one
says the *second* term always seems the worst for schoolboys at first. We all think
of you, and pray for you—and I am sure you do not forget to pray for yourself,
darling. Try and be brave, and cheerful, and the very trying will do you good.

Temple Grove stood in its own grounds between Mortlake and Richmond Park, a once grand mansion forming the core of the school, with here and there a reminder—such as an artificial mound topped with a gazebo—of more stately days. It was used many years later by Monty as the setting for 'A School Story' (in *More Ghost Stories of an Antiquary*):

The school I mean was near London. It was established in a large and fairly old house—a great white building with very fine grounds about it; there were large cedars in the garden, as there are in so many of the older gardens in the Thames valley, and ancient elms in the three or four fields which we used for our games. I think probably it was quite an attractive place, but boys seldom allow that their schools possess any tolerable features.

The Headmaster was Ottiwell Charles Waterfield—'Olympian', Monty remembered, 'both in appearance and manner'. Waterfield was tall, well-built, well-dressed and bearded, with eyes of exceptional brilliance and penetration. Arrayed in full silk gown, he was a figure of utter magnificence. 'I have never in my life been so afraid of a human being as I was of him,' confessed Arthur Benson, later to become one of Monty's closest friends.[2] An Eton Colleger and a Kingsman, Waterfield had taught briefly at Eton but was clearly not a man to relish the prospect of prolonged subordination. At Temple Grove he was supreme—'the one central and all-important *fact* of the place, pervading and dominating visibly and invisibly the school and all its concerns'.[3] But he did not rely simply on force of personality to keep order; he also believed in the efficacy of corporal punishment (and the threat of it) and in class acted on the principle that if a boy did not know his lesson it was tantamount to an insult. Arthur Benson judged him to have been too severe, but in his dealings with Monty (who was never, apparently, flogged) Waterfield showed himself capable of both sensitivity and restraint. As a teacher, he had the capacity to *interest* his pupils and to make the inspired connections that can bring a lesson to life—reading aloud from William Barnes's Dorset poems, for instance, to illustrate the difference between Doric and Ionic Greek. He was also an accomplished and sometimes inspiring reader of English literature.*

Temple Grove is described, but not named, in the first chapter of

---

* He is so celebrated, as Mr Acland, in E. F. Benson's *David Blaize* (1916), which is set at Temple Grove ('Helmsworth Preparatory School') and Marlborough ('Marchester').

Herbert James, Monty's father, taken at Livermere

Mary Emily James

The James family at Livermere, 1879. *Left to right*: 'Ber', Herbert James, Mary Emily James, Monty, Sydney, and Grace

Changing Eton by L. S. R. Byrne and E. L. Churchill, both Eton masters. The account is of interest, not only because Byrne was himself a pupil of the school in the 1870s, but also because the authors record their indebtedness to Monty for 'valuable reminiscences' of his prep school given to them personally shortly before his death. Life seems to have been rather harsher at Temple Grove than Monty depicted it in *Eton and King's*. It was difficult to keep warm in winter, while in the summer water was rigorously denied to the boys on 'health' grounds: 'Those who did not seem to the matron in charge to be overheated might get half a cup of water during the hot afternoon, but those who appeared panting and dishevelled were turned dry-lipped away.' The food is described as being 'so uneatable that boys brought in pieces of paper, wrapped up their dinner and hid it in the grounds or threw it down the drains, except during one term when rats ate a large hole under one of the tables and waited in hordes for the food eagerly passed down to them.' Mention is also made in Byrne and Churchill's book of the curious ritual of bath night, 'when boys were placed in rows in a set of shallow metal saucers and watched by the maids until they had scrubbed themselves thoroughly'.[4]

As his mother had predicted, Monty felt less homesick after his second term, although Temple Grove was not the sort of place one ever felt really happy at and he never showed any indications of sentiment for his prep school.

Soon after arriving he sent Grace his opinions of some of the masters. Mr Prior, the writing master, was dismissed as 'a pig'; Mr Geoghegan, on the other hand, was 'pretty fair'—perhaps because he stood up to Waterfield, which few other masters did, and had the romantic distinction of being one-armed. When he reached the First Class Monty was taught by William Rawlings, to whom he generously attributed a good deal of his scholarly grounding.

The work at Temple Grove was of course geared to the requirements of the public schools, which meant that the curriculum was dominated by Latin and Greek. The school had a reputation for sound classical teaching and in this respect Monty had cause to be grateful to it. The first of the monthly progress reports sent to his father was generally satisfactory, apart from his mathematics, described as poor. Waterfield, claiming he could find no fault in Monty, only warned that 'he ought to know more in order to make an Eton scholar'. By March 1874 J. H. Edgar, Waterfield's second-in-command, reported that Monty was gradually gaining his proper place in the school, although he was sometimes inattentive and was prone to dreaminess in English and history lessons. By the end of that year he had earned a glowing report from Waterfield, who thought he had rarely seen a boy make more rapid progress up the school or work with such apparent ease—except in mathematics, in which Monty was still falling below the required standard.

But then in February 1875 he dropped to eighth (out of eleven) in the division order; his Greek was only 'tolerable' and his Latin 'fair'; even his conduct had apparently deteriorated. Waterfield complained of endless excuses for not showing up work and believed that Monty found school work irksome after the Christmas holidays. On one occasion 'he declared that he had corrected a translation and mislaid it. He was made to produce it—and had only written three words.'[5] Waterfield did not punish the boy, considering he had the right to reap the benefit of a previously good character; but he warned that this kind of behaviour could jeopardize Monty's chance of gaining a scholarship at Eton. Monty characteristically shied away from talking about the matter to his father, who was naturally concerned. 'The last thing I should like to do', he told Herbert, 'would be to cause you to write another letter of the same kind as the last, but I don't like to touch upon it.'[6]

There were other minor confrontations with Waterfield, and at some point he was reported for bullying, which Waterfield said he would have disbelieved had he not examined the victim's bruises for himself. There was another incident towards the end of his time at Temple Grove, when he and a chum of his, Hubert Brinton, 'humbugged' another boy, though the only consequence was 'to make us feel rather silly in our own eyes and so be more careful in future how we carry on a bit of fun'.[7]

Waterfield may have been right in believing that Monty found school work irksome after the holidays. At Livermere he had time to devote to his 'hobbies' and he was already industriously accumulating knowledge of subjects that had fascinated him from an early age. Routine school work would certainly appear dull by comparison. One of Arthur Benson's earliest memories of Monty at Temple Grove was of being shown 'an immense list of Roman saints, with mysterious symbols appended', and Monty seems to have acquired the habit of systematic note-taking before he went to school—a letter probably written in his first term asks his mother to send 'that little plaid-covered note-book of mine (Gracy will know it) which contains most of the precious results of my hagiologic researches'. He particularly enjoyed collecting martyrdoms of saints, 'the more atrocious the better', and curious biblical legends. An undated letter to his mother is decorated with 'splendid specimens of original art'— including 'St Frederick after death' (a severed head dripping with blood), a martyr 'having his eyes screwed out from behind' and 'An ancient sagacious Abbot with one hand cut off'.

He was fascinated by what he called 'Archaeology', which involved exploring all the churches he could in the holidays and writing copious notes on them. He wrote excitedly to his father just before the summer holidays of 1874 to say that he wanted 'above all things to make an Archaeological search into the antiquities of Suffolk, to get everything I can for my Museum, and last but not by any means least, to get home'. He was also beginning to acquaint himself with research into documentary sources. 'I want to prosecute my archaeological studies at the Guild-hall Library [sc. in Bury] in the holidays,' runs another letter to his father. 'I s'pose you have not bought a share in it yet?' And he added a postcript: 'I should like awfully to see Cambridge's manuscripts etc.'

Another area of interest was the accumulation of what he called 'odd classics', such as Aelian, a clue to whose appeal for Monty is given by Lemprière: 'In his writings he shows himself very fond of the marvellous . . . ' He was certainly beginning to indulge his taste for the fantastic and the supernatural—for instance, we hear of him 'going diligently on with Erckmann-Chatrian', two celebrated nineteenth-century French writers of ghost stories. But the supernatural coalesced with his more 'scientific' researches in his eager scramble for knowledge: 'I want to know what LEPRECHAUNES and CLURICAUNES are. They are a kind of supernatural beings but that's all I know about them . . . I am making notes of traditions in a note-book . . . I have collected about 200 apocryphal works Old and New Testaments. Of course there are a good many more to be got. There used to be seventy-two Old Testament apocryphal works. Of these I can only find fifty-seven.'

In this way he began to lay up what was to become a quite extraordinary—and legendary—store of miscellaneous antiquarian knowledge. He flitted from one pet subject to another with a restless, almost insatiable desire *to know*. There seemed no rationale behind this compulsive acquisition of facts; it was, and was to remain, simply a pleasure and a fulfilment. 'I have no doubt', he wrote, 'my Divinity

papers at Temple Grove and my Sunday Questions at Eton were a sad
blend of ignorance and blobs of misplaced erudition; but to me it was
all fresh and delightful. Nothing could be more inspiriting than to
discover that St Livinus had his tongue cut out and was beheaded, or
that David's mother was called Nitzeneth.'[8]

In the school library he found Curzon's *Visits to Monasteries in the
Levant* (1849), which he believed first inspired him with a curiosity
about manuscripts; but he also read more conventional fare: *The
Water Babies*, school stories by Ascott R. Hope, the tales of R. M.
Ballantyne, the adventures of Tim Pippin (which he found absorbing
even in middle age), and *At the Back of the North Wind* by George
Macdonald, who always remained a favourite author.

On Sundays the junior boys were read to, by Mr Edgar or some
other master, from a work of an improving character, but Waterfield
himself read aloud to the boys of the First Class in his drawing-room.
Monty clearly enjoyed these occasions:

To see Waterfield in a milder light, to feel that he unbent to some slight extent,
was highly interesting. Besides, he was a very good reader. Stanley's *Lectures on
the Jewish Church*, Farrar's *Life of Christ* (in which I remember his sharply
criticising faults of taste) and the *Pilgrim's Progress* were the books I heard him
read. Some of us who knew the text of the *Pilgrim* were agog to see whether in
the episode of Doubting Castle he would give us the author's words and say,
'that lock went damnable hard'. When he came to the point, he checked
slightly, and said 'desperate hard'.[9]

On Saturday nights the choir (of which Monty was a member) would
meet to practise a few part-songs, after which they consumed cake and
a curious kind of pineapple jam. But for the most part there was little
sense of real freedom at Temple Grove, apart from the occasional
exploration of the outer shrubberies and groves beyond the playing
fields as a reward for coming first or second in the monthly
examination, or the treat of going to Richmond with a friend on
half-holidays.

It was Arthur Benson's recollection that there had been plenty of
pleasant and companionable boys at the school, amongst them Monty
and Edward Grey (Lord Grey of Fallodon). Grey was one of Monty's
two rivals for academic honours (the other was 'a nice boy called
Goldschmidt', as he was called in *Eton and King's*, whose mother was
Jenny Lind). In the end it was Monty who secured the undisputed
headship of the school. As Grey wrote: 'I would use my brain to make
the best use of whatever was put to me, simply to excel in competition,

without having interest in the subject or any natural aptitude for it. Monty James had both . . . '[10] The only lasting friendship of Monty's Temple Grove days was with Arthur Benson, though they did not get to know each other well until both went to Eton.

Unlike his brother Sydney, Monty never saw the attraction of exercise and unnecessary physical exertion, though he was by no means averse to rough and tumble and always claimed that in his youth he could run forty yards faster than anyone. But he had no taste for organized games, accepting his lack of the competitive spirit wryly: 'We have been playing a match this afternoon—the Ist class versus the IIIrd and IVth. I made one run and was bowled. Our side licked of course, because I was there.' But his unique standing in the school—being both an uncommon specimen and unpretentiously 'one of the others'—was recalled by Lionel Byrne, who wrote to him in 1981:

When you first went to Eton and left me behind at Waterfield's my regret was so sharp that it is with me still, and it came not merely from the welcome relief you so often afforded in the monotony of cricket by losing your spectacles in the middle of the pitch, but because you stood towards many of us even then in the position of a philosopher, stored with infinite knowledge, to whose friendly aid appeal was never vain.[11]

His health was generally good, although, as later in his life, he was constantly being urged to take more exercise. He had a bout of illness (measles, apparently) towards the end of 1875, during which he complained to his mother of sore and bleeding lips: 'They put GREASE (ugh!) on my lips which doesn't do them any good whatever, and I believe they're sore from having no cold water to drink.' With 'nothing to read, do, say or think about', he amused himself during his convalescence by composing a piece of mildly satirical nonsense. His target was a visiting missionary (he was clearly familiar with the type, his father being devoted to the interests of the Church Missionary Society) and his tedious procrastinating manner as he addresses a Juvenile Missionary Society meeting:

'He had always been "engaged in active service in Timbuctoo" for upwards of five years. His personal appearance was as follows. He had on correct clerical costume (C.C.C.) and never had more than half a dozen hairs on his head, sometimes less. They'd been pulled out by the natives (so *he* said). I always thought it was his wife!'

He then went on to invent an episode fashioned round a rather disapproving view of Freemasons (his father's, perhaps), who are seen as regularly consorting with demons: 'Well, so the Freemasons set the doorkeepers at the door to look if there was any one coming. So then they took off their jackets and waistcoats and toggery and they made the Demons light a fire in the midst of the room and they danced round it. Suddenly one of them turned round and saw me!!!!!! The tortures I underwent that night would have undermined Hector's constitution.'

His report in June 1875 put him second out of eight. Waterfield wrote: 'He will make a good scholar some day—at present he is liable to failure through inattention.' In July, Waterfield took him and some others to Eton to sit the scholarship examination. Monty recalled that he had been 'amazed and impressed' by the beguiling composition of Long Walk, School Yard, Lupton's Tower, the Chapel, and the rest: 'Yet . . . I cannot pretend that I was at once spellbound, or vowed that it should be Eton for me or nothing.'

It seems ironic, with hindsight, that the boy for whom Eton was to mean so much for so long was not at all perturbed by the prospect of missing an Eton scholarship and going elsewhere. 'I think on the whole', he wrote at the time, 'I should like Charterhouse better than Eton.' There was also talk later of trying for Haileybury and Winchester, though Waterfield seems always to have been determined to try and get Monty into Eton.

Across from the old Christopher Inn, where the Temple Grove boys were lodged, the south-facing buttresses of Eton Chapel could be seen beyond the churchyard, and atop the Chapel were those cupolas and golden vanes that later gave Monty 'a quite peculiar thrill' whenever he first caught sight of them. His mature opinion was that 'No more thoroughly incongruous, no more completely successful addition to a Gothic building was ever made', and they always remained for him 'the most significant, the best remembered feature of Eton'. On this, his first visit he merely wrote: 'The Chapel is awfully jolly outside, but I didn't see the inside . . . '

The Temple Grove candidates had to put up with some hostility as they came out of the scholarship examination from a mob of Lower Boys, who jeered, made 'unfeeling remarks', and even offered physical violence in the form of kicks. There was also a 'dreadful explosion' when Waterfield found out that Monty had put the subject of a sentence into the ablative absolute. 'The examiners are the Provosts of Eton and King's,' Waterfield told Monty's father sternly. 'This sort of thing will make their hair stand on end with horror.'

Monty's name was on the list for College, but not high enough to secure one of the few vacancies that year. And so he had to return to Eton the following July, accompanied this time by the placid Mr Edgar, to sit the scholarship examination once more. From Livermere came a letter to assure him that his father's heart was with him and to hope that he was 'not altogether like the butter at breakfast, but vigorous and ready for the fray that is coming'. Another letter from home counselled him to take care with his handwriting (always a sore puzzle for other people) and to watch out for ablative absolutes. 'I think the exam got on very well,' wrote Monty when it was all over. 'O.C.W. did not go up with us, but J. H. Edgar did, and said he thought I did very well, which is encouraging. But of course nothing is yet certain. We shall hear tomorrow or Monday. I am in unenviable suspense.'

The suspense ended in triumph. Monty's name was second on the list for College and he entered Eton as James, KS (King's Scholar), in the autumn of 1876.

CHAPTER 3

JAMES, KS
Eton 1876–1877

There were some days lurid with disaster, and anxiety, many days
of super exaltation, not many that were wholly drab and brown . . .
And every year, whether I knew it or not—and in my last two years
I certainly did know it—I was being more and more firmly bonded
into the fabric of the place, more and more sure that for me Eton
was the hub of the Universe and College the hub of Eton.

M. R. James, Speech at the Old Collegers' Dinner, 1923

THE King's College of our Lady of Eton Beside Windsor was founded
in 1440 by Henry VI, most devout and unworldly of English kings, with
the twin intention of combating heresy and promoting education. Like
William of Wykeham's earlier foundation at Winchester, Eton was to
be linked to a sister college at the University—in Winchester's case, to
New College, Oxford; in Eton's, to King's College, Cambridge. At
Eton, the Provost, Fellows and seventy King's Scholars (Collegers)
formed 'the College' and inhabited the ancient buildings clustered
about School Yard and the Cloisters. Around the foundation scholars
developed a much larger number of paying boarders, the Oppidans,
who were typically from affluent families and who were organized into
separate houses beyond the College buildings.

Collegers and Oppidans came together in many aspects of school
life, but their experience of Eton was fundamentally different. 'I have
read your book [*Eton and King's*],' an ex-Oppidan contemporary, C. E.
Chambers, wrote to Monty in 1926. 'It held me. It emphasizes the
extreme difference between Colleger and Oppidan. More than ever I
felt the gap yawning . . . We have been at two such entirely different
schools that it is impossible we should hold similar views.'[1]

College, in spite of the squalid and brutal portions of its history, had
a certain romance about it. By Monty's time, the distinct identity of
Collegers within the Eton community, symbolized by their gowns, had
developed into a definite *esprit de corps* based partly on the academic

supremacy that College had by then assumed, partly on the sense of a continuing corporate tradition stretching back to the ideals of the Founder. An Oppidan house, said Hugh Macnaghten, a Colleger of Monty's period, reckons by years, whereas 'College reckons by centuries, retains the impress of the Founder and abides'.[2] Monty, though he was without Macnaghten's sentimentality, shared this sense of inheritance and distinction to the full. Eton meant a very great deal to him throughout his life; but College, perhaps, was everything.

In comparison with the school his father had known, Monty entered what is recognizably modern Eton. The unsatisfactory state of the teaching at Eton and the administration of its endowments had been the subject of debate for some years before things came to a head in 1860–1. The *Edinburgh Review* printed a fierce attack, accusing the Provost and Fellows outright of misappropriating revenue,[3] and such was public feeling that a Royal Commission was set up almost immediately to inquire into the revenues, management and studies of the nine great public schools.* A year after the passing of the Public Schools Act in 1868, Eton produced proposals that were finally to abolish the ancient powers and privileges of the Provost and Fellows, who were replaced by a new Governing Body.

Dr James John Hornby had become Head Master on the last day of 1867, replacing Dr Edward Balston, who had been unable to face the changes envisaged by the Commissioners. Hornby had been deliberately chosen for being an Oppidan Oxonian (instead of the usual pedigree of College and King's, Cambridge) who had not formerly been an assistant master. It was something of a symbolic act, signifying Eton's willingness to begin cutting itself loose from the old constrictions. Although not in the least inclined to build a new Eton from the ashes of the old, Hornby was initially seen as a reformer and became nominally responsible for implementing the comparatively moderate recommendations of the Royal Commission. Under him the curriculum was widened, the teaching of French, mathematics and science was put on a regular footing (though all three continued to remain outside the main classical thrust of the curriculum), and a number of other long overdue reforms were carried out.

As far as College was concerned, conditions had been slowly improving prior to the Commissioners' arrival. The completion of

---

* Charterhouse, Eton, Harrow, Merchant Taylors', Rugby, St Paul's, Shrewsbury, Westminster, and Winchester.

New Buildings in 1846 had finally transformed Long Chamber, now known simply as Chamber, which was reduced in size and partitioned off to provide rudimentary accommodation in stalls for the fifteen junior Collegers. The remaining fifty-five scholars enjoyed the comparative luxury of individual rooms in New Buildings, and over them all was set a Master in College, the first being C. J. Abraham.

Dr Hornby had been Head Master for nearly nine years when Monty came to Eton. He was a striking figure in his day—'the absolutely perfect type of an Eton Head Master ... Immaculately dressed, and of fine presence, he possessed a natural dignity which even impressed boys totally lacking in reverence for all other institutions of the school.'[4] He was a sound classical scholar of the old school and a Christian gentleman, benign, courteous, and urbane. Unfortunately, his views were narrow and inflexible, and as time went on he began to seem to some like 'an apathetic, comatose man, who took things as lightly as he could'.[5] In fact his work-load had gradually become intolerable, since he insisted on carrying on the Head Master's traditional teaching in addition to heavy administrative duties, and he confessed to Hugh Macnaghten that he had been on the point of a complete breakdown before he finally resigned in 1884.

Hornby's reign was intemperately condemned by one of his masters as 'an inert and colourless regime, during which the tone and discipline of the school were perceptibly lowered'.[6] This was certainly not true of College, which positively flourished during Hornby's time as Head Master, when an absence of compulsion from above produced a voluntary and exceptional spirit of industry amongst the Collegers. Indeed Hugh Macnaghten speaks of 'a tradition of strenuousness among the Collegers of the 'seventies', though he felt that he himself had worked to little real effect. Still, Macnaghten was inclined to believe that 'the ten years 1873–83 were the greatest decade in the recent history of College' (he was writing in 1924). The *Eton College Chronicle*, reviewing Macnaghten's book *Fifty Years of Eton in Prose and Verse*, agreed with him, looking back to the years of Hornby's rule as a golden age, when 'if it was bliss to be a boy at Eton, to be in College was very heaven'.[7]

*   *   *

Having been formally admitted by the Provost, Dr Goodford, Monty was able to put on his Colleger's gown and officially write the letters 'KS' after his name. He then took possession of his stall in Chamber, at the north-west end, which contained a bed, a bath, an armchair and a 'burry', described by one old Colleger as 'a very useful article of furniture, made up, like a chimaera, of three parts, a bookcase above, a chest of drawers below, and a writing desk in the middle'.[8]

Like all new boys, Monty was required to fag, though as a Colleger taking a high place in the school it was only for a year. His fagmaster—the Sixth Former who had a personal call on him—was Arthur Ryle, the brother of Herbert James's godson. His duties were not onerous and largely consisted of making Ryle's tea and toast, calling him for early school, filling and emptying his bath and running miscellaneous errands, but they were carried out efficiently. When Monty fell ill during his first half (the Eton word for a term), Ryle had to find an unsatisfactory temporary substitute and was glad when the 'frail reed' recovered.

Monty's tutor was Henry Elford Luxmoore; the day in September 1876 when he first entered Luxmoore's drawing-room with his father was, he said, 'one of the very few pivot days of my life'. Luxmoore received his new pupil with great pleasure, telling Herbert James: 'I hope it may hereafter be a subject of congratulation that he entered Eton.' Though the friendship with his tutor was a constant and deeply valued fact of his life from 1876 to 1926, serving to anchor him still more to the Eton of his boyhood, Monty refused to panegyrize or even describe Luxmoore (who was still alive at the time) in *Eton and King's*—'my tutor would not like it'; and even after Luxmoore's death he was only slightly more forthcoming about the man who, to some degree, assumed a paternal role towards him for fifty years of his life.

Luxmoore, the son of a north Devon vicar, had entered College as a boy in 1852. From there he had gone up to Pembroke College, Oxford, as a Rous Scholar, returning to Eton as a master in 1864. To begin with, he had been intensely unpopular—hissed by Collegers in Hall, and booed by Oppidans; but he had persevered, being well aware that he was 'grievously lacking in the cordiality which puts boys at their ease'.[9] He struggled against his inhibitions and in time was counted amongst a small number of Eton masters who were, in their various ways, developing a new attitude towards the boys in their charge and attempting to break through the conventional barriers separating master and pupil.

The impetus had come largely from William Johnson (Cory), Herbert James's contemporary at Eton and King's. But there were obvious dangers in cultivating relationships with 'sweet-hearted enthusiasts', and despite his brilliant successes Johnson was held responsible for some indiscretion. He left Eton suddenly in 1872 and never broke silence.

The way pointed by William Johnson was followed, with characteristic embellishments, by his pupil Oscar Browning. For sixteen years Browning, known universally as 'O.B.', tried to encourage intellectual interest on a wide front at Eton, as a counter to what he saw as the prevailing philistinism. Literary celebrities like George Eliot and Walter Pater would come to his house; musicians would come down from London; he put his library at the disposal of the boys; he encouraged discussion; above all, he strove to humanize and broaden the life and aspirations of Eton boys and to stand in a confidential and effective moral relationship to them. But he, too, came to grief. In 1875 he committed what is usually described as a technical blunder (concerning the number of his pupils) and was dismissed by Hornby. There was a great uproar, but in the end Oscar Browning shook the dust of Eton from his shoes and migrated to Cambridge, to carve out a legendary place for himself at King's, where we shall meet him later.[10]

Like Oscar Browning, Luxmoore had also been a pupil of William Johnson's. He had a strong puritan streak in him, but also a deep vein of idealism, and in time he began to attract boys who were sensitive enough to appreciate the values he cherished. He was deeply influenced by Johnson, on the one hand, and by John Ruskin, his spiritual master, on the other. He also nourished a passion for the beautiful ('Luxmoore was our artist,' wrote Percy Lubbock. 'I am not sure that we had another').[11] At the same time, as the photographs of him show, he had a certain severity of outlook: he appeared to crave for, and find comfort in, a species of asceticism and confined his romantic longings by religious, moral and intellectual restraints. He never married and remained at Eton all his long life.

This was the man who was to have direct oversight of Monty while he was at Eton. Division masters came and went: 'my Tutor' remained. The ideal form of the tutorial relationship was described by Luxmoore himself in 1918:

Of the tutorial system the gist is this. From entrance to leaving the boy should be attached to the supervision of one master 'in loco parentis'. The tutor and the new boy, working together many hours daily, get to know each other pretty thoroughly, and, if each be a good sort, they become real friends. Then, all through the school, the tutor would supervise his pupil's work and have charge of his literary training.[12]

Monty, even as a young Colleger, was too independent-minded to be 'trained' in a narrow sense; but Luxmoore may be said to have confirmed and deepened some of his natural prejudices and values, as well as encouraging him to strive after what was best in all things. Monty's view of the responsibility the present must assume towards the past, for instance, was endorsed by a similar respect for historical continuity in Luxmoore. A more negative influence, perhaps, was Luxmoore's antagonism towards science, which may have encouraged, if it did not directly inculcate, a comparable attitude in Monty. As M. D. Hill, who taught biology at Eton, wrote of Luxmoore: 'There could rarely, if ever, have been a man of his intellectual calibre who so little understood the position and scope of Natural Science in our civilization, or its future potentialities. He was in some sense a medievalist, and I always had a feeling when talking to him that he would gladly have burnt me at the stake for the good of my soul.'[13] To some extent, Monty's intellectual outlook was similarly limited.

Though there were many areas of coincidence, Luxmoore and Monty certainly did not agree on everything, and in general Monty continued throughout his time at Eton to develop his own highly individual lines of intellectual enquiry. But the personal bond between them was strong. For his part, Luxmoore wrote frankly in 1882, just as Monty was leaving Eton for Cambridge: 'As I have told you before, failing in so much I want and wish to do, it is an unspeakable consolation to have your friendship and affection, and to feel that opportunity has not been all lost. Reflection whispers that it is little credit for a schoolmaster to have "got on" with his best boys, who would indeed have got on with anyone, but still it remains a tangible consolation and happiness, and what I shall do without you I don't know.'[14]

*   *   *

Monty's first half at Eton was cut short by an attack of food poisoning and he did not return to school until towards the end of February 1877. He had to work hard to catch up with the rest of his election (the batch of scholars elected in any one year) but he appeared nonetheless to be in a generally buoyant mood. 'Dear Parents,' he writes, 'Your affectionate offspring takes up his pluma with the full intention of telling you all he can. He is well and takes his drinks regularly. He takes his porter into Hall and drinks it at dinner. He thinks that on that point you need not be anxious.'

His first schoolroom was a small building, 'rather like a Dissenting Chapel', in Gasworks Lane, presided over by H. G. Wintle, a genial and engaging figure with a supposed resemblance to Verdant Green, the Varsity hero invented by 'Cuthbert Bede'. It was Wintle who set him his first set of Sunday Questions (questions, nominally on divinity, set on Sunday and shown up to the division master on Monday). In one such question, on the meaning of the word 'Communism', Monty later presented what he called 'the following flight of eloquence':

In more recent times the word has been applied to the opinions of an abominable set of people who rendered themselves objects of abhorrence to every well balanced mind in the last Franco-Prussian War, by destroying a vast number of priceless treasures of art and antiquity by means of petroleum and other equally detestable compounds.[15]

If this was an early expression of Monty's characteristic reaction to barbarism, it was not long either before he began to weave in 'a side and a half of Apocrypha' when answering Sunday Questions, a practice to which his division masters were obliged to become accustomed. Some of his masters were to remain lifelong friends— Walter Durnford, A. C. Ainger, Henry Broadbent and Edward Austen Leigh* amongst them. Others, like the Revd R. F. Rumsey ('a confirmed ritualist') he had no time for. He recalled earning a written punishment from Rumsey within his first fortnight at Eton for cribbing mathematical extra work from a neighbour, W. S. Godding, in Chamber: 'The offence was not repeated, but my distaste for Mathematics was not lessened.'[16]

Godding was one of the first friends he made, but he soon palled and became 'most awfully loathsome. It is quite impossible to protect him. He is given to tears and such, and goes about with Oppidans.'†Another friend, Ion Thynne, shared walks and some of his scholarly tastes with him; but there were no intimate attachments, and certainly nothing comparable to the experience of his contemporary Arthur

---

* Austen Leigh, a great-nephew of Jane Austen, was one of a large family of brothers, all of whom Monty became friendly with. He was known at Eton as 'The Flea', for his fabled ability to draw blood with the birch, and Monty's imitation of Austen Leigh's extraordinary voice and pronunciation became a standard item in his later extensive repertoire of impersonations.

† Monty and Godding appear briefly in G. Nugent-Bankes's *A Day of My Life, or, Every-day Experiences at Eton*, published in 1877 while the author (an Oppidan) was still at Eton.

Benson.[17] There was no sign in Monty of any emotional hunger that might drive him to seek out, like Benson, a passionate relationship with another boy. The Cambridge portion of *Eton and King's* contains the bare record of a great many friendships, not passionate, but several of them of enduring significance in Monty's life; but the part that deals with his boyhood and adolescence at Eton—his most impressionable years—is a chronicle of a different kind, revealing the development of a deep personal relationship, not with any of his contemporaries, but with Eton itself. 'These last few weeks have been passing quickly and agreeably for the most part,' he told his father towards the end of his first year. 'Eton is simply heavenly in the Summer Half. Evenings are a terrestrial Paradise, especially in the Playing Fields and at Romney Locks.' The spell had been cast.

Rejoining his election after his illness, he soon took first place in the division. 'The work is obviously too easy for him,' wrote F. H. Rawlins, his division master, in March 1877, 'but he is not careless . . . His one fault is unpunctuality. I am much pleased with him on the whole.' The Master in College, H. A. Chignell, with an opportunity for observing Monty at even closer quarters, wrote a gushing commendation of him to Herbert James: 'It is long since I have had a boy here whose very presence gives me so much satisfaction and pleasure . . . His tutor never ceases to say kind things of him. I think we both envy you such a son.'

CHAPTER 4

THE LEARNED BOY
Eton 1877–1880

MRJ's preparatory school was the old-established Temple Grove ... I was there myself twenty years later, but do not remember any stories of him: but in college at Eton, where I also followed him at the same interval, there was still a legend of him as the learned boy ...

Sir Stephen Gaselee of M. R. James

WHEN Monty returned to Eton after the summer vacation of 1877 it was with the consciousness of possessing a new status. He no longer had to fag and could write home with the slightly superior voice of experience: 'The nine new people this half are nothing very remarkable and very bad hands at keeping up a fire. Punishment with a siphon will be henceforth adopted in Chamber, since Sixth-form object to the previously established custom of chastisement with a brush for a bad fire.'[1]

December, however, brought a severe blow to his pride when he heard of his performance in trials (terminal examinations). The places were read out in Chapel, to great excitement: '1 Brooks. 2 Brooke mi.* 3 Wood mi. 4 Hitchcock mi. Ugh! 5 James ... ' He was put out at being beaten by Hitchcock, whom he detested, but he knew that his mathematics, science and his slow handwriting had let him down. He signed himself 'Your devoted offspring, exceedingly disgusted with himself for his trials'.

But all in all, he was enjoying Eton life immensely and began to savour a sense of real independence that was unlike anything he had experienced at Temple Grove, or perhaps even at Livermere. He started to explore the School Library, where he was pleased to find all the publications of the Camden Society, as well as the *Journal of*

---

* Alan England Brooke, KS, later an eminent biblical scholar and Provost of King's. He was Rupert Brooke's uncle.

Philology. His letters home throughout 1878 show intellectual excitement, abundant good humour and an increasing contentment with his
environment. In Middle Division he conscientiously began to read
German with Luxmoore ('It is always useful,' he wrote) and put the
increased amount of free time he now had to constructive use, both in
regard to school work and to his private interests. 'Altogether,' he
confirmed to his parents, 'I am happy.'

In general literature he read widely: Isaac D'Israeli, Max Müller,
Lord Lytton, Wilkie Collins (much admired: *The Moonstone* was, quite
simply, 'the best novel in the language') and Charles Kingsley, whose
poems he rated highly. On Dickens he 'fastened like a leech'. 'Not
many whole months can have passed since', he wrote in his
recollections, 'without having recourse to some part of those writings. I
put Charles Dickens in the forefront of the accessions to my pleasure
which Eton gave, for it was wholly new.'

At Temple Grove he had been encouraged to inquire freely of his
parents on religious matters, although his mother had told him that
many of his questions would have to remain unresolved. But at Eton,
with his horizons rapidly expanding, he had little time, and perhaps
little inclination, to dwell upon the state of his soul. Chapel services at
this period did little to encourage the spiritual sense: Monty's main
source of interest was the fabric of the Chapel itself, mixed with mild
curiosity and amusement at the ministrations of venerable but decrepit
Fellows, survivors of pre-Commission days, or the idiosyncrasies of
preachers. Services, on the whole, meant merely 'a little folding of the
hands to sleep. You wrapped your gown about your arms, your head
sank into its folds, and your thoughts travelled whither they would till
you became unconscious.'[2]

Games, like Chapel, were unavoidable. The Wall Game had some
appeal for Monty, probably because it was a uniquely Etonian game
and of especial significance to Collegers. It was College's duty to beat
the Oppidans at the Wall on St Andrew's Day (30 November).
Though Monty never played on that day of days, he was twelfth man in
1881 and always claimed that 'but for a bad knee and a crumpled
ear—both accruing from friction against the Wall (I still have the
ear)—I should have played for College that year'. The Field Game had
less allure: 'Nobody told you what to do, but they were very free in
telling you what you did was wrong.' Fives he seldom played. Being
well built he might have made a useful wet-bob (rower), but he found
the charges for boats prohibitive—a reflection of his always precarious

finances. As for cricket, he never discovered that it was a recreation: 'My innings was a form—a shortened form—of service that must be gone through; fielding a salutary discipline, keeping intellectual pride in its due place.'

He usually went up to London for the Eton and Harrow match at Lord's, though less for the cricket than to call on his brother Ber, who was studying at the Charing Cross Hospital, and to browse contentedly in his favourite second-hand bookshops. At J. M. Stark's shop in July 1878 he was shown a number of treasures, including a copy of part of *Jerusalem Delivered* with Tasso's autograph, a Testament of Job and a fifteenth-century manuscript Book of Hours. Stark later sent him manuscript fragments and engravings, which were pasted into a scrapbook. He seems to have begun sending for booksellers' catalogues in November 1877, writing to his sister Grace: 'I hope father will not be alarmed. I shall not get any hurtful publications from Mr Stark.' The following autumn he describes being 'in the midst of two new and lovely catalogues procured from David Nutt . . . Certainly catalogues are an enticing form of literature.' One amusing consequence of his handwriting (described as 'execrable' by one division master) was that the catalogues would arrive with the most extraordinary addresses, 'all honouring me with a "Revd". And one calls me Games and another represents me living at Kew Buildings'.

In October 1878, obviously feeling confident of his specialist knowledge, he devised a hoax that foreshadows the invention of spurious documentation in his ghost stories:

I forged an interesting manuscript on a fragment of old paper, which was stuck on one of the real manuscripts, containing revelations as to the whereabouts of two chests full of gold which were buried at Rome in the Via Appia in 1569. I completely deceived Chignell with it. He was going into raptures over it, which I checked by informing him it was in my own handwriting. He hastily changed the subject by attempting to sneer at another manuscript. I was again down on him. It was a genuine one. My tutor was much disappointed on discovering it to be a forgery. He then began to insinuate that he had not believed it, which was not true.[3]

Sometimes this self-assurance became something like cockiness: 'In Translation I made no mistake,' he wrote towards the end of that year, describing trials, 'but introduced a new interpretation of one passage which may stagger the Examiners. I argued it hotly with the Tutor, and he could not answer me.'

The following March a more serious project than the forgery had suggested itself:

Yesterday I found in looking over my note books, and aided by a subtle process of reasoning terminating in absolute certainty, that a manuscript fragment at Bury, No 135 in S James Library on the right hand corner as you go in, bottom shelf, a white vellum book, contains the Preface to and the beginning of a Latin translation of Plutarch's Life of Sertorius in a hand of the 9th or 10th century.[4]

He worked up his deduction into an article, which was sent to C. E. Doble, editor of *The Academy*. Doble replied encouragingly and in July a short communication, 'A Latin fragment of Plutarch's Sertorius', appeared in *The Academy*, dated from Eton College and signed 'M. R. James'. Luxmoore disapproved of this 'publicity', as he called it, but said nothing to Monty. To Herbert James, however, he warned that Monty should be careful 'not to anticipate maturity or let business be encroached upon'. He also thought that Monty should be on his guard against what might do him 'social harm, if misinterpreted as conceit'.[5] Monty hoped for a series to follow the Sertorius piece, but this prospect quickly receded when a second article was declined by Doble as being 'scarcely critical enough for our purpose'.

Luxmoore's warning about 'social harm' came only a few months after what was the main upset of Monty's otherwise smooth passage through College. There had been a minor row in November 1878, when about ten boys, including Monty, were complained of by Chignell to the Head Master for harassing a boy called Brooks. Hornby had been angry, but as no harm had been done peace was soon restored. Luxmoore, puzzled by Monty's involvement, could not make out 'where he has the time or the interest for folly if what I see is his genuine self. One has not to be long a schoolmaster to find out that very good boys do very foolish things at times, but in that case sympathy goes with them, and in this the feeling of the ordinary Collegers was the other way ... I only feel as if the boy was rather more of a problem than I thought.'[6]

But this incident was only a prelude to a much more serious one in March the following year. Monty claimed in *Eton and King's* that his version of the incident, which was one on which he had often been challenged, was the true one, but in fact it leaves out a good deal.

Back in January 1879 Monty had told his sister Grace that he was learning Ethiopic 'without a grammar and with only an alphabet and glossary, which I recently purchased in an Ethiopic reading book'. The book was August Dillmann's *Chrestomathia Aethiopica* (1866), which he had acquired from one of his booksellers. The first item in it was an apocryphal text, *The Rest of the Words of Baruch*, and as a new apocryphal book was already 'meat and drink' to him, he was fired to prepare an English version of the Ethiopic original. In his recollections, he describes how he stimulated an interest in Ion Thynne and how they 'together' translated *Baruch* and sent it up to Queen Victoria at Windsor Castle with 'a very polite letter to Her Majesty, beseeching her to accept the Dedication of our work'. But the letter was intercepted by the Queen's private secretary, Sir Henry Ponsonby, and sent to Dr Hornby, 'intimating, I believe, that we should be the better for some personal correction'. They were not beaten, however: 'Only verbally were our foolishness and impertinence pointed out to us.'

This account omits two key factors. Firstly, Monty was unwell at the time. At the end of March he apologized to his father for not writing with the excuse that he had been 'slightly disarranged in the intellect', due, he said, to the 'combined effects of too much reading and too much East Wind'. Secondly, in addition to what seems to have been mental and physical strain, there was a 'badgering tendency . . . to think of nothing but the Queen'. The start of this strange fixation had been the wedding of the Duke of Connaught and Princess Louise Marguerite of Prussia on 13 March in St George's Chapel. 'I lived last week quite in an Atmosphere of Royalty,' wrote Monty soon afterwards. 'I went to see the bride arrive at S.W.R. station . . . Next day the Prince of Wales and one of the young Princes said farewell to the Head and Provost just under my window. I was about the only one who witnessed the scene, which I watched through my faithful spy glass.'

The following day he went to the wedding itself: 'The crowd in the street opposite the castle was vast. The Queen looked very nice indeed and smiled benignantly . . . We followed all the Royal carriages from the gates with loud cheers . . .' In the same letter he reported that 'Ethiopic is progressing. Beautiful. We have nearly finished Baruch.' Soon afterwards he became distinctly unsettled: '*Symptoms*. Disability to read or work, or sleep, or converse coherently . . . *Best Remedy* (which I couldn't get) Playing on a Piano, or other Instrument of Musick. *Actual Treatment*. A tonic of unknown composition and feeble effect.'[7]

The strangest symptom of all was this 'badgering tendency' to think of nothing but the Queen and other royal personages. He became fascinated by 'the representation of the Royal Pages (two of whom are at Eton) in the picture of the Wedding in the Illustrated, and every day since then till Saturday, I had to go to the Reading Room to pore over them'. He could not remember being in such an inane state of mind before. He was excused work and allowed to go out when he liked: 'Light literature appeared idiotic. Heavier books I could not comprehend. I think the last straw that broke my back was reading a lot of the Orphic Hymns (fifty of them) at a sitting'—but, he added, 'they taught me a good many words so I will not repent of my evil ways'.

He could imagine what his father would say: ' "See what comes of reading too many different things. Keep to one thing at a time." Of the propriety of which advice I am painfully aware.' Altogether, in the jargon of his boyhood, it had all been 'unmitigated rot' and he told his father that he would not go through it again for pounds—'in fact for nothing except the office of Groom of the Stole or Page of Honour, which have been the burden of my thoughts for the last week, but from which thank goodness I am a little recovered and begin to take a glimmering interest in other less chimerical topics.'

In the midst of this derangement the Baruch translation was sent up to the Queen and Luxmoore had to try and make sense of his pupil's extraordinary and uncharacteristic behaviour. 'I was made rather uneasy', he told Monty's father, 'by your boy's complaining on Monday that his head failed him at work and he said he had a fixed idea and could not rid his brain of "the Queen" and could not sleep.' Then came the note from Sir Henry Ponsonby: 'The Head Master is exceedingly annoyed at the conceit and bad taste of the proceedings,' Luxmoore went on, 'For myself I am only afraid that it may be an effect not a cause—I hope that this fixed idea he spoke of is not the cause of the letter. If it were not for the joint production I should be almost afraid it were.' Ponsonby apparently thought the letter from Monty and Thynne was an impertinent joke. 'Of course it was not that,' said Luxmoore. 'Still he ought to have asked some one before he did such a thing, and the Head was really put out. I thought I had better tell you this. I expect if the other boys get hold of it they will not spare their chaff, and that perhaps is the best way of treating it.'[8]

It fell to Sydney to go to Eton and try and sort things out. Herbert wished him to tell Luxmoore about Monty's 'Apocryphal proclivities and also of a former wish on the lad's part to publish some Apocryphal translations', and to see both Monty and Hornby. 'I think you would do better with Hornby,' Herbert told Sydney. 'I am a bit nettled with him for both the last and present proceeding. He had much better have dealt personally with the boys. NB Be gentle with the Head so as not to prejudice him more against Toby.'[9]

By the beginning of April things had blown over somewhat and Monty tried to set the record straight in a letter to his father, signing himself 'Your badgered MRJ':

As far as I can see you have all got hold of the idea that I have been ill in consequence of writing to the Queen whereas I wrote to the Queen in consequence of being ill, which makes a considerable difference I think . . . Please understand that I should never in a normal and healthy condition of mind have thought of writing to the Queen. As it was, however, I looked upon it as quite a common sort of thing, and do so still, I must say. I did not see the remotest necessity for going to my Tutor about it anymore than about writing to you, and almost dismissed it from my mind as soon as it was sent . . . Besides, I was more than half ashamed of having written.[10]

The Baruch episode, which underlined the dangers of Monty's precocious intellectual energy, was a temporary aberration and he soon recovered his equilibrium. As with the Brooks incident, there seem to have been social repercussions, hinted at by Luxmoore, who reported early in April that in talking to some senior Collegers he had found them 'rather colder in their appreciation [of Monty] than I expected'. His school work, however, was not affected and he acquitted himself well in trials at the end of the year against several older Collegers. Luxmoore was glad Monty had showed he could do so much, for he thought him 'rather undervalued in College. He is not of course a boy's boy nor a very forceful character, but I think he ought to have his fair range of influence and I have never quite seen to what fault on whose side it is owing that he appears not quite to get it.'[11] At least Luxmoore was glad he could not detect in Monty 'the coolness, the intellectual assumption or the contempt of schoolboy duty' evident in some of the best Collegers; but he was careful to warn, as he had done before, against 'prematurely transplanting' Monty's private studies 'into a time when the grounding ought to be ensured which will make them all the better afterwards'.

Those studies were becoming quite astonishing in their scope and detail. The earliest of Monty's surviving notebooks date from 1878 and 1879 and contain notes, epitomes, and lists on such topics as Chaucer, Bury Library, St Mark, the Acts of Andrew and Peter, the Sybilline Oracles, the *Dictionary of Christian Biography*, miscellaneous notes on Apocrypha, a translation of the Psalms of Solomon, notes on the Kabbalah and the Ten Sephiroth, saints, and, in January 1879, 'A Complete List of all Apocryphal Books (belonging to Both Testaments), Lost and Extant, with references added shewing in what Former volumes of notes may be found either Notices, Fragments, Abstracts or Translations of each Book.'[12]

In his leisure hours he explored local churches, some of which did not pass muster with an already settled opinion. Old Windsor church was 'a most Frightful Edifice . . . rendered Execrable by Restoration': its painted walls produced in Monty 'the effect of nursery wallpaper'. Langley, by contrast, offered a library that was ripe for rummaging in: 'I found a noble printed fifteenth-century Service Book with lovely hand painted initials and two or three manuscript leaves. I had thoughts of gagging the old person who takes care of the library and departing with the best books, but thought better of it.'[13] He contented himself with copying out the catalogue.

The most significant awakening came in the autumn of 1879 when, as he described in *Eton and King's*, he and his friend Henry Babington Smith 'succeeded in wheedling the keys of the Fellows' Library out of Vice-Provost Dupuis'. College Library, built between 1725 and 1729 to replace the old south gallery of the Cloister, has been justly called one of the most beautiful libraries in the world.[14] To Monty, soon after discovering it, it was 'a delightful place. Quite what a library should be.' Apart from two sixteenth-century Collegers no other boys seem to have gained access to College Library until Monty and Henry Babington Smith prevailed upon Vice-Provost Dupuis. By February 1881 Monty was using the library regularly. He got to know F. St John Thackeray, a master who was then writing a series of articles on the history of the library for *Notes and Queries*. Monty reported that he was able to do some 'deciphering' for him.

It was in the superb setting of College Library at Eton that Monty James first browsed 'untrammelled', as he said, amongst an important manuscript collection. He counted it as 'another of the great gifts of Eton' and his later catalogue of the collection, published in 1895, was a sincere token of his gratitude. 'The least I could have done in return', he said in the Preface to the catalogue, referring to the indulgence of the College authorities, 'was to put at their disposal such knowledge as they had helped me to gain.'

CHAPTER 5

SIXTH FORM
Eton 1880–1882

Now one of them's wed, and the other's dead,
So long that he's hardly missed
Save by us, who messed with him years ago:
But we're all in the Old School List.

J. K. Stephen, 'The Old School List'
(*Lapsus Calami*, 1891)

THE great event of the summer of 1880 was a trip to France, with two other boys, organized by Luxmoore as a reward for Monty gaining a place in the Select (runners-up) for the Newcastle Scholarship, Eton's premier academic prize. The holiday marked Monty's introduction not only to 'the sacred soil of France', but also to medieval glass and sculpture on a large scale. From Paris (never one of his favourite cities as an adult) he wrote home in high spirits from the Hotel Castiglione, describing the magnificence of the streets and the forest of gas lamps in the Place de l'Etoile. They had a brief taste of bohemianism in a café, 'where people sang and there was some Trapeze Gymnastics at which Ma's hair would have curled, and we drank coffee song lay (without milk), quite dissipated'.

That September Monty took his place in the Head Master's division, as the lowest member of Sixth Form. Dr Hornby's regular system of calling boys up to construe provided him with the opportunity for private study during school, as Sydney James recalled:

I remember meeting my brother . . . then a Sixth Form Colleger, outside Chambers* with a huge pile of books on his arm. I asked him what the lesson was; he said:
    'Thucydides.'
    'Are all those books Thucydides?'
    'No, none of them. I was called up last school.'
The books were on the Ethiopic language, or some equally recondite subject.[1]

---

* The matutinal meeting of assistant masters with the Head Master.

From Haileybury, Sydney had gone up to Trinity, Cambridge, and after taking his degree had spent some time as private tutor to John Fortescue, the future Royal Librarian at Windsor and historian of the British Army. ('It is fifty-two years', Fortescue told Monty in 1930, 'since your brother Sydney told me with reverence and awe that he was as naught compared with his younger brother.') Sydney had come to Eton as an assistant master in May 1879, soon after the Baruch incident. One result of his presence was that he could add weight to Luxmoore's regular admonishments to Monty to take more exercise. Between them, they pressed Monty (who wanted 'more opening of pores', according to Luxmoore) into the Rifle Corps, which he joined with apparent willingness, considering it 'an important step'.

A significant social development had been the furthering of Monty's acquaintance with Arthur Benson in the autumn of 1879—'a very superior party,' he wrote of Arthur. 'I like him extremely. His chief topic is the Collegiate Church, and Ecclesiastical Constitutions generally.' With Benson there were 'great times': evenings in the Winter and Easter Halves in Arthur's room, or with Arthur's friend Herbert Tatham, when the object was to talk—'*not* canvassing the problems of Life and Being, no, nor yet the probabilities of some one getting or not getting their colours, but of what we liked in books or did not like in our neighbours; of buildings, churches, novels, incidents in Chapel, vagaries of masters . . . '[2]

Arthur displayed a good deal of architectural knowledge that impressed Monty, who learned from him to appreciate St Paul's and the City churches, in particular the organ cases of the Wren period, which were always appearing on Arthur's scribbling paper, 'in proportions ever more colossal'. Church music was another shared enthusiasm. Henry Broadbent had taught Monty how to read tenor and bass parts in hymn tunes, and practical experience had been gained at (Sir) Joseph Barnby's Sunday Evening Musicals, at which a miscellaneous body of boys and masters sang through standard items from the *Messiah*, *Elijah*, *Saul*, and Spohr's *Calvary*. With Arthur Benson, and two other friends, Willy Boyle and Hugh Childers, Monty committed chants to memory, to be warbled in parts round high table in Hall on summer evenings. They would also go up to St George's to enjoy the music there: Monty's preference was for Lenten anthems, heard on dark afternoons in February or March, during which he sat in the stalls entranced.

Monty's friendship with Arthur Benson doubtless helped his

election to the Literary Society in the spring of 1880. In November of that year Arthur, then President of the Society, invited Ruskin to come and speak. The great man had just returned from a tour of northern France and chose to lecture on Amiens cathedral. Monty had heard Ruskin speak once before at Eton, but this second lecture had been revelatory: 'For the first time I learned what might be read, and in what spirit, in the imagery of a great church: and what the thirteenth century had to say to the nineteenth. I say I then learned it first; yet I doubt if in so saying I do justice to my tutor, who, a faithful disciple of Ruskin (and long Master of his Guild),* had at the very least prepared my mind to absorb that lesson.'[3]

Monty's papers to the Literary Society included one on 'The Occult Sciences', a rambling résumé of the history of magic that reveals, if nothing else, plenty of obscure reading. The main authority is Collin de Plancy's *Dictionnaire Infernal*, 'an appalling book', as Monty called it, which he had seen and desired in July 1879. Interest in the occult and in the more lurid sort of folk-tales continued to be a subsidiary theme of his private researches. In February 1878 he had come across Walter Map's hotch-potch of tales, *De Nugis Curialium*, which contained 'some extraordinary stories about Ghosts, Vampires, Wood-nymphs etc'. He also seems to have begun either writing his own ghost stories or else reading other people's to his friends, for he had written in December 1878: 'I must depart for a while, as I am engaged for a "dark seance" i.e. a telling of ghost stories, in which capacity I am rather popular just now.' The *Eton College Chronicle* (hereafter simply the *Chronicle*) thought Monty's paper on 'The Occult Sciences' displayed 'surprising knowledge', though it had to be curtailed owing to its length; the following week Henry Babington Smith read a paper on Paracelsus, after which Monty, with still more curious knowledge to impart, told a story of a demon in a tree.

Also through Arthur Benson, Monty became involved with the *Eton Rambler*, the first number of which appeared on 4 May 1880. The editorial by Arthur stated that the paper aimed 'to supplement the Chronicle in throwing open the pages of a periodical to all the literary talent which must exist, though at present latent, at Eton'. Herbert James seems to have feared in the *Rambler* yet another inroad on his

---

* The Guild of St George, founded by Ruskin in 1871. Members were required to give a tithe of their incomes to philanthropic purposes. It was originally called 'St George's Company'.

son's time at an important stage in his Eton career; but Monty replied
reassuringly: 'I have nothing to do with it except in the way of getting
subscribers and contributing when I can. I am glad to say I had nothing
in the first number which was very feeble . . . I appear in the next
number in the shape of an essay. I think it is rot, but the Editors appear
to like it.'

The essay he refers to is called 'Ghost Stories'. It began with the
supposition that

Everyone . . . has an innate love of the supernatural. Everyone can remember a
time when he has carefully searched his curtains—and poked in the dark
corners of his room before retiring to rest—with a sort of pleasurable
uncertainty as to whether there might not be a saucer-eyed skeleton or a
skinny sheeted ghost in hiding somewhere. I invariably go through this
ceremony myself. Of course we all know there are no such things,—but some
one might be going to play us a trick, you know; and anyhow, it's best to be
quite sure. People do tell such odd stories.

Such, he went on, was the substance of most people's expressed views
about ghostly phenomena, though sometimes in debate 'one audacious
mortal opposes—rarely more. I pity that rash individual when he seeks
his couch.'

He continued the theme of ghost stories in the fourth number of the
Rambler, drawing attention to the lack of a really adequate collection of
supernatural tales, veridical and fictional. If he were to compile such
an anthology he would exclude the well-worn (' . . . in 18—, Mrs C—,
a respectable lady residing in the small town of D— . . . ', and so on);
he felt that the teller of supernatural tales 'should assume the tone of
one who believes in the truth of what he is relating'. The narrator
should also occasionally stoop to the incredible, 'by which I mean the
sort of tale which deals in blood and bones, and sheeted spectres, and
other phenomena in the nature of walking undertakers' advertise-
ments'.

The bulk of this article consists of an anecdote, for which Monty
claimed to have 'perfectly unexceptionable evidence, possessing, as I
do, an intimate acquaintance with the sources'. This claim to
authenticity may be doubted: the later ghost stories contain a number
of ingenious devices designed to enforce the suspension of disbelief in
the frankly incredible. This appeal to 'unexceptionable evidence'
is probably an early example of this. There are other proleptic touches:
the skeletal form in its tattered shroud, its skinny, clawed

hands, the fact that the incident takes place on the north side of the church (cf. the burial of Mrs Mothersole in 'The Ash-tree'), the leaving of a small but sufficient loophole for reason (it *may* all have been a dream). On the other hand, it is possible that Monty may have been told something that he believed in. Whatever the source, the story is worth quoting in full:

A 'belated wanderer' arrived at a country village too late to procure a lodging for the night. As the season was summer, and the night fine, he determined to sleep out-of-doors, and actuated by some inexplicable impulse, he pitched his camp in the churchyard. He laid himself down under a buttress on the north side of the building, and in blissful ignorance of the fact that he was surrounded by the graves of murderers and suicides (who were there, as is often the case, buried on the north side of the church), he fell asleep. After a while he awoke with a dim and unpleasant consciousness that something was pulling at his clothes. Rather startled by this, he hastily got up and looked around him. Above him the moon was shining, through the windows of the tower, and the bells stood out sharply and clearly against it. Beyond the churchyard he could see hills and woods, and in the valley below him a broad mere on which the moon was shining. So after admiring the view for some minutes he was just composing himself to sleep again, when the moonlight caught an object nearer to him—almost at his feet in fact. Nothing less than two glassy eyes belonging to a form that crouched there in the long grass. It was covered with what looked like a stained and tattered shroud, and he could dimly discern its long skinny clawed hands, eager, as it seemed, to grasp something. Further particulars did not possess sufficient interest to detain him. The terms 'walked', 'ran', or even 'proceeded' are scarcely adequate to express the pace at which he put distance between himself and the churchyard. Suffice it to say he left.[4]

*   *   *

At the end of 1880 Monty told his tutor that he had never been happier, which Luxmoore thought augured well for Monty's academic success at Eton. He was still worried, however, about his pupil's tendency to stray from the high road of the old classical tradition. He told Herbert James: 'He dredges the deeps of literature for refuse, as I told him after his very amusing and clever paper on "fabulous animals". But it may be fairly answered that out of the seeming refuse comes the evidence on which one bases the cosmic histories, and I hope he will so use it hereafter.'

Certainly Monty showed some impatience with routine chores: 'I have to do a Theme (Latin) of the usual stock type . . . wherein you are expected to write enough idiomatic and patriotic Latin platitudes to cover three pages or more of paper.' There was some wilfulness, too: 'Last Sunday I introduced the Head Master to the Acts of Thomas in my Sunday Q[uestion]s. I always begin on every one with the Acts of Thomas. They are a healthy and imaginative production, though slightly tinged with Gnostic vagaries.'[5]

With this determination to proceed on his own terms went a slightly supercilious attitude towards certain of his seniors—Edward Peake Rouse, for example, who had the misfortune of trying to teach him mathematics. 'He is a sort of fiend,' wrote Monty.

Rouse is hanxious that we should learn by 'eart the Sixth Book of Heuclid. But it will be of no use to us hereafter . . . We will have none of him: but I fear capitulation must be the final result. We have made application to be removed from his reach but he does not see 'ow the School would go on if discipline were broken through like that, so will not let us go.[6]

A similar tone is taken in a letter of December 1881: 'I have been to several beaks lately. On Sunday to [E.D.] Stone to tea. Poor dear man. His society is sometimes very depressing. He has a large family and is painfully conscious of it though he is very fond of them. That little idiot Vaughan [another master] was there too. He is really an exceedingly virtuous little man, but I can't abear his conversation.'

He now had a fag, R. E. Myddelton-Biddulph—'slow but makes very good toast'—and a number of activities confirmed his increasing social prominence in the school, although they also took up a good deal of his spare time and placed severe strains on his limited resources. He often tried unsuccessfully to persuade his father to let him draw on his savings: 'If not', as he wrote on one occasion in October 1880, 'I must apply to you, please, as I have three societies, Literary, Natural History, and College Pop, to pay, besides supporting the mess* in a certain degree.'

College Pop was a debating club of senior Collegers, which took its name analogically from the more celebrated Eton Society, known generally as Pop (a word of doubtful etymology). Monty had been elected to College Pop in July 1880 but did not speak until September, when he advocated Home Rule in a debate on Ireland. (His rather illiberal conclusion was that the Irish were 'a radically vicious people'.) He determinedly opposed a motion in October 1881 that 'The distinctive dress of Collegers should be abolished', appealing for

* Contributing victuals to tea, or to Sixth Form supper.

loyalty to the Founder's wishes and arguing that to abolish the gown would be an act of simple ingratitude towards King Henry. The Founder's statutes, he said, had been sufficiently tampered with already, so much so that 'any miserable man—Bradlaugh or Huxley—might be Provost'. As for gowns, no one had the right in his view to do away with 'so ancient and harmless an institution'.[7]

One further College Pop debate may be noted, occasioned by A. E. Brooke's motion 'That we need not believe in ghosts'. It all depended, Monty said, on what one meant by belief; for himself, 'he could not but believe in anything and everything when in bed'. Further, did not Mr Brooke's scepticism indicate a tendency to disbelieve in a future state, and indeed in the Bible itself? According to Monty, something like ten out of every hundred ghost stories had some basis of truth in them: they were dismissed simply because people did not like the idea of such things happening.[8]

Monty was among the first members of the Shakespeare Society, founded in the spring of 1881 by two masters, Francis Warre Cornish and Frank Tarver, and Warre Cornish's wife Blanche. The Shakespeare Society was to mean a great deal to Monty, who resumed his association with it on returning to Eton as Provost in 1918, by which time Luxmoore had taken over the presidency from Frank Cornish. As a Colleger, Monty also read Shakespeare privately with Arthur Benson and Harry Cust (an Oppidan), and it was with Cust and Benson that one June night, after a meeting of the Shakespeare Society, he broke bounds, feeling that the night was too lovely for going straight home from the Cornishes. They wandered up the Slough Road, clambered over the Wall, and roamed as far as Sixth Form Bench, where they sat and looked at the river and listened to the Guards' Band at the Castle playing 'The Lost Chord' to Queen Victoria as she sat at her dinner. 'I have never forgotten the atmosphere of that June night', he wrote in *Eton and King's*.

It was with Benson also, aided by some other friends, that Monty concocted a paragraph that was inserted in the *Boy's Newspaper* under the heading 'News from Schools':

ETON SECOND ELEVEN. The first match of our cricket season was played in the college playing fields on Saturday, the 7th. Mr Macnaghten's Eleven scored 87 and Mr Remington White-Thomson's 108.

Mr White-Thomson's side owed their victory to the splendid innings (62) of A. C. Benson, Esq., our composition Master, and Little (56). The bowling of the Hon. E. Wood and Sir M. James was very noticeable . . .[9]

'A cruel hoax perhaps,' Monty admitted, 'but they are forever mis-stating Eton facts and matches, so that they have made themselves quite fair game.'

In September 1881 he succeeded Arthur Benson as President of the Literary Society and soon afterwards was elected to Pop, confirmation that he had now reached the highest levels of Etonian society. Pop had been founded in 1811 ostensibly as a debating club, but gradually eligibility became associated with boys of 'social weight', often sportsmen.[10] In time, Pop became a ruling élite: 'If you were in Pop,' wrote Eric Parker, 'the whole of the Eton world was yours.'[11] Monty spoke in his first Pop debate soon after his election, supporting St Clair Donaldson, a fellow detester of mathematics, on the question 'Whether Classics or Mathematics are the most desirable branch of education?'

Two Pop debates in particular show how early his opinions were fixed on certain issues. The first concerned the restoration of ancient buildings. Monty, appealing to the authority of Ruskin, insisted that ancient buildings belonged to the men who built them: 'it was only our duty to preserve them for posterity if we could do so without altering them. *Restoration* was unjustifiable, *reparation* was beneficial.' He instanced Eton Chapel, declaring that the removal of the Corinthian stalls and organ loft and the irreverent treatment and partial destruction of the medieval wall paintings (which he was later to be instrumental in uncovering) were among the worst crimes of the century. The second debate once more emphasized Monty's loyalty to the Founder. It concerned the post-Commission Governing Body, which was dismissed as 'rather an unnecessary institution' and a 'flagrant violation of our pious and royal Founder's wishes'.[12] This *pietas* towards the artefacts, buildings, and institutions of the past never weakened.

*   *   *

As Monty James's last year at Eton approached, Luxmoore was able to report: 'He seems very happy and very wholesome, and he is now an influence in College and increasingly useful.' With his friend St Clair Donaldson, Monty was co-editor of the *Chronicle* for 1881–2, at a wage of fifteen shillings per number. It has been possible to identify some of his anonymous contributions by consulting the L. V. Harcourt set of the *Chronicle* at Eton, which has partial attributions, probably in

Harcourt's hand.* Of these 'literary aspirations' Monty wrote in *Eton and King's*: 'Some devastating attempts at humour are to be found—but I hope no one will look for them—in my numbers.' Though the humour perhaps deserves his irony, some of the pieces are of interest in relation to his mature ghost stories, for they reveal his exceptional gift for linguistic mimicry. One of them, for instance, contains extracts from a fictitious fifteenth-century Etonian's diary; another purports to be a transcript, in Latin, of a document found in a copy of Durandus' *Rationale Divinorum Officiorum*.

In January 1882 he sat the scholarship examination for King's and was bracketed first with an outstanding mathematician. The standard, Herbert Ryle (who had been elected to a King's Fellowship in 1881) told Monty's father, had been high, 'Montie [sic] more strong and rough than polished as a scholar, as you have often said.' Writing to Herbert James, J. E. C. Welldon, a Fellow and tutor of King's and one of the examiners, had only one criticism to make of Monty, which was that he wished his style were equal to his knowledge: 'Nobody can examine him and not conceive a great respect for his ability, yet I thought his work would often be more telling if he did not seem to fling down his information in a slapdash, almost defiant manner, without much effort to order or marshal it.'

Just before Easter, Monty sat the Newcastle examination for the third time. 'As you may imagine,' he told his father, 'I have not much news, having spent fourteen hours of the last two days in writing.' As everyone had probably expected, he took the Scholarship, allowing Luxmoore to remark that 'he could not have got more Eton distinction'.

At Easter, as a reward for winning the Newcastle, Luxmoore again took Monty abroad, this time to Florence. Monty travelled down to London from Suffolk by train, 'accompanied by heat and babies', and met his tutor at the Savile Club. At Sens they inspected the cathedral and its treasury: 'We saw there the finest tapestry in the world I should think. Flemish, an Adoration of the Magi and other large pieces which took my tutor's fancy very much as tapestry is his peculiar vanity.' On their first Sunday in Florence Monty attended the English church but was highly critical of the reading and the preaching. The walk to the

---

* Lord Harcourt, who donated his collection of some 2,000 books on Eton to the school in 1916, wrote to Monty in 1897 to enlist his help in identifying *ECC* contributors for 1881–2.

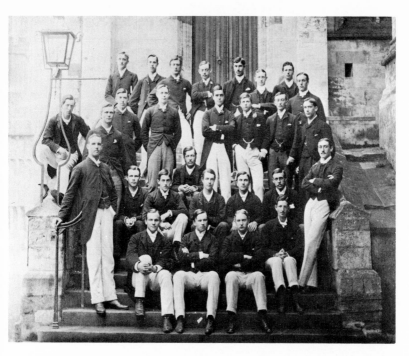

The Eton Society (Pop), 1882. Monty sits alone in the middle of the picture. To his left, seated in the second row, is Henry Babington Smith and to Smith's left in the front row is St Clair Donaldson

Monty and friends in Greece, 1883. *Left to right*: Sydney James, Stuart Donaldson, Walter Durnford, Cecil Baring, Monty, and St Clair Donaldson

Monty as Peithetairos in *The Birds*, 1883

TAF (Twice a Fortnight) group, Cambridge, June 1887. Monty is standing third from the left, with his hands on Ted Butler's shoulders. H. B. Smith sits on the far left, with Lionel Ford next to him. St Clair Donaldson stands second from the right

church had been 'absolutely bewildering. There is I suppose no place anything at all like Florence.' He visited the Bargello and was captivated by Donatello's David; he also saw 'the most hideous wax representation of the plague. People dying and dead ... and decomposing in all stages.' They met Herbert Ryle and his 'young woman ... He separated from her when he saw us and greeted us with perspiration on his brow.' Monty watched Ryle with amusement: 'He could not be away from her two minutes but ran off at once. We have not seen him since.' The return journey was enlivened by an avalanche, which briefly inundated them as they crossed the Simplon.

As the last of Monty's school-days slipped past, the pleasures of that final summer at Eton were doubly sweet: 'Clad in a simple towel, one baked on the Acropolis* and looked at the Castle shimmering in the heat, and, with the smell of the river in one's nose, was conscious of complete happiness.' With spirits not yet damped by the sadness of leaving Eton he made a series of illegal explorations on the roof of St George's Chapel: 'Walking on St Barnabas' day through the Cloisters at Windsor I saw a ladder leading to the roof of the said cloisters. Wood who was with me said "You won't go up that ladder." I said (with characteristic boldness) "I will." So I went up and looked around. I approached the East window of St George's and poked it with my umbrella.' A week or so later he returned with another boy and explored more fully, purloined a mop, and left it protruding through the battlements. 'We explored all the aisle roofs except the Eastern half of the North aisle, and very nearly effected an entrance into the Queen's private pew of which the outer door was open. (P.S. If the lock had been a little less stiff we should have done it. *And there would* have been a row.)'[13]

The Fourth of June, the day when Eton celebrates George III's birthday, brought Speeches (declamations by Sixth Formers before the Provost, Head Master, and guests, who included that year the Prince and Princess of Wales). Monty's performance of Horace's *Ibam Forte* apparently brought the house down and made it difficult for H. B. Smith to follow him with George Eliot's *Spanish Gypsy*. He also took part in a scene from Sheridan's *The Critic*, and one from Molière's *Le Bourgeois Gentilhomme*. Finally, on his own, he recited Milton's 'Lycidas'. This last, the *Chronicle* pronounced, 'lost nothing of its

---

* Part of the river bank opposite the Windsor racecourse where there was a raised diving platform.

exquisite grace and unapproachable pathos from the recitation of James, and its introduction sounded, not too loudly, a chord to which all hearts were responsive.'

The reference here was to a recent tragedy: the drowning of Seton Donaldson, St Clair's younger brother, on 24 May, the first fatal boating accident at Eton for forty years. 'Every one who knew anything of the three brothers must feel it most deeply,' Monty told his parents. 'Their family has always been most united . . . How St Clair will stand it I cannot think.' St Clair, in fact, was 'nearly mad', as Sydney James told Harry Cust.[14] (It had fallen to Sydney to break the news to the eldest Donaldson brother, Stuart, also a master at Eton.)

Seton Donaldson's death affected Monty profoundly, even though he hardly knew the boy. In spite of this, the memory of the incident and its effect on him remained with him for the rest of his life. 'A few', he wrote in his obituary notice of St Clair in 1935, 'will remember vividly the tragic death of his younger brother Seton.'[15] There is no indication that the tragedy seeded religious doubts in Monty's mind: rather, his belief in the ultimately loving intentions of the Creator seems to have been strengthened. What does emerge is that, following this unlooked-for intrusion of death, he began to develop a sense of his own unworthiness—a consciousness that he lacked deeply rooted principles. Seton Donaldson became a pattern of what Monty felt his life ought to be. By all accounts, Seton was just the kind of boy to bring to mind an acute sense of one's own shortcomings, especially if one had been brought up, as Monty had, to believe that rectitude and godliness were prerequisites of salvation. As the *Eton College Chronicle* put it in its obituary number on 1 June: 'Of how many of us could our friends say that we have never been known, in word or deed, to swerve from the course of Christian purity and honour? In saying this of SETON DONALDSON, we merely state what we believe is a fact.' Monty's inability to sustain this level of uprightness is clearly expressed in a letter to his friend Henry Babington Smith, written from Livermere a month or so after he finally left Eton:

It seems strange, but I find it ever so much easier to backslide here than at Eton. I seem to have no principles or object in life at all here and I am sorry to say am much more inclined to be irreverent and so on than where others were ready to join. It only shews how little real principle one had to guide one there [i.e. at Eton]. I expect an idea analogous to that of 'scoring off' people—the idea that others didn't like to see one act differently—had its effect—conceit in another form.[16]

With Dr Hornby's permission, Monty went down to Bere Court, the Donaldsons' home near Pangbourne, to do what he could to help the family in their grief. Lady Donaldson, a widow since 1867, serene, serious, and dignified, lived with her sister, the Baroness von Brandt, and a companion, Miss Adie Browne, whom Monty seems to have become quite fond of. Monty felt drawn to Bere Court and the high-minded Donaldsons. In January 1883, just before his second term at King's, he described Bere as 'just the place to set one up morally—and goodness gracious, how I want some such process at present . . . Lady Donaldson makes you feel you would cut your throat in five minutes if it would afford her any relief.'[17]

St Clair was a few months younger than Monty, but they had both entered Eton in 1876, St Clair as an Oppidan. He was a good sportsman but had academic ability as well, gaining a place in the Newcastle Select in 1882, the year Monty was Scholar. Even at Eton he seemed destined for a Church career, holding prayer meetings in his room and generally exuding an aura of natural piety that was an immediate bar to what was then considered 'mean or loose language'.[18] It was perhaps the strength of St Clair's principles that most impressed—and attracted—Monty, who saw St Clair as 'an example which every one who came into touch with him loved and yearned to follow'.[19]

Monty wrote a public tribute to Seton for the *Chronicle*—a piece of unusually mature and resonant prose:

And we, whom he has left behind, however bitterly we mourn, as comfortless, yet know that for us, too, there *is* comfort, and that we shall meet again. We know that by that dark path our dear friend passed forth into the very centre and fulness of Eternal Day; for the Lord God giveth him light, and he shall reign for ever and ever. We know that he, having fought the good fight, and having overcome, hath entered into the temple of his God, whence he shall go no more out. We know that his eyes are looking upon the King in His beauty, and that they shall evermore behold Him in the land that is very far off.

Verily, it is well with him now.

In private, he sought expression for his feelings in verse addressed to 'dear St Clair', 'truest of brothers'.[20] As he wrote many years later in *Eton and King's*: 'The name of Seton Donaldson remains among the sacred things.'

Two letters from Arthur Benson, by then an undergraduate at King's, are of importance for filling in some of the background of what

was for Monty a significant moral crisis. 'One of the thoughts that
came upon me most and made the leaving of Eton so hard to bear',
wrote Arthur, 'was how little one had ever done: and of course it is all
the harder for you now, when you see how much the unobtrusive and
unseen efforts of one, hardly known in the school, have done.' Arthur
went on:

Though I neither wish or care to pay compliments, I cannot help feeling that
your example is doing as much or more for good than most in College now—as
I *know* it did in my last year . . . I don't say this in the least merely to please
you—but I am sure that in some cases, it is best to tell the truth. And I do not
believe that a conscientious and religious life, however unassuming, is thrown
away in a community.[21]

Arthur's other letter gives further indication of Monty's involvement: 'One's last year at Eton is not generally very improving, I think,
except for the downfall which follows it, but most last years are not so
momentous as yours. It is the sort of trouble which must come later,
but leaves a much deeper impression the earlier it comes.'[22]

But Seton's death could not wholly blight that last blissful summer
at Eton, which brimmed over with simple pleasures—walks, expedi-
tions, easy and affectionate companionship, afternoons on the river,
gooseberries and tea at Cookham. Over everything hung the haunting
magic of those final summer nights, when Monty would lie in bed in
the top Tower room of New Buildings:

I don't know what I thought about when I listened to the Weir and the clocks
and the chimes, and smelt the perfume of the lime-blossom in the Long Walk,
but if I had been capable of writing poetry, I daresay I should have written it
then. A still summer night in one's last half at Eton! I ought to have been filled
with great projects for the public good, and wonderings as to what I was going
to be and do. But I am sure there was none of that, only a sense of how kind a
mother Eton was . . . [23]

The thought of only three more Sundays at Eton was horrible and he
felt rather helpless in the face of the 'leaving depression'. On 7 August,
Luxmoore wrote his last report to Monty's father:

I have no doubt of his continuing to do well. He loves knowledge far more than
marks and prizes, and loves something better than knowledge, which is better
worth having . . . This school time has both vivified his conscience for higher
things and at the same time opened his eyes to the value of lower things . . . He
has been useful in many ways at Eton, to others besides himself, specially
useful to me. I am very grateful to you for the charge of him.

Monty's birthday that year was not, he said, a particularly cheerful one. He said his goodbyes, though he would be seeing several of his friends at Cambridge in the autumn, and set off to camp with the Rifle Corps at Ashridge Park, Berkhamsted, where there was a private chapel whose glass was later to figure prominently in 'The Treasure of Abbot Thomas'. From Ashridge he returned briefly to Eton and faced 'the dreadful business of packing up'. He told H. B. Smith that 'It was worse leaving one's room I think than almost anything else'.

'Well, dear old boy,' his father had written in July, 'years come and years go, but it will take a long time to get the taste of Eton out of our mouths—and for you, at least, there is not much of bitter in that taste.'

Nor was there.

CHAPTER 6

KINGSMAN
King's College, Cambridge, 1882–1883

It occurs to me occasionally like a bad dream that we have left
Eton, but I don't often think of it.

M. R. James to H. B. Smith, 27 August 1882

FOR much of August 1882 Monty was in Switzerland, climbing with
Stuart and St Clair Donaldson, though he admitted to Henry
Babington Smith that: 'I don't think if I was by myself I should be an
eager Alpist.' At one point there was an appalling drive in a kind of
covered wagon:

There was a man like Wintle ten years younger without whiskers, and two
Brocas-cads* in the coupé who aggravated us intensely. Inside was a fat man
who spat, two dirty Italian men, and a dirtier Italian woman, and dirtiest of all a
cutaneously afflicted baby of the same race . . . Towards the end of the day the
Italian woman produced pears and began imparting them to her infant as a
pigeon does. I nearly succumbed.[1]

In Constance their hotel was a former monastery and exhibited all
manner of abominations: 'The church is the dining room—what would
Ruskin say!' It was at Constance that Monty had the most pathetic
dream he ever remembered—'about bringing Seton back to life—
wonderfully vivid'. They spoke little of Seton, but it was clear to Monty
that he was often in Stuart and St Clair's thoughts. Stuart seemed to
derive less benefit from the trip than St Clair, who was 'quite a
different person—revived in a most extraordinary way'.[2]

Back at Livermere once more there was lawn tennis and rowing on
the mere to while away the remaining few weeks of the summer
holiday. Monty also amused himself by playing on a barrel organ in a
neighbouring church, reading Blake, and visiting Ely:

* The term 'cad' gradually began to die out at Eton around the turn of the century. It
was applied to all sorts of boys (and men) from the town. The Brocas lay on the Eton side
of the river and took its name from the family that formerly owned the land.

I knew it before but it is always delightful, a stupendous church with pure Norman west front. They have dealt very cruelly with it inside of course. There is one tomb in particular, Bishop de Luda's . . . which a late Dean has had painted all over one side with patterns resembling a cheap lodging house wallpaper on red and arsenic green grounds: in some smaller tracery openings he has inserted pieces of glass such as you have in the windows of WC's . . . I examined all of it very carefully and came to the conclusion I had never seen anything so heartless or so useless.[3]

Towards the end of September, Sydney James and Henry Broadbent arrived at Livermere. There was already 'an amusing young Scotchwoman (what a hideous word) in the house whom we took pains to impress with the idea that whatever she did she must not laugh at Broadbent. We then put her opposite to him at dinner and her misery and efforts to suppress mirth afforded much pleasure.'[4]

Just before Monty went up to Cambridge that October, his father was urged to accept an important King's living, Prescot in Lancashire. Sydney seemed rather keen on the idea, whilst conceding that Prescot would be 'a beastly hole' to live in. Grace, on the other hand, was considerably relieved when her father eventually turned the offer down. 'We ain't going to Prescot after all,' she told Monty, who was by then in Cambridge. 'It is a beastly squalid place, and the house in very bad repair, and the atmosphere nasty . . . I wish I were not a consideration in the matter, but I cannot help not being stronger, and fortunately it is not only on my account that Father declines.'[5]

Worries about Grace's health also led to the suggestion that she and Mary Emily should spend six months in the south of France, though in fact this idea was eventually discarded. Monty therefore went up to King's in some uncertainty as to whether or not the family would be leaving Livermere for Lancashire and rather put out by the idea of Grace and his mother having to be away for so long.

The prospect of his new life in Cambridge did not seem to elate him. Indeed, after receiving a telegram asking him to write a leader for the *Chronicle*, he gave in to a wave of nostalgia for the life he had left behind. 'Don't you feel very morbid at the idea of Eton having begun without you and everybody enjoying themselves there?' he asked Henry Babington Smith. 'I quite wished this morning that I was playing in College Wall game—veritably wished it.'[6]

*   *   *

King's College, like Eton, had undergone significant reforms between the time Herbert James had been there and when his son Monty arrived, as a self-assured and academically distinguished freshman in the autumn of 1882. For over four centuries after its foundation by Henry VI, King's had remained umbilically linked to Eton—sequestered, exclusive, and increasingly infertile: a closed corporation with the right to award the BA degree without a University examination. Agitations that were eventually to prevent King's from becoming a sterile cul-de-sac had already begun before the Royal Commission of 1850–2 started its work and before the accession of Richard Okes as Provost in 1850. Okes was sympathetic to surrendering the degree privilege, which was actually effected on 1 May 1851, before the Commission reported.[7] In 1861 the outcome of another Royal Commission fixed the number of Fellows and Scholars at forty-six and forty-eight respectively. Twenty-four of the new scholarships were reserved for Eton, the rest thrown open to boys from other schools. From 1869 all Kingsmen were required to read for Honours, a unique requirement in Cambridge at this time. As one historian of King's has put it: 'It gave notice that the kind of man who came up simply for sport and other amusements, as many did in those days, should look elsewhere.'[8]

As a result of these and other reforms, King's began to assume a new position amongst Cambridge Colleges, and a new era in its history began. Yet another Royal Commission settled the Statutes of 1882, under which Monty James lived, and set the seal on what was called 'New King's'. But the centuries of being tied to Eton had left their mark. The most valuable legacy of the old order, resulting from a shared experience of Eton, was a tradition in King's, 'knit up with its history', as Monty wrote, 'that the relation between elder and younger should be closer and more familiar than it is in many other places'.[9] Amongst the resident Fellows, Henry Bradshaw in particular developed this traditional cohesion into a prime attribute of the new College as it began to admit non-Etonian 'outsiders'. Monty followed Bradshaw's example, seeing it as one of his principal duties as a don and College officer to make himself accessible to the junior members of King's. More than this, he perpetuated the sense of an enfolding corporate spirit by the example of his own indomitable loyalty to the foundation.

Another consequence, however, of the long association between King's and Eton was the growth of tension between Etonians and outsiders as the numbers of the latter increased. These were the 'rifts' guardedly spoken of in *Eton and King's*:

Some Etonians were suspicious of non-Etonians, feeling, perhaps, that their old sacred preserve was being laid waste by revolutionaries . . . I could tell unedifying stories of collisions such as youth rather welcomes and enjoys. Our elders saw, and regretted, and did all they could to heal breaches: but of course some irreconcilables on both sides stood out.

When Monty was an undergraduate, the Etonians in King's were associated with the so-called Best Set, the leading light in which was Arthur Benson. On the other side were the 'Scallywags', typified by Nathaniel Wedd, who came up to King's in 1883 from the City of London School. It was natural for Monty to fall in with his fellow Etonians, and to some degree he assumed the general outlook of the Best Set. For instance, during the Lent Races of 1884, he reported that 'Wedd the steerer ran us into the bank . . . What could you expect with an Agnostic from the City of London School on board?' This was ungenerous, but the more reprehensible attitudes of the Best Set were fundamentally at odds with Monty's instincts as a peacemaker and he shed them soon enough. He freely admitted, speaking on behalf of his largely Etonian circle, that, 'we were all inclined to look askance on that part of non-Etonian King's which showed (as we thought) an inclination to cast aside tradition. One cannot deny that there was an Eton clique. I think it was inevitable, in that stage of the development of the college, that some cleavage should exist.'[10]

It was also inevitable that there should have been residual unease at the influx of non-Etonians amongst some of the dons. The Provost himself, Dr Okes, though he had acquiesced in the admission of non-Etonians, persisted in doubting that they could really be considered as Kingsmen. This was understandable in a man of Dr Okes's age and background. A younger man, Arthur Tilley, Junior Tutor in 1883 and a rather fastidious ex-Colleger, was another who never felt quite at home in the company of outsiders, but his attitude is harder to defend. He cuts a sorry figure in a celebrated incident, described by Wedd: 'One evening after dining with a company of undergraduates that included Goldie Dickinson,* Tilley ran up to Arthur Benson's rooms, threw himself into a chair and said, "Oh, do give me a cigarette! Thank God my bounders' dinner is over!" ' Benson, 'to whom', commented Wedd tartly, 'such a remark was most agreeable', relayed Tilley's words to others and soon King's 'thrilled

---

* Goldsworthy Lowes Dickinson. Went to Charterhouse and entered King's as a Scholar in 1881.

with indignation'.[11] It was not the only time that an indiscreet remark from Tilley caused trouble, as we shall see.

*   *   *

M. R. James, then, arrived in King's, the only Etonian of his year, for the Michaelmas Term of 1882, and settled himself in rooms in King's Lane (known as 'The Lane', but also 'The Drain') on Number 2 staircase, amidst a rambling collection of tenement buildings, now demolished, that lay between King's and St Catharine's.

He was immediately able to call on an abundance of friends and acquaintances from Eton. At King's, there were several ex-Collegers he already knew, including William Boyle, Hugh Childers, Marcus Dimsdale and, of course, Arthur Benson; but his closest friends, St Clair Donaldson and Henry Babington Smith, were at Trinity, the other main Etonian enclave in Cambridge. At Trinity also were Harry Cust and Herbert Tatham, amongst others. The following summary, in a letter of 25 October, documents a typical week during his first term at King's:

Since Thursday my movements have been erratic, including Friday. Breakfast with Little, I think, lunch at St C[lair]'s. Thursday evening by the way I spent at Baring's. Present himself, Cust, Loder and St C. The usual rag supervened and we had great sport altogether. Saturday I can't remember, except reading and tubbing. *Sunday* a walk with H.B. [Smith] and St C, when we inspected Peterhouse, Christ's, Emmanuel and Jesus Chapels. Monday a blank. Mathematics and Translation paper. Tuesday lectures. Lunch at Leathes, H.B., St C, Benson and Thomson. The afternoon saw me in the University Library . . . Today has seen me doing Mathematics and verses. H.B. and Benson to lunch and a walk with Boyle in the afternoon towards Trumpington where we discovered Elizabeth Woodcock's monument.

Of his many friends, he was particularly attached to St Clair Donaldson. St Clair, as one friend recalled, was 'tall, very fair, with a light moustache, a lithe frame and rather specially square and solid shoulders . . . simple, strong, resolute and gentle'.[12] Another friend summed him up as 'a noble soul in a perfectly proportioned body'.[13] Monty looked forward tremendously to his parents knowing St Clair and hoped that the two families would become 'as intimate as they ought—being both so exceedingly choice'. He took a keen interest in the fortunes of the Third Trinity boat in the University Fours, principally because St Clair rowed stroke, but also because the whole four consisted of Etonians; and he shared his friend's disappointment when doubts as to St Clair's fitness prevented him from rowing for the University. Throughout his first term, Monty tried to see St Clair once a day. They were both elected to the Pitt Club, a concentration of the socially acceptable that Monty described as 'a nice (Eton) institution' and 'a delightful refuge'; and he was pleased to be able to entertain Lady Donaldson, Miss Donaldson and Miss Browne, who appeared early in the term to supervise the furnishing of St Clair's rooms. They came to tea while St Clair was rowing and presented Monty with 'some very choice plates and candlesticks'. Though Seton Donaldson's death had deepened the friendship between Monty and St Clair, it was by no means a solemn relationship, and horseplay—always a feature of Monty's closest friendships— was not infrequent: 'I then called on St Clair . . . He eventually came to my rooms and I speedily originated a rag by hanging his hat on the coal scuttle. Marshall and Thomas thought my book cases were falling and came to see if they could render any assistance. We were at that moment somewhat mixed on the hearthrug.'

On a typical day, which began with a struggle for Monty to get out of bed, there was Chapel at 8 a.m. (compulsory, unless you 'signed in' at the Porter's Lodge before that time) followed by breakfast, after which there might be lectures. In the afternoon, most people took some form of exercise. For Monty, this usually consisted of long walks: a brief period of 'tubbing' (rowing) came to an abrupt end in sleet on a piercingly cold day, when 'the feelings of repulsion for the Cam and its surroundings which had long been festering within me broke out'. He did, however, take lessons on what he called 'a high bicycle'. The machine was presumably of the penny-farthing type and he found it 'a hopeless position . . . The man held me all the time. I am certain I shall never learn it.'[14] It may be that the impetus had come from Henry Babington Smith, who two days earlier had recorded in his diary: 'Rode on a bicycle for the first time after a considerable lapse of time. Got on all right—or rather found getting on the most forgotten part.'[15] Monty persevered, and in time the bicycle proper became his main form of exercise and a much valued pleasure.

Tea would be taken in King's or with friends in Trinity, followed by Chapel at five—not compulsory this time, unless Monty, as a scholar of the College, was required to read the lesson. Hall was at six, with coffee and conversation afterwards; then work, and then abroad once

more to see friends, sometimes until the early hours of the morning:
'At the end of the *séance*, on a fine night, you would perambulate the
court. It is at twenty minutes to two a.m. that you may hear in late
October the wild geese coming over King's.'[16] On Sundays, when
morning Chapel was at ten, there might be a breakfast party and
usually an informal lunch. In the evening, a variety of gatherings—an
Oscar Browning 'At Home', a 'Hell' in Harry Cust's rooms in Trinity,
or perhaps, most agreeably, just a meeting of 'half a dozen familiars'.
As he cheerfully conceded, his ideals of University life had always been
'sadly monastic'.

In between his recreations, Monty worked hard. He claimed to have
derived no benefit from formal lectures and preferred to work to his
own plan, which was 'to read everything, not dwelling on minutiae'. He
gained an insight into 'the mind and atmosphere of Greece and Rome'
that was very precious, 'and the process of acquiring it was blissful'.
His advice to contemporary youth in 1925 was: ' "You ought to aim at
being able to take the general sense of a page of Greek or Latin as
easily as that of a page of French." '

An unavoidable hurdle of that first term was the Previous
Examination, better known as the Little-go, an elementary test for all
intending Tripos candidates (corresponding to Responsions at Oxford). It was an annoyance more than anything else, but still, at the end
of November, it seemed 'dangerously near and very dreadful'.
'Tuesday morning,' he wrote when at last it came on. 'Paley [Paley's
Evidences of Christianity] in the Corn Exchange, a dull farce. They treat
you like the beasts that perish in the Little-go. In the afternoon they
made me pay a shilling for being five minutes late. The afternoon
paper was Euclid.' The next day he had to face an Algebra paper
sitting under a leaking roof; but there was consolation afterwards in
meeting Sydney for tea at Harry Cust's and adjourning to King's
Chapel, where the Anthem provided Handelian balm in the form of
Zadok the Priest. 'I have just finished the Little-go,' he told his mother
on 12 December, '—disgusting beyond all description. We are
examined in the Corn Exchange, a hideous place with a glass roof
which sins against all imaginable rules of architecture and is really so
ugly as to make one miserable.'

There was little left of the term after the Little-go (Monty took an
undistinguished Class II). By the early part of December he had said a
reluctant goodbye to St Clair and was preparing to pay a long-
contemplated visit to Arthur Benson at Lis Escop, Truro, where

Arthur's father, Edward White Benson, had been Bishop since 1877.* He showed some consternation at the prospect of Bishop Benson's probable translation to Canterbury happening during his visit: 'What would one say? "I congratulate you" or "Well, I'm sure" or, with Sarah [a family servant], "The hidear of such a thing".'[17] Mr Gladstone's formal offer of the Primacy did indeed arrive during Monty's stay—in fact on Christmas Day. 'It certainly was a very embarrassing situation,' Monty wrote to H. B. Smith. 'I did *not* say "I congratulate you". What I did say must be left to imagination.' From Lis Escop Monty joined Grace in Torquay for the rest of Christmas Day, the plan to winter on the Riviera having been abandoned. Torquay he thought a beautiful place, and not really like England; whilst there he visited a 'highly Ritualistic Church' and derived some amusement from what he called 'the most scandalous hymnbook I ever saw', in which was a hymn to St Anne praising the saint as the 'long expected day' that had dawned on a benighted heathen world. He seemed a little indignant that the hymnal professed to be Church of England.[18]

From Torquay he went to Bere Court for a night, though he had planned to stay longer. He told H. B. Smith: 'I am afraid Christmas brought with it other than cheerful thoughts. I do not know that I ever felt half so mean and small as when brought face to face with Seton's memory.' A postscript wished Babington Smith a happy new year: 'It seems unlikely as far as one can see that it can bring either of us as much good as last, but who knows. Anyhow, last year will not be forgotten.'

*   *   *

At the end of January 1883 Monty and Babington Smith were elected to the Chitchat Society, founded in 1860 and to which Sydney James had also belonged. Monty described the typical form of meetings in a prefatory note to the Minute Books:

They were held at 9.45–10 p.m. on Saturdays at the rooms of the reader of the paper, who provided coffee, a cup, and *whales* (anchovy toast). Minutes were read and a snuffbox (presented by F. W. Maitland) passed round . . . of which all members were supposed to partake. It will be found by various entries in the minutes that Mr Tilley was recalcitrant in this matter. A paper and discussion followed and out-college members departed at or about midnight.[19]

---

*   Monty had already met Bishop Benson at Eton in July 1881. Lis Escop is the setting of E. F. Benson's story 'Pirates' (in *More Spook Stories*, 1934), where it is called 'Lescop'.

It was generally supposed that the Chitchat was the main recruiting ground for that more celebrated sodality The Apostles. The theory was that a newly elected (and unsuspecting) Chitchat member would be taken out for an afternoon stroll by an investigating Apostle and discreetly examined as to his suitability for membership. 'You might be found wanting,' Monty recalled, without a trace of regret. 'If the experiment was ever tried on me, as to which I am in doubt, that certainly was the result.'

The claret cup, snuff and 'whales' were ritual trappings borrowed from The Apostles, but the Chitchat had only modest intellectual pretensions and its papers were rather more of an excuse for conviviality than a *raison d'être*. The first of Monty's many papers was given in May 1883, on 'Useless Knowledge'. Over the next few years he read others on a wide range of subjects, from 'The Beginnings of Christian Fiction' and 'Church Portals' to 'France' and 'Sheridan Le Fanu'. 'The Beginnings of Christian Fiction' was probably one of a number of subjects on which he had seized in desperation when obliged to give a paper; but, as he said, he took encouragement by looking back at what the Society had been offered in the past: 'When I read for instance that . . . we have sat still and listened to an effusion on the aesthetic aspect of Ethics or the standpoint of Determinism—I feel that my subject is likely to appeal as much to your inner sense now as either of these subjects would have appealed to mine.'[20]

The Chitchat was to be one of Monty's regular social pleasures for the next ten years or so and was important in establishing him as the centre of an ever-widening circle of friends and admirers. It expired informally in 1897, 'of inanition'. A later offshoot, dear to Monty's heart, was the TAF (Twice a Fortnight), though his association with it did not begin until the autumn of 1886. The name had been coined by J. K. Stephen* and the idea was for a weekly gathering of friends from King's and Trinity, meeting on Sunday evenings instead of going into Hall, which, Monty said, was intolerable on Sundays.[21] Like the Chitchat, and indeed the Best Set in general, the TAF consisted of well-defined social types and was well stocked with Etonians and Harrovians. From the start, Monty was the central figure and by 1890, when he quietly dissociated himself from its exclusiveness, it had

---

* J. K. Stephen, an occasional member of Monty's circle of friends, was a brilliant and much admired Etonian and Kingsman who died insane in 1892, at the age of thirty-three. He was a cousin of Virginia Woolf.

become what one member called the 'Love-feast of the Clan'—an apt image for the vivid group of which Monty was the undisputed head:

The clan of friends met, so to speak, under the informal hegemony of Monty James ... When dinner at the TAF was over, Monty ... might be induced to read about the birthday-party of the Kenwigses [from *Nicholas Nickleby*], with a cigarette sticking to his upper lip, where it bobbed up and down to his articulation, until a shout of laughter on the reader's part over Mr Lillyvick's glass of grog, cast it forth on to the hearth-rug.[22]

Conversation at the TAF was what Monty was pleased to call 'trivial'. There was a good deal of mimicry, with Monty as the leading performer; and there were rags. Cyril Alington, later Head Master of Eton and Dean of Durham, omitted from a description of the TAF 'for reasons of piety' St Clair Donaldson's recollection of writhing on the floor 'with Monty James's long fingers grasping at his vitals'.[23]

Year by year new friends joined the fold. In King's, these included Leo Maxse and Walter Headlam from Harrow, Dighton Pollock from Wellington and Lionel Ford from Repton; at Trinity there were William Bridgeman and John Stirling-Maxwell, both Etonians. As Lionel Ford wrote of Monty: 'He was the centre of our group, never seeking people out, but letting people find him, and then with apparently endless time at their disposal.'[24] Monty and Ford remained good friends until Ford's death in 1932. Of their almost daily meetings as undergraduates Monty wrote simply but sincerely: 'One knows that more than most things they gave a relish to life, made for affection, and closened friendship.'[25]

For a brief period from 1883 Monty was drawn into the Cambridge circle of Prince Albert Victor (known as Prince Edward or Prince Eddy), the eldest son of the Prince of Wales. Prior to the Prince's residence in Trinity at Michaelmas 1883, J. K. Stephen had been enlisted to supplement the coaching of Albert Victor's tutor, the Revd J. N. Dalton, and to introduce the young man to companions of the right sort, many of them friends of Monty's. Henry Babington Smith and Harry Cust were among those summoned to Sandringham who subsequently formed a kind of Etonian escort to the Prince while he was at Trinity. Monty received reports from his friends during the summer of 1883 to the effect that Prince Eddy was 'rather dull but well disposed'.

The 'Pragga' is mentioned several times in Monty's letters. In January 1885 he dined with him in his rooms in Nevile's Court: 'As is usual on these occasions we played a good deal of whist afterwards. It is very difficult to engage the Pragga in conversation for any length of time, but he is very easily amused.' In June of that year the Prince actually called on Monty unannounced during a visit by Grace: 'He is not at all formidable,' Monty wrote, 'but I hate presenting people to him.' After leaving Trinity, Prince Eddy sent him 'a very good engraving of his physiognomy', and in March 1885, having already met 'the younger Pragga', the future George V, Monty was introduced to the Prince of Wales himself.

Amongst the King's dons Monty soon made the acquaintance of Henry Bradshaw, paying his first call, apparently, in December 1882.* Bradshaw's role in the development of New King's has already been touched on; in addition, he had been University Librarian since 1867 and by 1882 was a scholar with an international reputation—a world expert on early printed books, a palaeographer and a specialist in, amongst other things, liturgical history. Around him gathered 'a curiously assorted coterie of Cambridge youth',[26] including many 'outsiders'. In his rooms in Wilkins' Buildings he would hold court, often caressing the hand of some favoured intimate. As his biographer, G. W. Prothero, Senior Tutor of King's from 1881–92, wrote:

All sorts of men used to meet in his room. He never seemed to select his friends; they were drawn to him by some mysterious affinity, having nothing in common but their liking for him. Athletes and students, senior classics and pollmen ... distinguished persons whose name was in every one's mouth, together with the retiring and unknown, sat on the same sofa and forgot their differences in the halo of his presence.[27]

This combination of formidable scholarly accomplishment and 'charisma' was something Monty also had, and many came to see him as Bradshaw's legitimate successor. Monty paid tribute to both aspects of Bradshaw's greatness, though particularly to the pioneering methodology of his scholarship, in *Eton and King's*:

Beyond the personal influence which he exercised (and I have never seen anything more marked; it extended to forming the handwriting of his disciples) there was one great service he rendered to knowledge. He taught that the same methods of exactness and the same love of truth should be the rule for students of bibliography and of art which the great men of his generation were applying to natural science.

* Like Monty, Bradshaw had been to both Temple Grove and Eton. The Henry Bradshaw Society, for editing rare liturgical texts, was founded in his memory in 1890.

For the first time in his life Monty had found someone who knew a great deal more than he did about many of the subjects that had fascinated him since boyhood. 'What curious things did he not know?' he mused years later, the admiration still apparent:

It was he who told me of the devotion of King Henry VII for St Armagilus or Armel. In some sea-peril off the Breton coast the king, then Duke of Richmond (I imagine), had been told to invoke St Armel, and had been preserved. Hence the image of the saint in Henry VII's Chapel and elsewhere, and the occurrence of St Armel in many prayer-books of the time. He it was also who gave me a name for that curious repetition of the first word of an antiphon which is regularly found in the Roman service-books.

At their first meeting, Monty found Bradshaw 'very nice and delightful', and he was given a present—'an interesting pamphlet about Cambridge . . . I am going again soon as he wants to look at my rags of parchment, and then I shall take St Clair after that.' He did continue to call on Bradshaw, but later regretted that he had not done so more often, having been deterred by the difficulty of actually getting near to him: 'All sorts of dons and undergraduates might be there: some of them . . . simply sat there whole evenings and said nothing at all; others monopolised Bradshaw: whereat, as I was bursting with questions I wanted to ask him, I was discontented. It did sometimes happen, though, that one stayed late and got him almost alone. That was delightful.' Sometimes he would be called upon to tickle Bradshaw's palms, while the great man purred. A certain felinity also struck Reginald Brett (Lord Esher), who found Bradshaw's manner 'curiously caressing. He always reminded me of some tawny, heavily built cat.'[28]

It is certain that Monty did not deliberately set out to emulate Bradshaw; but it would have been strange if he had not recognized that his own interests and certain aspects of his temperament closely matched those of Bradshaw and that they would probably eventually place him in a similar position within the College. On the 'pastoral' level, Bradshaw's accessibility and sympathetic qualities perhaps exerted as great, if less conscious, an influence as the technical impact, acknowledged by Monty, of his working methods as a scholar. In this respect, some words at the beginning of the section on Bradshaw in *Eton and King's* could equally apply to Monty himself: 'You felt there was nothing little about him, and the reverence and love he inspired needed no explanation.'

Just as open to undergraduate contact was Oscar Browning, but unlike Bradshaw, Browning had absolutely no distinction as a scholar and his immense egotism made him something of a *bête noir* to Monty. After the Eton disaster, Browning had moved into one of the best sets of rooms in King's and begun living on a scale that he could ill afford. With undergraduates, as with his Eton boys, he tried to be both friend and mentor, offering them a pot-pourri of activities—a Dante Circle, a Mozart Club, his famous Political Society, and his equally famous At Homes. He worked hard for the study of History in King's and built himself a small but successful personal empire in the Day Training College for teachers, which he founded with Henry Sidgwick and of which he was first Principal. But he never achieved high College or University office: he antagonized too many people, and his good intentions were often smothered by financial ineptitude and by his artless snobbery. Above all, he transgressed by the steps he took to avoid the degrading fate of not being known; and yet he had a noble vision of what King's could become, and in many ways was a positive liberating force.

'No young person', wrote Monty, with commendable candour, 'so prejudiced (if you like) in favour of Eton—I would rather say, no one so grateful to Eton—as I was, could judge at all fairly of Oscar Browning.' It was Browning's custom to take Etonian freshmen for walks and then pour out disparagements of Eton while extolling 'the day-school and its least superficially attractive products, in a way which robbed one of all desire to know the rights of the matter'.[29] Monty was 'collared' in this way; indeed Browning's attentions became persistent. 'If you like,' Monty told his father sardonically early in 1883, 'I will procure you an invitation to lunch.' He also found Browning's attempts to press him into the Union unwelcome, telling H. B. Smith: 'I heard from my tutor yesterday. O.B. had been at him to get me to join the Union and speak there, but nary.'

For Monty, it was Browning's attitude towards Eton that placed him irrevocably beyond the pale. How could he be expected to think well of a man who constantly abused the foundation to which he gave his deepest loyalty?

Eton, O.B. was sure, had treated *him* very badly, and therefore it must be a very bad place. *We* didn't care what had happened to him seven years before—who would?—and we knew that Eton had given us a vast deal of what we prized most. We were much fonder of Hornby, who had dismissed him, than we were of O.B., and to hear both Eton and Hornby abused, in what I must say was a very tiresome way, was not our idea of enjoyment.[30]

As for the other senior members of the College, little was seen of the Provost, the aged Dr Okes, and only occasional glimpses were caught of the handful of Fellows elected under the Founder's Statutes who were still in residence. The Vice-Provost was Augustus Austen Leigh, a brother of Monty's former division master at Eton and one of the principal architects of New King's. Austen Leigh was modest, kindly and rather dull and Monty's main contact with him as an under-graduate was through '"letters of regret" that I had not fulfilled the alternative duties of going to Chapel or "signing in" at 8 a.m.' Eventually, Monty was gated (i.e. confined to College) for 'persistence in this evil-doing'. More approachable than Austen Leigh was the jovial and delightful Fred Whitting, Bursar and later Vice-Provost, who, having no roof to his mouth, seemed to strangers to be speaking in an unknown tongue. The prize eccentric in King's was perhaps J. E. Nixon, Junior Dean and a Classics Lecturer when Monty went up. Nixon generated a rich corpus of legend amongst Kingsmen. His mind, said Monty, worked 'like a clock with the pendulum taken off'.

The following incident is typical. Journeying forth on his tricycle one afternoon . . . he came to sad grief at the bottom of the Madingley hill, was picked up and brought home and laid up for three weeks. When restored to health, he went forth again on the mended tricycle, accompanied by his friend George Chawner, to survey the scene of the disaster. 'It was just here,' he said, 'that it happened. I was merely doing like this . . . ' His recollection was doubtless accurate. Over went the tricycle again, and three weeks more in bed were the result.

Monty's memories of Nixon in *Eton and King's* take up ten pages. As he said, to the tale of Nixonisms there was no end.

*   *   *

Early in 1883 Monty suffered from an attack of palpitations, which naturally worried his parents but did not seem to cause him much concern. His tutor, J. E. C. Welldon, writing to Herbert James, thought him 'delicate', although 'intellectually and morally he is all I could wish'. Perhaps it was with Monty's health in mind that Sydney soon afterwards offered to take him to Greece for the Easter vacation.* Stuart and St Clair Donaldson and Walter Durnford were also to go,

---

* The date of the Greek trip is erroneously given in *Eton and King's* (p. 150) as 1885.

and in the event Cecil Baring (Lord Revelstoke's third son, an Oppidan in his last year) also joined them. Sydney magnanimously offered to stand fifty pounds towards Monty's share of the cost, whilst Durnford and Stuart Donaldson agreed to make up the balance between them.

Monty's mother began to apply her mind to those aspects of the trip that most concerned her. On Sydney's instructions she put together quinine (ready-weighed into two-grain doses) and a bottle of Eno's Fruit Salts; on her own initiative she packed 'a box of vaseline—and I intend to add Eau de Cologne . . . Please answer about the flannel belt, that I may set about it, if I am to make it—and if you think of any small useful things to add tell me of them. Have you good socks and stockings enough?'

Thus prepared, Monty and the rest set off in March. From Brindisi they took a steamer to Corfu, Patras and Corinth and made their way to Athens, where they met the archaeologist Heinrich Schliemann. They chartered the services of a dragoman, Apostolis, 'a man of infinite resource'; it was he who provided the travellers with what he called a great delicacy—described by Sydney as 'a large cuttle-fish, stewed in some viscous fluid and surrounded by what looked like brown rosettes, which turned out to be its suckers. It defeated us.'[31] Their itinerary included Delphi, Thebes, and Eleusis. Monty was captivated by the landscape as much as by the architectural and archaeological treasures they had principally come to see. 'What is the name of a place somewhere near Andritzena', he wrote later, 'where the Alpheus river bursts out from under a rock, and a large wild fig-tree grows over it? Labda, I am told. That is the spot I should feel inclined to haunt, and that is the kind of picture which in the end one treasures most.'[32] On their return he wrote to Walter Durnford and Stuart Donaldson to thank them for their subsidies. 'The small sum contributed by me', replied Durnford, 'is a very inadequate return for the pleasure of your society (rather neat that, I think, but oddly enough true) and the knowledge ranging from Pausanias to Privies imparted.'[33]

The succeeding summer term brought Monty's first May Week at Cambridge. He found it 'hideously demoralizing. I cannot work, not that there is much else to be done in the mornings.' The invasion of female relatives disturbed his equilibrium, though he unbent so far as to row the mother and sister of a friend down the Cam. More typical of his attitude is his reference to a 'Miss Holden with the soapy eye.

Tilley is much fascinated by her. I, not.'[34] He never came to terms with May Week: 'I am hanged if ever I stop here again during it,' he wrote in June 1885, when he registered his disapproval of 'the dreadful bustle and dissipation of this most detestable week' by playing funeral anthems by Handel during the King's Ball and watching with displeasure at 'ladies trapesing about the court all day'.

With the autumn of 1883 came preparations for the Greek Play. One of the main events of Monty's first term had been a production of the *Ajax* in Greek, the first Greek Play at Cambridge. As several of his friends had taken part in the *Ajax*, and as his own theatrical talents were probably already well known, it was perhaps inevitable that he would be involved in the following year's production. The choice for 1883 was *The Birds* by Aristophanes, with 'delicious' music by Hubert Parry. Monty was cast for the longest part, Peithetairos,* and work began in earnest that October, often in Monty's rooms (by now a large set on the ground floor of Gibbs' Building that had been previously occupied by Arthur Benson). 'I don't suppose I ever spent a more consistently amusing term,' he recalled. 'There was shaking of heads over the inroads into my working time, but in the end nobody seemed one penny the worse.' (His father's was chief amongst those shaking heads, but Monty wrote him one of his reassuring paragraphs.)

The costumes had been designed to represent 'with some degree of ornithological accuracy both the structure of the wings in general and the form of the beaks of the individual birds'.[35] The scenery was suitably spectacular: a bird's-eye view of the earth as seen through the clouds formed the wings and gave the audience the impression that they were looking down a funnel of vapour, across which the chorus of birds would fly at intervals.[36] The play was performed at the Theatre Royal at the end of November and beginning of December. Harry Cust provided some anxious moments, for not having committed his part to memory, he was forced to rely on opportune whispered prompts from Monty and to fill in the lacunae 'with improvisation in an unknown tongue'. But the production was enthusiastically received and widely reviewed, both in and outside Cambridge. Monty's performance was generally recognized as outstanding. 'Mr James', said one reviewer, 'performed an astonishing feat in thus reciting eight hundred lines of Greek with perfect familiarity, and almost without a

---

* He subsequently played small parts in the 1885 production of the *Eumenides* and the 1887 play, *Oedipus Tyrannos*.

moment's hesitation from beginning to end. His admirable acting was the backbone of the performance.'[37]

Through *The Birds* Monty considerably enlarged his acquaintance with those senior members of the University who had been involved with the play, amongst whom were A. W. Verrall, Henry Jackson, Charles Waldstein and J. W. Clark. John Willis Clark of Trinity, known throughout Cambridge as 'J', was a turbulent but attractive character with whom Monty was to fraternize over France, libraries and Sherlock Holmes. An old Etonian, Clark was a compelling mixture of irascibility, good humour and downright naughtiness; but he was also a delightful companion, a much respected figure in the University and an accomplished scholar with a wide range of interests, from zoology and the theatre to early printed books and hunting. He is perhaps best remembered for completing the *Architectural History of the University and Colleges of Cambridge*, begun by his uncle, Professor Robert Willis. While still an undergraduate, Monty was given the proofs of the part dealing with Eton and King's to read and correct. He was enormously flattered and in carrying out the task gained 'a new view of the way in which scientific method could be applied to the study of the history of buildings'. The *Architectural History*, published in 1886, was dedicated to Henry Bradshaw. Clark's influence on Monty's working habits was probably as important as Bradshaw's; it was, moreover, transmitted through a friendship of some seventeen years, whereas the relationship with Bradshaw, never a particularly close one, lasted only from the latter part of 1882 until Bradshaw's death in February 1886. As with Bradshaw, Monty admired Clark for his readiness to mix with his juniors, many of whom were entertained by 'J' and 'Mrs J' at their home in Scroope Terrace and, from 1885, in Scroope House.

The Birds also led Monty to the Amateur Dramatic Club (ADC), of which J. W. Clark had been treasurer since 1880. Though his father disapproved, Monty got a good deal of pleasure from the ADC, which was then something of a 'jolly, cheerful club', as one member put it, rather than a focus for serious theatrical activities.[38] A typical offering was *The Overland Route*, in which Monty played Sir Solomon Fraser, 'an elderly Anglo-Indian who, wrecked on a desert island, loses his dentures and is reduced to sad straits'.

After the final performance of *The Birds* the cast assembled one snowy morning in the garden of Christ's College to be photographed in their costumes—Monty wearing his 'wedding dress (and nothing else)'. For him, the play and its preparations created what he called 'a halo in memory' and was linked in his mind with the spectacular Krakatoa sunsets then being seen in Cambridge. 'There has been nothing since', he wrote, 'like the sight we used to see as we came out of evening Chapel and looked across the lawn to the belt of leafless trees and the blazing sky.'

CHAPTER 7

A DON IN THE MAKING
King's 1883–1887

> Of the Founder we may have but a dim conception: we can at least
> be sure that his spirit was so righteous and gentle that he would
> have rejoiced in the felicity of his chosen.
>
> M. R. James, *Eton and King's*

IN the four years from 1882 to 1886, besides taking Firsts in both Parts
of the Classical Tripos for his BA degree, Monty fulfilled every
expectation of him by winning a number of prestigious awards.
Together with the emoluments from his Newcastle Scholarship and
his Eton Scholarship at King's, the proceeds from these went a long
way towards financing his university career.

In November 1882, in his first term, he won the Carus Undergraduate Prize for knowledge of the Greek Testament, against strong
competition and in spite of the fact that before the examination he had
felt that the field was 'a hopelessly wide one, for a person who finds
comfort in details'. The following January he gained a place in the
Select for the Craven Scholarship, taking the Scholarship itself, worth
£80 a year for seven years, in 1884. 'I do give you great joy of your
success,' his father wrote with unconcealed satisfaction, 'whilst I am
sure that we shall both of us give thanks where thanks are due.' A note
arrived from J. W. Clark with a postscript that perhaps had Herbert
James in mind as much as anyone: 'How about "The Birds" wasting
people's time—diverting attention from their proper academic aims,
etc, etc!'

One of the two available Bell Scholarships, reserved for sons or
orphans of Church of England clergymen, was secured in 1883; in
December 1884 he was awarded one of the two annual Jeremie
Septuagint Prizes, involving intensive study of the Septuagint text of
the Old Testament; and finally, the winning of the senior Chancellor's
Classic Medal for 1886, gained after he had taken his degree, provided

a triumphant conclusion to Monty's conspicuously successful undergraduate career.

He seemed strangely unmoved by this succession of glittering prizes. What excited him, as it had done at Temple Grove and Eton, was 'finding out about things that interested me.'[1] The pursuit of what interested him continued and developed unobtrusively beneath the surface of his always busy and sociable life, and a good deal of the groundwork for his later scholarship was the result of work done in his spare time between 1882 and 1887.

In March 1883, for instance, he revisited Ely, where Archdeacon Chapman was an old friend of his father's, and began to examine the Lady Chapel sculptures in detail—a mass of figures, set in a rich arcade, decapitated or otherwise mutilated during the Reformation. Monty determined to identify the sculptures, a task hitherto unattempted, and on this visit 'did' about half of them—a formidable display of knowledge, as any visitor to the Lady Chapel can verify. He established that the imagery was based on apocryphal legends of the Virgin and told his father that he intended writing a monograph on them. In fact his researches continued for some years, a paper eventually being presented on the identification of the subjects in August 1892.

The incomparable glories of King's Chapel, of course, were always available to him for study. His interest centred on the windows. Early in 1883 the results of a detailed investigation were relayed with gusto to his father: 'One of the angels—a delightful being in himself—holds a sword with the following very unseraphic inscription: "Egredere egredere uir sanguinum et uir Belial" [2 Sam. 16:7, 'Come out, come out, thou bloody man, and thou man of Belial']! It is of course apropos of the adjacent representation of Shimei cursing David, but it amused me.' Later on, in June, he explored the chantries on the north side of the Chapel and eagerly described some typical detective work:

I found an interesting collection of scraps of lettering which render it certain that those grisaille figures in the Brassie Chapel which you like so much are only relics of a complete series of prophets and apostles. The apostles had each their clause of the creed and the prophets their corresponding prophecies. This pleases me extremely. Another thing I will tell you about the windows at the risk of repeating myself from some former letter. The window about Emmaus has as usual four explanatory scrolls, two of which ought to refer to the N[ew] T[estament] subject and two to their O[ld] T[estament] types*

* A biblical event that symbolizes or foreshadows a later one.

above. As it is, all four are out of the Acts about the Lame Man, Ananias, and
so on. Well, further on there is a window in which all these subjects out of Acts
are represented. Of course you would expect to find the Emmaus scrolls here,
imagining that they had been shifted. But not so. The right scrolls out of Acts
are repeated. The only explanation is that another set of windows like ours
were being made at the same time, and that two copies of their scrolls were
inadvertently inserted.

As often happened, Monty's scientific researches stimulated his
imagination, resulting in a story, 'A Night in King's College
Chapel', about a student of the windows who falls asleep and is locked
in for the night, whereupon the figures in the windows come to life and
begin to talk to each other in very un-biblical language. ' "I may only
be a Type,"' complains Reuben, '"but I ain't goin to be put upon."'[2]

By December 1884 Monty had also begun to work systematically on
the illustrated manuscripts at the Fitzwilliam Museum, writing to his
mother that month: 'I hope to get through half the collection—about
65 out of 130—before I go down. They are mostly what are called
Hours of the Virgin with a few of the services, the Seven Penitential
Psalms and Litany and the Office for the Dead—which formed the lay
people's prayer book.' He gained access to the Fitzwilliam through the
Director, Charles Waldstein, who had been on the Greek Play
Committee for 1883 when *The Birds* was produced.* Waldstein was
also Reader in Classical Archaeology, in which Monty was specializing
for Part II of the Tripos. Monty got on well with him and enjoyed at
one remove the influence of Henry Bradshaw, who had been
instrumental in bringing Waldstein to Cambridge. For Bradshaw,
Monty later wrote, Waldstein had 'an admiration and a reverence
which continued undimmed till the end'.[3] Waldstein began to coach
Monty in the Michaelmas Term of 1884, but as far as the Tripos was
concerned Monty was alarmed at the amount of time he was having to
give to archaeology: '*Sculpture, painting, coins, inscriptions, mythology,
gems*—each of these implies a good deal of reading'.[4]

He had time enough at any rate to press on with his researches at the
Fitzwilliam. Luxmoore, who was shown round the Museum by his old
pupil early in 1885, was pleased to see Monty 'getting his finger into
the University pie in this way and making himself felt as useful already'

---

* Waldstein (an American-German-Jew) became a Fellow of King's in 1894. He was
knighted in 1912 and changed his name to Walston in 1918.

and he reported to Herbert James that the dons at King's were also loud in Monty's favour. Monty seems already to have had an unofficial position at the Fitzwilliam in respect of the manuscript collection, but this was formalized and extended, at Waldstein's instigation, in October 1886, when he was appointed Assistant Director (at the age of twenty-four). He described the appointment offhandedly as 'a post of £100 a year as bottlewasher . . . entailing a very limited attendance'.[5]

Work on the Fitzwilliam manuscripts went on steadily. By May 1887 he had completed descriptions of about 6,000 illustrations (by his own reckoning) and was also working on the illustrated books at Trinity. More importantly, he had realized what needed doing and had conceived the grand ambition of describing the manuscript collections of every college library in Cambridge. It was an ambition few could have formed, and even fewer achieved.

*　　*　　*

Throughout these years Herbert and Mary Emily James watched over their youngest son with unfailing solicitude and insisted on hearing from him regularly, even when (as Monty frequently complained) there was a dearth of news. His letters were eagerly awaited. 'Mother and I had a "rag" this morning over your letter,' his father writes in 1884, 'which she *would* seize! It ended by my putting her head through one of the dining-room windows. The glass was *not* the hardest of the conflicting substances, and the shattered remains with the cold air which plays through them are a monument [to] cerebral solidity.' From his mother, Monty received complaints that no mention was being made in his letters of fresh air and exercise, or that he smoked too much and did not take in enough 'good wholesome food'. Herbert James's concern, naturally, was with Monty's academic progress, but this was always placed in a broader spiritual context, with each academic success being seen as a further instance of God's mercy. In October 1882, when his father was sixty, Monty received a letter thanking him for his birthday greetings:

All loving thanks to you, my dear son, for your good wishes. *Sixty years* marks a great milestone in one's life, and I desire that the rest of it shall be lived as it should—for God's glory. I have much to learn, much to unlearn—God only knows how much. But . . . I have infinitely much to be thankful for, and not the least for my mercies in *you* all. I do desire to thank God for all He has done for you children, and specially for you my son.

Monty's father probably hoped he would take Holy Orders fairly soon after graduating. St Clair Donaldson certainly seemed to think this course was likely when he wrote to Monty in September 1883 about Edward Lyttelton, a contemporary of Sydney's at Trinity, who had been teaching at Eton since the previous year: 'He came almost straight from Cuddesdon where he had been reading Theology and doing brain-cracking, as you and I will have to do someday.' A year later, apropos of his brother Stuart's impending ordination, St Clair wrote: 'My own ordination—and yours (is it not?) is beginning to seem close . . . ' Herbert Ryle took priest's order in 1883; Sydney James received deacon's orders the same year and entered the priesthood in 1897. Edward Lyttelton and Stuart Donaldson were ordained priest together in September 1884, and St Clair took the same step in 1888, which drew from Monty the enigmatic comment: 'Dear, dear, it will be the most considerable acquisition the Church makes this year, I should think.'[6]

The examples of all these probably strengthened the general expectation that Monty would sooner or later make a formal commitment to the Church; but from the start he was beset by doubt—not spiritual doubt, but a fundamental uncertainty about his qualifications. 'It is much joy to me', wrote his father in November 1882, 'that your thoughts are being lifted higher and higher. Don't give way to any false shame about admitting your ignorance or non-experience of Christian life or doctrine . . . no truly Christian heart will ever despise those who feel their weakness and are looking out for light and strength.' The moral insufficiency in himself that he had felt following Seton Donaldson's death seemed to persist as a general sense of unworthiness. On strictly doctrinal grounds, too, Monty was perhaps moving away from the firm evangelical principles on which he had been nurtured towards a broader 'Churchmanship'.* His father may have sensed an incipient divergence of views. He urged Monty to go and hear the sermons of Handley Moule, a leading Cambridge evangelical, since Moule was 'singularly clear in his statement of doctrine'.[7] Herbert was clearly aware that there were difficulties and used Monty's birthday as an annual rallying point. His letter for Monty's twenty-first birthday in August 1883 shows him hopeful that

---

* He never, though, entirely threw off a suspicion of Catholicism, in spite of an interest in Catholic liturgy. In 1909, as Provost of King's, he refused to let Elgar's *The Dream of Gerontius* be performed in Chapel. According to Arthur Benson, he considered it 'too papistical'.

the commitment to Christ will eventually be made, and he reminded Monty that there were things 'higher and better far than mere intellectual advancement':

You have had your stirrings of heart, and your desires after spiritual good, and though you may feel that you have not yet attained to all that you could desire, yet it is something to have had right impulses which have not altogether been disregarded.

And now, with a new year, and new epoch, as it were, let these impulses have their right issue.

You know *where* they would lead you and *how*. Follow them up. Let them have their healthful effect in bringing you nearer to God in the person of His Son.

The same hopes were repeated in succeeding years; but as time passed, Herbert's anxiety that Monty might not after all take the longed-for step became more apparent—most forcefully in the birthday letter for 1886: 'I want—God knows how much and how deeply I want—to see you coming out more and more for Christ, and taking your place as a rallying-point for others. Do, my darling son, let yourself be fully persuaded of His real true love for you, and of His readiness to fill your whole heart with the purest of all pure joy.'

There was never open conflict between father and son over the ordination question, but for some years it may have contributed to the occasional bouts of low spirits Monty suffered from. To St Clair Donaldson in 1884 he apparently confessed some of his doubts. 'I do not wonder at what you say about yourself,' replied St Clair, 'for, I fear, we cannot hope to live up to our highest moments all our life. Let us rather thank God that we have been allowed to stand together on a height from whence we can see the Promised Land. We shall have to wander a great deal before we get there, but the memory of what we have seen will surely be a help.'[8]

What, then, would Monty make of his life if ordination was resisted? Perhaps it is appropriate to quote here the frank evaluation of himself he made in 1922:

It is a constant puzzle or if not puzzle, surprise, to me that I have never shared the ambitions or speculations about a career which ordinary people have, and ought to have, choice of profession, home of one's own, and all such. I believe there never was a time when I have had more of a programme than to find out all I could about various matters and to make friends. Positions and objectives have been the same ... It has not been a case of amiable modesty, but something more like indolence or if a long word is better, opportunism.[9]

Whether he took Holy Orders or not, Cambridge and an academic life seemed virtually certain. Even before Monty went up to King's it had seemed obvious to Arthur Benson that here was a don in the making: 'I doubt if you will ever leave [King's] for the rest of your life,' Arthur had written, 'and only wish it was to be my lot.'[10] But if Monty, halfway through his undergraduate career, had no clear idea of what he intended doing, others besides his father were forming distinct expectations of him. His tutor Welldon foresaw a great future for him, as St Clair Donaldson reported:

He [Welldon] says . . . that it lies in your power, if you choose, to do work both for Science and the Church, such as has not been done for years. In Archaeology you are to teach Cambridge. In Theology you can bring to bear what is sorely needed—great knowledge (which you know how to use) and a wide grasp of universal history. You are one of the very few, for instance, who can work out a scheme of 'Comparative Religion' . . . with ability and devotion.

Now, you know that I don't tell you all this simply to please you, or even to encourage you. Indeed I am not sure that praise bringing such responsibility is enviable. But it is right you should hear what a man who knows thinks you can accomplish, if you like.[11]

It was indeed an awesome—indeed, possibly a numbing—responsibility for a twenty-two-year-old undergraduate to contemplate. Welldon may have been over-ambitious for his pupil; but as things turned out, Monty James, for all his 'indolence', achieved scholarly distinction effortlessly, and almost in spite of himself.

*   *   *

At the beginning of May 1884, just as Monty was about to sit Part I of the Classical Tripos, the Provost of Eton died. The question of Dr Goodford's successor was naturally of the keenest interest to Monty, who stood with the conservative interest in favouring Dr Hornby's automatic succession. There had been an amusing diversion when his friend Leo Maxse wrote a letter to the *Pall Mall Gazette* recommending Oscar Browning for the provostship. 'O.B. suspects nothing and is highly pleased,' reported Monty, who had been disgruntled at the suggestion (which he believed had emanated from Browning) that T. H. Huxley should succeed Dr Goodford. 'However little respect for Henry VI the Governing Body may have', he said, 'I don't think people would stand a lay Provost at once—not to say a secularist, and a coarse nineteenth-century stinks man like Huxley don't do.'* But Hornby was duly appointed Provost on 1 July and Edmond Warre took over as Head Master at the end of that month.

After taking a First in Part I of the Tripos, Monty relaxed with a hired piano and some Coptic apocrypha. His immediate plans included a trip to France with Hugh Childers on a double tricycle, the first of many French holidays on wheels. The machine had solid tyres and Monty and Childers sat side by side to propel it, 'with infinite labour', through the hot June days. In spite of the labour, broken spokes, horses that shied at their approach, the *pavé*, and the 'invocations' of market women, the holiday was 'singularly delightful':

The bathes in wayside streams: the drinks, the foods: the wide prospects from the tops of hills at night (for we often ploughed on till very late), the smell of vineyards in flower in early morning: the sighting of the next cathedral tower above the poplars, and the subsequent deciphering and noting of all its sculpture and glass—which sounds like bathos, but is nothing of the kind. I have not often been more acutely alive in mind and body.[12]

Part II of the Classical Tripos, taken in the summer of 1885, marked the effective end of Monty's undergraduate career, and he again took an expected First. To mark the event he gave a dinner for his friends—St Clair, H. B. Smith, Lionel Ford, Willie Boyle, and others. The principal absentee was Arthur Benson, who had by now left Cambridge and was teaching at Eton. Monty was at Eton himself in July and reported 'bathing with Broadbent this morning and subsequently socking at Webber's', as well as carrying out some researches in Fellows' Library.

At the end of the month M. R. James, BA, set off for Silvaplana in Switzerland as tutor and travelling companion to Lord Paisley, eldest son of the Marquis of Hamilton, who was then an Oppidan in Walter Durnford's house. Back in June, Cecil Baring had sent Monty some background information on Paisley's character and concluded that he would be 'amenable enough to discipline without having to put a hook up his nose'. By the beginning of September Monty and Paisley were in Munich, having already seen Salzburg, which, said Monty, had been rich in churches 'of that particular style which makes me quite ill'. They had also visited a salt mine, where they were required to put on 'a

---

* The comment on Huxley recalls Monty's pronouncements in College Pop (see p. 42). In fact, Eton's first lay Provost since Sir Henry Savile in the seventeenth century was to be Monty himself.

hat and coat and trousers and leather flap behind . . . The females appear in a cap and coat and white trousers, which thrilled me with horror but they seemed to like it. I could have spent hours in whizzing down the wooden slides (but you only do it twice) . . . ' In Munich he found a Memling in the Old Pinakothek and some other early Dutch and German painters whose style he approved of. Paisley, being fond of 'savage curiosities', visited a Japanese exhibition. 'They rather bore me do Jap things,' confessed Monty, 'but with certain reservations I can be happy anywhere and was so among the Japs on this occasion.'[13]

He returned to King's in the autumn for a fourth, and then a fifth year, to work on his Fellowship dissertation. He still had no systematic plan for a career, but it was clear that if he wished to stay at King's for the time being he must do his best to obtain a Fellowship, which would settle things for six years at least. The moustache he had sported since 1882 was shaved off, and he called on his acquaintances posing as someone else and hoping to deceive them. He pushed on with his manuscript investigations at the Fitzwilliam, took part in an ADC production, and agreed to become Librarian of the Union, a newly created office that principally involved ordering books. But he gave the post up the following year, his enthusiasm for the Union never having been great:

If membership could have resulted in giving me any confidence as a speaker, why, then I missed much-needed opportunities of improvement. From any other point of view I don't feel much regret. The elections to office used periodically to cause excitement in Union circles: some men were quite wrapped up in Union politics. If they enjoyed it, so much the better: to me the game of political intrigue on a small (or large) scale has never been interesting.

Early in 1886 he received a telegram from Sydney telling him that Edmond Warre wished him to come to Eton for a month to take the place of a master who was ill. Two days later Monty wrote home from Eton 'in the new capacity of Usher'. He had faced a class before, having briefly taught French at the Albert Institute in Cambridge in 1883. He had also taken a Sunday School class in the town, which had been 'not altogether a stirring success':

I was in a room by myself with eight largish youths, and they preferred the consumption of the early green apple that perisheth to paying any attention to the pearls of eloquence I was casting before them. I accordingly sought to bring the painful scene to a conclusion as speedy as was consistent alike with the entire preservation of self-control and the decencies of scholastic inter-course.[14]

M. R. James in his D.Litt. robes, 1895

H. E. Luxmoore

A. C. Benson, *c.* 1915

J. W. Clark

Oscar Browning

Apart from having to get up for Early School, Monty found teaching his Eton division (which included a future friend, R. C. Norman) rather easier than he had imagined; but teaching had no allure for him, and he showed no inclination to pursue it as a career. In his free time he walked with Arthur Benson and other friends who were then teaching at Eton, worked in College Library, and generally enjoyed himself. It was while he was at Eton, early in February, that Henry Bradshaw died peacefully at Cambridge. He was found one morning sitting in his armchair, his spectacles pushed up on his head, still wearing his evening dress. Monty could not be present for the funeral but was in Cambridge just before it. 'Surely', he wrote, 'never was a society so broken with grief on a like occasion than which I found at King's and Trinity'. It was Monty who composed the Latin inscription on Bradshaw's memorial tablet in King's Chapel. It was, he said, the best phrase he could devise, 'but no mere phrases could do justice to the memory of Henry Bradshaw'.[15]

Though Monty had been asked initially to fill in at Eton for a month, he remained there for the entire half. The Easter holidays were to be spent in Rome, with Luxmoore, A. C. Ainger and an Oppidan called Robert Norton. Returning briefly to King's before leaving, Monty was taken off for over an hour by Oscar Browning 'for the purpose of abusing Eton'. Browning reappeared the next morning and sat on Monty's bed 'jawing like all possessed' about the people they ought to call on whilst in Italy. But Palm Sunday found Monty far away from Oscar Browning, in Milan Cathedral—all banners and incense, with an exquisite view of the Lombardy Plain from the roof. Then came Pisa—the Campo Santo, and Benozzo Gozzoli's frescoes of Genesis; Lucca, and a gorgeous Fra Bartolomeo; and then Rome, in time for the Maundy Thursday office, which Monty observed with detached antiquarian interest.

St Peter's astonished him, and the Pantheon was magnificent. They returned to St Peter's, after seeing the Colosseum and the Lateran, to find it deserted and lit by only a dozen wax candles—'most impressive'. On to Orvieto and to 'various sweet little churches; the last had thirteenth- and fourteenth-century frescoes peeping through the plaster all over it—only uncovered here and there. What a joy to scrape for a day.' Northwards from Florence they encountered a memorable sunset, 'a silver crescent in a pink sky over purple Apennines and a pale green over that'. And so on to Lake Maggiore, with its chestnut trees and narcissi. From there they made their way over the Simplon, where Monty was delighted to see the scene of their former avalanche under brighter circumstances, and then home.

*   *   *

By this time, there were several additions to Monty's already considerable circle of friends, and the number steadily increased each year. Two of these were Harrovians: Edward (Ted) Sanderson, whose parents kept a well-known preparatory school at Elstree which Monty frequently visited, and Edward (Ted or Teddy) Butler, the son of Henry Montagu Butler, a former Headmaster of Harrow recently elected Master of Trinity, Ted's college. Monty was instantly captivated by Ted Butler, describing him as 'the admirable Crichton of this age . . . a tall dark youth, straight as a poplar with curly hair and dark eyes . . . I think he is quite a magnificent being, not spoilt by his success.'[16]

Other new friends included Owen Hugh Smith at Trinity and Vincent Yorke at King's. Both were Etonians and both were to provide Monty with comfortable and congenial vacation hospitality at their respective homes, Mount Clare near Roehampton (where there developed in the 1890s what Monty called the 'usual Sunday', a weekend gathering of friends in July) and Forthampton Court near Tewkesbury. Arthur Benson's brother Edward Frederic came up to King's from Marlborough in 1887 and naturally gravitated towards Monty's set. Monty was less friendly with the youngest Benson brother, Robert Hugh, who was at Trinity, though he was a member of both the Chitchat and the TAF.

The first draft of his Fellowship dissertation, begun in the summer of 1885, was 'practically finished' by October 1886. The subject was the Apocalypse of Peter, known to scholars then only by its title and a few fragmentary quotations. Apocryphal literature had been 'the obvious department' for Monty to choose: 'I had cherished for years, I still cherish, a quite peculiar interest in any document that has claimed to be a Book of the Bible, and is not. Nowadays [he was writing in 1925] I suppose it would be proper to say that I have a complex about it.' As for his dissertation, he wove, out of almost nothing, 'a web of considerable size'; it was almost as if he were posing a deliberate challenge to his knowledge and scholarly ingenuity. What primarily interested him (apart from the sheer pleasure puzzles always gave him) was the line of descent from the Apocalypse of Peter down through the later Apocalypse of Paul to the apocalyptic visions of the Middle Ages (including

Dante's *Divina Commedia*). This reminds us that, in spite of his classical background, Monty was essentially a medievalist: to a large extent his work on apocryphal documents was a means of deepening his appreciation of Christian art and of the architecture and literature of the Middle Ages. Apocryphal literature provided the medieval artist with a fund of stories and images that was, literally, a closed book to later ages. Monty's work in this area thus contributed to the study both of Christian origins and of the artistic, literary and philosophic inheritance of the medieval mind. As he wrote of apocryphal documents in his *Apocryphal New Testament* (1924):

If they are not good sources of history in one sense, they are in another. They record the imagination, hopes, and fears of the men who wrote them; they show what was acceptable to the unlearned Christians of the first ages, what interested them, what they admired, what ideals of conduct they cherished for this life, what they thought they would find in the next. As folk-lore and romance, again, they are precious; and to the lover and student of medieval literature and art they reveal the source of many a puzzle. They have, indeed, exercised an influence (wholly disproportionate to their intrinsic merits) so great and so widespread, that no one who cares about the history of Christian thought and Christian art can possibly afford to neglect them.

The main conclusions of his dissertation, a handwritten copy of which survives at King's, and his conjectures about the structure and scope of the lost Apocalypse were later confirmed by a fragment discovered at Akhmîm in Egypt in the winter of 1886–7, just as the dissertation was being completed.*

While working on the Apocalypse of Peter Monty was also devouring manuscript catalogues 'in the hope of stumbling on some unnoticed text in my line of business'. One of these was the 'romance' of Joseph and his wife Asenath (Genesis 41:45, 50; 46:20). The story was known only via partial texts, but as a result of scanning catalogues for manuscripts that might have laid unconcealed for years through being wrongly titled, Monty found two Latin versions of Asenath in Corpus Christi College, Cambridge, and a fuller Greek version in the Bodleian at Oxford. He communicated his discoveries to a French

---

* Three days after the Greek texts of the Akhmîm fragment (containing parts of the Gospel of Peter and the Apocalypse of Peter were first seen in Cambridge, on 20 November 1892, Monty and his friend J. Armitage Robinson lectured on them in the hall of Christ's and that year published together *The Gospel According to Peter and the Revelation of Peter* (CUP).

scholar, Pierre Batiffol, who was then working on an edition of
Asenath from Greek manuscripts in the Vatican Library. Batiffol's
edition appeared in 1889, dedicated to Monty, and their correspondence over Asenath was, as Monty put it, 'the propitious beginning of
acquaintance with foreign scholars'.[17]

With the dissertation finished, Monty planned a trip to France at
Easter 1887 with two friends, Willie Bridgeman and George
Duckworth. He hoped they could get as far as St Bertrand de
Comminges in the Pyrenees, if the weather, as was likely at that time of
the year, did not render it inaccessible. Just before leaving for France
he was flung into some uncertainty about the trip by an extraordinary
story which he urged his parents to keep 'extremely close—absolutely
secret, in fact'. An Albanian called Alexitch had turned up in London
with a fabulous tale of having discovered an intact Greek temple,
hidden by a landslip and covered by a projecting rock, and there were
moves afoot to send Monty and Henry Babington Smith out to
investigate. 'On the whole', wrote Monty, 'it is one of the most exciting
things I have heard—beats King Solomon's Mines. But if it once gets
abroad, there will be no chance for the preservation of the things as the
Germans will get at them or the Turks break them . . . It makes a
pretty story, doesn't it?'[18] But suspicions as to Alexitch's trustworthi-
ness were apparently confirmed and Monty was able to set off for
France as planned.

On 15 March a note from the Bursar's Clerk at King's had informed
him of his election to a Fellowship. It had been a unanimous decision
by the electors. His mother wrote on the 16th: 'Padre's news last night
was delightful, though not altogether unhoped for! I give you my
lovingest congratulations, dear, with my earnest prayers that you may
go on, and prosper, as in the past, so in the future—both in the earthly
and the heavenly race!'

Monty was formally admitted as a Fellow in King's Chapel two days
after his election, on 17 March. 'So Montague Rhodes James has had
a final touch put to him,' wrote Ted Butler, 'and is now complete and
on the same level as O.B.'

CHAPTER 8

FELLOWSHIP
King's 1887–1889

MR MONTAGUE RHODES JAMES
'Faultily faultless, icily regular.'

There are some lives whose brilliancy and cleverness serve to
dazzle rather than to lighten the eyes of the critic and biographer.
It is a well-known scientific fact that excess of light is much more
impenetrable than the thickest darkness.

'Those in Authority', *Granta*, 31 May 1889

THE Fellowship made no radical changes in the pattern of Monty's
life. Lecturing was the main innovation. He was elected to a College
lectureship in Divinity, for two years in the first instance, at a stipend
of £100. 'The proper stipend is £200,' Augustus Austen Leigh, the
Vice-Provost, had told him, 'but this is rather too much to give on a
first appointment.' But Monty could never think that lecturing was his
forte. 'It was certainly never one of my pleasures,' he wrote in *Eton and
King's*. Infinitely more important to him, from the start of his life as a
don, was his relationship with the junior members of both College and
University. He took especial care to make freshmen welcome. His
election in the Easter Term of 1887 to the presidency of the Pitt Club,
for instance, pleased him 'chiefly because it will ensure my seeing
something of the new people each year'.[1]

In May, as well as 'mending up' his dissertation, he conceived the
notion of forging 'a fourteenth-century English account of the
Parthenon by a traveller of the time'. The result, he claimed, had
deceived Waldstein and was published that year as 'Athens in the
Fourteenth Century. An Inedited Supplement to Sir John Maun-
deville's travels' in a slim pamphlet by Macmillans and Bowes. The
instigator, according to the title-page, is 'Professor E. S. Merganser',
whose eccentric English is a delightful *tour de force*:

I shall from the upset beg to excuse me, for all these that through misluck and an overweening forknowledge of the English speech mistakenhoods may befall me, my goodheart readers. Ever must my plea of an amateur be that I have in my studies of the foresaid only so far as the early twelfth yearhundreds beginning bestrided. And this last, is it from out today's times forgettinghood or our much to be bewailed speechshapelearningness's unwisdomship, is to a nineteenth yearhundred period's togethergatheringreceivingsaloon sad unbefitted. Man can hope, the alltimes speechshape will not long—

At this point the owner of the manuscript, one George J. Barker, interrupts and finishes the preface, after which the spurious transcription begins: 'The cite Atenes is treuli to sein a feyr place and a Cristeyne, but not aftir oure lawe for y do you to wete, that in that place men han no regarde vnto our Lorde Pope; but thei paien reuerence vnto the Patriarke of Byzance that is to seien Constantinope.' I begin to fear', wrote Monty, apparently well pleased with himself, 'that anything I do find will be discredited.'[2]

It was with his brother Ber that Monty had developed the character of the ubiquitous Barker, originally portrayed as a Suffolk village tradesman:

Herbert [Ber] was Johnson a butcher, and Monty was a grocer called Barker . . . A jealous and intense rivalry was understood to exist between these two characters; they crabbed each other and made the darkest insinuations; Barker would suggest to Johnson that he tampered with his weights, to be accused in turn of putting sand in his sugar. All this began in private school days, and was renewed whenever they met.[3]

Monty's friends came to know this *alter ego* well. Barker was argumentative; Barker was voluble; Barker was slow on the uptake; Barker could be almost anything Montague Rhodes James was not, as S. G. Lubbock wrote:

Barker would often take a rich, elemental interest in some entertainment which must have been stupidly dull to M. R. James; and the worst sort of film would be enlivened by the running comment that Barker whispered into one's ear—in an accent which was Suffolk, of course, in origin, but later on had surely acquired the peculiar *timbre* of Cambridge.

In the Michaelmas Term of 1887 Henry Babington Smith was granted £150 by the Special Board for Classics in order to undertake archaeological research in Cyprus, on the condition that anything he found would become the property of the University and that he must furnish a report of the results of his researches.[4] But at the last moment he took a government post and the Special Board, believing the opportunity was one 'of unusual interest and importance', recommended that Monty should go in his place. 'Here the College comes in,' Monty told his parents. 'I do not intend to do anything in the way of leaving them without their complete sanction. If they give it, I think I must go . . . the Fitzwilliam Syndicate and the University Council are all in favour of my going and supposing the College consent, I should find it very difficult to draw back, in fact it would be stultifying myself.'

His father was concerned that absence from Cambridge might unsettle his work at King's, but the College gave its approval to the venture. Though the Master of Clare made a fuss in the Senate about Monty's being granted leave of absence from the Fitzwilliam so soon after his appointment as Assistant Director, all was settled by the end of November. 'We are looking out one or two portable nostrums for you', wrote Herbert, 'in the shape of Fever Tincture and Sweet oil for viper bites . . . Don't forget good useful boots, and belly-band of flannel, admirable prophylactic against diarrhoea, chills, etc.' He also offered £10 towards expenses and Sydney wrote to say that he would be willing to lend £40 or £50 if there was a prospect of repayment within a reasonable time.

Monty left England on 11 December, reporting progress thus far to his parents on the 12th:

So far all has gone well, and I do not find that with the exception of brushes and soap I have left much behind, except that I should prefer having some more books . . . From Paris to Brindisi I had the same companion throughout, a Greek. I thought it probable that he would murder me, and so made myself unusually agreeable, supplying him with cigarettes when his own failed and entering into comparisons of Demosthenes and Cicero much in favour of the former . . . Just before Brindisi the Levantine asked if I had any arms about me, and on my replying no, produced, ah heaven, a revolver from his pocket. But his intentions were honest, and I took an early opportunity of assuring him that if I disappeared, the Continent would instantly be plunged into all the horrors and miseries of an European war.

On board ship from Brindisi he made 'two pals' amongst the English passengers, but dismissed the rest as 'a singularly scrubby lot'. He was particularly irritated by a woman who played 'the worst kind of music, an imitation of Haydn—perhaps Haydn himself. It could not be worse. And the beast was knitting during dinner.' He arrived in Cyprus without further incident on 22 December and drove to Limasol to meet his brother Ber, who had been stationed on the island with the RAMC since 1883.*

The director of the expedition was Ernest Gardner of Caius, the same age as Monty and a co-performer in *The Birds*. The party was also joined by D. G. Hogarth, a Fellow of Magdalen College, Oxford, who later became T. E. Lawrence's mentor. 'I knew nothing of the digger's art at the beginning,' Hogarth wrote of his part in the 1888 excavations at Old Paphos, 'and very little at the end. Our leader had studied in the Egyptian school of Petrie, but the rest of us were so raw as not to know if there were any science of the spade at all.'[5] It was as well, therefore, that they were able to call on the instincts and local knowledge of their foreman, Gregorio, of whom Monty wrote appreciatively in *Eton and King's*.

Gardner had brought his wife with him; she turned out to be something of a thorn in Monty's flesh: 'She is a plaintive and affectionate Newnhamite recently married to him. How I hope she won't come up here today. Nobody could mean better, but the irritation she causes me is entirely disproportionate to the causer (or causeuse).' A few weeks later he was feeling less charitable: 'A lady in this kind of place [he was writing from Old Paphos] has to rough it considerably and I should say her 'elth would not permit of it for long. You will see that I consider her somewhat of a nuisance. She objects to smoking, with far less reason than you, for what is one to do of an evening if not smoke? [*sic*] when you have read all your books and are playing piquet?'[6]

But he got on well with Hogarth—'a good sort I think'. After some preliminary digging at Leontari Vouno he joined Hogarth at the main site of Old Paphos to excavate the famous Temple of Aphrodite. They shared a room there and Monty came to prize him as 'a real acquisition':

Upon my word I don't know what I should do if the Gardners and I were alone here. He (Gardner) is terribly one-sided, though he tries to be like other people and to be sure he is not the kind of man to quarrel with: but I could easily quarrel with Mrs G, who dresses in terracotta and thinks she can argue. She is Scotch, used to teach in the High School at Oxford, used the phrase internally subjective lately, and takes rather a pride in being unconventional.[7]

* It would thus appear that S. G. Lubbock's story of Monty and Ber greeting each other on the pier at Nicosia as Barker and Johnson is inaccurate as far as their meeting place went (*Memoir*, p. 28).

Monty retained 'the brightest recollections' of Cyprus and was struck by the wonderful mixed flavour of the island, a compound of 'a kind of Hellenic civilization with three or four later ones—ancient Greek inscriptions built up into cottage walls, Burgundian Gothic churches, a Turkish bath paved with tombstones of French knights, beautifully carved Venetian pulpits in the churches, beautiful minarets rising out of fourteenth-century Gothic towers, hideous little Greek churches with more hideous wall paintings.'[8]

Much of his time was spent deciphering inscriptions, an occupation that had seemed dull to Luxmoore but which naturally appealed to the puzzle-solver in Monty:

The best fun we have here is with inscriptions. There are a good few scattered about the village and we have dug up some more . . . We often spend an hour with our noses down to the stone, and the thing comes out like a puzzle, letter by letter. One or two of the blocks you would swear were perfectly illegible. Sometimes you can't say whether they are inscribed at all at first sight, but if you spit at them and wack them and so on it is wonderful what a lot comes out.[9]

At the end of March he began to set his sights on home: 'I shall be sorry for some things to leave these works, but we have very nearly finished here . . . I shall be very glad when I see my ome and frens once more.' Some of these friends had kept in touch during his sojourn in Cyprus. J. K. Stephen sent out a copy of his new weekly paper, *The Reflector*; St Clair wrote; and so did Ted Butler, who, while relaying the latest transgressions of Oscar Browning, had complained that 'Everything here is beastly. Sunday we had a TAF in King's and adjourned to your rooms afterwards, but your rooms without you are not at all what rooms ought to be . . . ' Monty left Cyprus early in April. The report of the excavations appeared later in the year in the *Journal of Hellenic Studies*.*

Judging from his letters home, Monty was in good spirits throughout his stay in Cyprus, but he seems to have left England in a low mood, with the emergence once more of self-doubt being compounded by homesickness. He confided in Lionel Ford, who wrote to him in Cyprus at the end of December:

* Monty supplied an account of the work at Leontari, wrote the immensely erudite section on 'The History and Antiquities of Paphos', and collaborated with Gardner and Hogarth on the inscriptions section and on the findings from the Paphos tombs.

Dear old chap, I know the kind of feeling that comes over one in a railway carriage, when each moment carries one further away from all that one loves. I don't wonder at your being despondent and thinking of your unworthiness. Only you mustn't say that your life is wasted: if there was nobody except me left of your many friends, I should know well enough it isn't so. How much I owe to you I can't say, but I do feel with all my might that in starting on what is probably my lifework* I start with aims and hopes which you have largely created.

Ford passed Monty's letter, which does not survive, on to Ted Butler, who also rallied round with a long and affectionate letter of encouragement:

Though I was very glad to hear something about you, I hated to see the way that you wrote about yourself, for I am quite sure that you are quite wrong: I mean as to your saying that your life must be a useless one. Why need it be? . . . You or others have often told me what a tremendous loss Bradshaw was to the college, and how many people felt the loss of his affection and sympathy, which are not found too commonly with our dons. I am quite certain that, if you like, you can do all that he did and a great deal more . . . You know yourself that you have as many, or rather more friends who really love and admire you than anyone else up at Cambridge and you only want a little more exertion to turn the good you already do into still greater.

Could simply being himself form the core of a useful life? Perhaps Monty, after receiving these sincere testimonials, did begin to see dimly that there were, in the broadest of senses, pastoral possibilities in his being a Fellow of King's. Even without Holy Orders, his Cambridge life, and particularly his position in King's, could after all become what his father would have called a 'useful' one. Herbert James, in fact, clearly recognized this, writing in 1891: 'You have much within your reach. By writing, by teaching, by influence, you can be, and I hope will be, a moulder of men, and do good work in that not very easy way.'

For the time being, however, the ordination question was still an open one. In the birthday letter for 1888 his father hoped that 'real *soul*-good, as well as real outward good and prosperity' would be Monty's and that 'with all the imparted knowledge may there be much of that which will bring you nearer to Christ, and help you bring others with you.' If Herbert James was slowly coming to accept the fact that Monty would not be ordained, Luxmoore, writing in February 1889,

---

* Ford went to Eton as an assistant master in January 1888.

still thought that the step would eventually be taken and asked outright whether Monty was 'quite satisfied to let the question of Holy Orders wait'.

The undercurrent of doubt and indecision persisted after Monty returned from Cyprus and he continued occasionally to fall prey to low spirits. In November 1888, a letter to his mother concluded: 'I do not think that I was anything but extremely sulky when I left home. These things will happen and all one requires is time, employment and tobacco.' A year later he wrote gloomily to Ted Butler, who replied: 'What you mean by saying that you are very near to losing the spiritual sense, I don't quite know and I don't think that you do either.' But these moods became increasingly infrequent as it became clear to all concerned that Monty would remain a lay member of the Church.

In August 1888 he took a short holiday with Arthur Benson, Herbert Tatham and Hugh Childers, cycling from Eton to Lincoln. Afterwards, he confessed himself 'much exercised'. 'I told them I could never go on a tricycle again. The exertion of going up hill tells on the legs too frightfully.' The trip was recalled by Arthur Benson: 'Tatham, Childers, M. R. James and I went from Eton by Buckingham, Towcester, Oundle etc to Lincoln, on bikes. MRJ on a trike, in *silk* stockings (black).'[10] There was another holiday in the autumn, when with his friend George Duckworth ('Ducky') Monty visited Talland House in Cornwall, the holiday home of the Stephen family. He met George's sister Stella and admitted to his mother that he found her extremely beautiful. Perhaps Stella aroused unwonted feelings in him, which may explain the curious remark made in a letter to his mother: 'I think I should have stopped a little longer at St Ives but it really was becoming dangerous.' As things turned out, Ted Sanderson became inflamed by Stella and Monty had to comfort him when the romance floundered. Mary Emily had been relieved that Stella Duckworth had been Ted's choice and not Monty's: 'I should be deeply grieved, and very anxious,' she wrote, 'if you married a woman who did not distinctly hold the Christian faith and hope. Miss D's surroundings, even, as I understand, her mother, do *not* hold this . . . I can but pray and trust that you will be guided in your own choice, whether it be an early or a later one.'[11]

*   *   *

On 25 November 1888 Provost Okes died, aged ninety. Augustus Austen Leigh, the Vice-Provost, had a clear claim to the provostship, but there were those who felt that a stricter adherence to the Statutes, which required that the Provost should be distinguished in either theology, literature, or science, would now be in the best interests of the College. A party, which included J. E. Nixon, signified its intention to vote for Henry Sidgwick of Trinity, Knightbridge Professor of Moral Philosophy. Monty thought this attempt was 'wrongheaded'. A new undergraduate magazine, the *Granta*, the first number of which appeared on 18 January 1889, was more forthright and castigated the moves to elect Sidgwick as 'a desire on the part of the discontented set amongst King's Fellows to force themselves into notice and administer a rebuff to the less self-asserting section of the community'.

In the event, Austen Leigh was elected with a comfortable majority. The new Provost preached his first sermon in Chapel to the undergraduates on 3 March 1889 and took for his theme the need for collegiate unity: 'We *must* live together, work together, play together; yet the very closeness of the connection, which ought to destroy jealousy and distrust, may only serve to strengthen them. It *will* do so, if there is no true fellowship.'[12] Behind Austen Leigh's words was the reality of a confrontation that had long been simmering in King's and that now threatened to come to the boil.

Towards the end of February Monty had told his father that 'The deans Nixon and Stearn are incompatible and one will have to go. The greater part of the College would like to get rid of them both and it is not inconceivable that Douty might be made one dean and myself the other. It is a formidable prospect and one which does not strike me as anything but a duty.' On 1 March the *Granta* printed an article on 'The Coming Dean' by Robert Ross, a King's freshman of Canadian origins. Having first recommended that the vacant post of Vice-Provost should be filled by Oscar Browning, Ross turned to the deanship:

A rumour has reached us on very good authority of another plan of the 'Stupid Party', as they are termed in King's. It is proposed to elect Mr Douty to one of the vacant Fellowships, and to confer on him the somewhat degrading office of Dean. That obsolete anachronism, attended as it is with so much odium and opprobrium, is naturally shirked by competent men in the college, and they are ready to make anyone Dean who is willing to do the dirty work.

The point at issue was that conferring a Fellowship on E. H. Douty, then an MA, would be to pass over much better qualified men; but tied up with this was a deeper question, which was taken up by an anonymous attack in the *Pall Mall Gazette*. This article made sneering reference to the Douty 'job': 'Mr Douty is understood to be a very good fellow, who is deservedly popular, "goes out riding with the dons, you know", belongs to the old social Etonian set,* and altogether is just the man who *should* be elected if the college is regarded as a kind of pleasant social club.'[13]

At the heart of the controversy, then, was the division between the Best Set and the outsiders, and sympathies began to polarize dangerously. A number of people wondered how Ross had known of the intention to elect Douty to a Fellowship and then make him Dean. Surely the information must have come from a senior member of the College? Arthur Tilley, for one, was sure that Oscar Browning was at the bottom of it all and wrote to him to protest at this 'gross violation of confidence' in discussing the Douty proposal amongst the undergraduates. Browning vigorously denied the charge, and in fact later received a subdued reply from Tilley expressing 'unqualified regret' for his former accusations.[14]

But Tilley did more than accuse Oscar Browning of spreading confidential information. At a dinner party soon after the *Granta* article on the deanship Tilley threw out the suggestion that Ross should be ducked in the College fountain. Things now began to get out of hand. 'On Friday night,' Monty reported, 'Francis Ford [Lionel's brother], Ted Sanderson and two or three other highly respectable people placed [Ross] in the College Fountain. They had talked about it for some time before and the idea pleased me a good deal, but I was rather afraid of the consequences, and hoped it had blown over.'[15]

The affair did not blow over, however, and soon the College was in ferment. Oscar Browning, 'nearly mad with rage', advised legal proceedings against the people who had ducked Ross, and Monty was asked by one of the *Granta*'s editors to hold a general meeting of the Pitt Club to expel Francis Ford, which he refused to do. The *Granta* naturally took up its position publicly against the ducking, though not until the 15th:

We were not desirous to bring prominently before the world the fact that there existed in any College in Cambridge six individuals so lost to every sentiment of good fellowship, so utterly oblivious of the honourable obligation that strength entails, so arrogant in demeanour and so mean in conduct as those

---

* Douty, however, was not an Etonian himself.

who took upon themselves to perpetrate the dastardly outrage which has caused a feeling of resentment amongst all right-thinking men.*

By this time Fred Whitting, the Bursar, had been elected Vice-Provost and the motion that would have given Douty a Fellowship and made him Dean was thrown out by one vote. Monty considered this 'a grave loss' to King's, but the College continued to boil: 'Oscar Browning, I suppose, told one hundred lies if he told one (and one I can pretty well swear to). That man, believe me, is the worst I know.'[16] But he had now decided that enough was enough and stepped in, as Nathaniel Wedd described:

The leading mind among the Exclusives, taking stock of the position, concluded that the lines of exclusiveness were wrong, and that for the future, he and all whom he could influence, would have no more to do with them. With great moral courage, he asked all the undergraduates to meet in the reading room, and there expounded the conclusion at which he had arrived, and his determination to act on different lines in the future.[17]

It was, conceded the *Granta*, 'an oration à la Mark Antony'—though it noted that Monty also urged all those present not to buy or read the next number of the *Granta*.[18]

It had indeed been an extraordinarily courageous decision on Monty's part, and his 'sermon' (as he termed it) was followed by a general reconciliation. He even had a tête-à-tête with Ross and found him 'quite reasonable and sorry for what he had done'. Personally, Monty had been in sympathy with those who had ducked Ross: they were, after all, his friends. But he felt that it had been 'a mistake in policy, in as much as it was regarded by the College at large as an act of revenge coming from the "Eton" set. That is the only thing that made it important.'[19] He had found it unpleasant enough throughout, but he believed 'the net results will be nothing but good (I spent a couple of hours with Wedd the other evening as one consequence)'.

Ross left King's not long afterwards, to become in time the 'foul-weather friend of Oscar Wilde'.[20] Feeling amongst the undergraduates ran strongly against Tilley, who was forced to resign the junior tutorship; but Monty's act of mediation, of which Bradshaw would surely have approved, considerably enhanced his reputation

---

* The same number of the *Granta* contained a challenge from five members of the paper's staff to the six perpetrators 'to combat in the manner of law-abiding Englishmen, with the gloves of the boxer'.

with all sections of the College and in May he was elected to the Council. It may even have confirmed a conviction in him that collegiate life offered ample scope for social good, and this perhaps neutralized any guilt he may have felt at not being able to follow his father into ordination.

As a direct result of the Ross affair Monty was made Junior Dean, with A. H. Cooke as his senior, towards the end of the year. Though just before his election Monty read a paper to the Chitchat in which he pointed out the inevitability of cliques, he now began to lay all shows of partisanship aside, and though there always remained a touch of exclusiveness about his inner circle of friends, he nevertheless quietly inspired loyalty to the collegiate ideals of unity and fellowship in large numbers of Kingsmen for nearly twenty years.

CHAPTER 9

THE DEAN
King's 1889–1892

'But what,' said Mr Swiveller with a sigh, 'what is the odds so long
as the fire of the soul is kindled at the taper of conwiviality, and the
wing of friendship never moults a feather!'

Dickens, *The Old Curiosity Shop* (Chapter 2)

'I HAVE not a great deal of news this week,' Monty told his father on
1 December 1889. 'The Deanship was conferred on me and Cooke last
Tuesday, but we do not enter on our duties yet—not till next Term
practically. There was not much hair lost, I am glad to say.'

There had been the possibility of trouble, when Oscar Browning
took up Nixon's cause and circulated a printed notice deploring
Nixon's removal from the deanship and claiming that, following the
ducking of Robert Ross, it had been owing to 'Mr Nixon's presence of
mind, good sense, and wise exercise of authority that a serious danger
was averted'.[1]

But Nixon himself took his deprivation graciously and the College as
a whole could feel confident that in the new Junior Dean they had a
man who would do his best to uphold the corporate spirit. Of all his
posts at King's, the deanship brought Monty closest to the undergraduate body and in many ways provided him with the happiest
portion of his Cambridge career. On 10 December he received a letter
from Ted Butler in Dresden:

I was delighted to hear of the deanery, though I suppose that some of the work
will be distasteful, but still a post of that kind may be made very useful, and you
will appreciate, more than most people, being associated with the chapel . . .
Dear old Montie, you have got a fine future before you at Cambridge, if you
like; and I know that you will like it . . . Goodbye, dear James, and very much
love to you.

Almost the first thing Monty did as Dean was to end his association with the TAF. It was a quiet but firm gesture, indicating the seriousness with which he took his new duties. 'It seems hard to imagine the TAF without you at its head,' wrote Ted early in the New Year. 'I see that it was the right thing to do, but you must feel a little being obliged to cut yourself off at all from the young set in this way.' But there was no lessening of Monty's contact with the young (quite the reverse)—simply an avoidance of any possible charge that he was encouraging social division in King's by openly associating with a particular clique.

The deanship made Monty responsible, amongst other things, for undergraduate discipline. In Cambridge as a whole there was still plenty of almost Regency rowdyism. An edict issued by the Senate in 1889 censured Gentlemen of the University for driving out of Cambridge on Sundays 'in dog-carts and other vehicles' and conducting themselves 'in a noisy and disorderly manner'.[2] Misbehaviour at the theatre was also common, as a letter from 'A. N. Other' ('on the boards') to the *Cambridge Review*, also in 1889, indicates: 'On Thursday it was bad. On Friday it was worse. On Saturday to call it blackguardly is hardly strong enough.'[3] But in King's the level of delinquency was generally low and confined to the release of animal spirits at predictable points in the calendar—after the Lent Races, or on Founder's Day (6 December), which Monty liked to get out of the way 'on account of the boys being noisy until an early hour'.

The Chapel—its fabric, services and Choir School—also came under the jurisdiction of the Dean; but in Monty's case, his intense interest in and devotion to King's Chapel led him to take an exceptionally active role in relation to its affairs. Two major projects were undertaken during his deanship. The first concerned the windows. By 1849 J. P. Hedgeland had cleaned and restored a number of them, but his work had been stopped in the face of growing opposition to his wholesale and often unwarrantable alterations. Nothing further was done until 1890, when Monty carried a proposal in Council to have all the windows photographed. 'The thing will be difficult, but well worth doing. We shall have to have a scaffold (with which the Fitzwilliam will supply us I think) and photograph the windows of each bay on either side from it.'[4] The photographs revealed the deteriorating condition of much of the lead in the fourteen windows untouched by Hedgeland, and in 1893 C. E. Kempe (a well-known glass painter), under Monty's direction, began repair work. It lasted until 1906, one window being treated every year:

A scaffold with many floors was put up, from which every part of the window could be got at with complete ease. This was moved from window to window as required. Great was the excitement, when a fresh window was thus made accessible, of going all over it, settling what mistakes must be rectified, what glaring modern patches should be taken out and replaced by neutral-tinted glass, and what ancient patches were worth removing and preserving; for it had been the habit of the eighteenth-century repairers to stop up holes with pieces of old glass that they had by them, and some of these were of considerable beauty and interest. I collected a large stock of them, had them leaded together, and kept them till some opportunity of using them to good purpose should occur.[5]

In 1899 Monty published his *Guide to the Windows of King's College Chapel*, which, in spite of its compact size, remained the standard authority for many years. He also read two papers on the subject to the Cambridge Antiquarian Society (to the Council of which he had been elected in May 1888).*

The second major project begun during Monty's deanship was the remodelling of the east end. This was a great deal less successful from Monty's point of view than the work on the windows, and the tedious wrangling over what was to replace the eighteenth-century 'Gothick' arrangement by James Essex rumbled on inconclusively for years. 'When you have to take counsel with a body of forty-six persons on a question of taste,' Monty recalled ruefully, 'unanimity is not easily secured . . . I should be loath to pass through the many stages of committees, reports, discussions, again.'[6]

In 1876 a boarding school for the College's choristers had been started and was subsequently installed in the West Road. Choristerships were offered for competition to boys from all over the country, and the choir, under the greatly loved organist A. H. ('Daddy') Mann, began to assume the reputation it has since acquired. It was part of Monty's decanal duties to assist at chorister trials. The competitors were required to read a few verses of a psalm to test their reading powers and to see whether any of them had 'an accent of more than ordinary poignancy':

There was every degree of attainment, of course, from the infant who traced the lines with his forefinger and audibly spelt the words out, to the one who shot ahead and had finished ten verses before you could tell him to stop. There

---

* 'On some Fragments of Fifteenth-century Glass in the Side Chapels' (November 1894), and 'On a Window Recently Releaded in King's College Chapel' (May 1896).

was also the shy one who subsided into tears: he had to be beckoned to your side, and there in the intervals of sobs he whispered into your ear, 'Wherefore should I fear in the days of wickedness', and the rest.[7]

Finally, five or six boys would be selected, taken into Chapel, and asked to sing a hymn of their choice: 'This would compensate', recalled Monty, 'for all the weariness of the morning: the child had ceased by that time to be nervous—"had strangely forgotten to weep"—and one was in no hurry to cut off the lovely sound.'

Monty found considerable pleasure in his connection with the Choir School and would usually play in the annual cricket match between the school and the Fellows. The choristers had to remain in Cambridge over Christmas, but they were well looked after. As one of them, Gordon Carey, later to become one of Monty's closest friends, recalled: 'There was a topical play, devised usually by Dr M. R. James and enacted for our benefit by him and others, in which certain College notables were for once identifiably guyed.'[8] Two such pieces, *The Dismal Tragedy of Henry Blew Beard, Esq* (with Monty taking the title role) and *Historia de Alexandro Barberio et XL Latronibus*, were both written by Monty in the mid-1890s for the amusement of the choristers and performed at the ADC, with music and lyrics by Dr Mann and E. G. Swain, the College Chaplain. The action was distinctly Grand Guignol in style: the climax of *Alexandro Barberio* (Ali Baba), for instance, was reached in the slaughter of Cassim off-stage, the remains being packed neatly into a suitcase. 'The opening of this suitcase', wrote Monty, 'I take to have been another of the memorable moments of the play.'

But Monty also offered the choristers something more, as Gordon Carey again recalled:

We were more conscious—very properly—of the laughter and fun provided, and shared, by him than of the store of learning that lay behind it. Yet surely there was a distant echo of the latter in his reading of a Lesson, more arresting than that of any other reader I heard in Chapel . . . and I can still recall him in the Chapel one whole-holiday morning, as he brought to life and meaning the stained glass of each of the windows in turn.[9]

To the undergraduates the Dean became just as accessible. 'I doubt', wrote one non-Etonian Kingsman to Monty in 1918, 'whether even you know how much confidence and affection you have inspired in widely different types of men.' Though to some Monty might have seemed to represent, in P. N. Furbank's words, 'the more *bien-pensant* and Etonian element' in King's,[10] it was still true, as Gurney Lubbock said, that no undergraduate ever found M. R. James 'too busy to talk to them, play games with them, make music on that very clangy piano, and entertain them with his vast stores of knowledge, his inexhaustible humour, and his unique powers of mimicry'. The atmosphere of his rooms was deftly evoked by Charles Tennyson, who knew them and Monty at the turn of the century:

There were no invitations and no obvious effort at hospitality. Whisky and soda water, cigarettes and tobacco, were on the table. The host lay back in his chair, smoking. He seemed to have no fear of silences, but spoke low and intermittently, turning from one to another and presenting to each in turn the friendly transparency of his large round spectacles. Now and then he would throw back his head and laugh with a sharp barking sound at some quip or anecdote. Sometimes he would let fall a dry witticism as he padded softly across to the mantelpiece to fetch a spill or fill his large curving pipe at the tobacco jar.[11]

Tennyson also supplied a sense of Monty's physical presence at the end of his deanship, as he approached his fortieth birthday: 'He was tall, dark and rather heavily built, with straight black hair and features which were clear cut without sharpness or aquilinity. He moved silently and with deliberation, spoke softly, seldom laughed but often chuckled . . . ' One interesting sketch of Monty is to be found in Arthur Benson's essay 'Sociabilities' (in *From a College Window*, 1906), where he is described under the name 'Perry': 'He is always accessible, always ready to help any one. The undergraduate, that shy bird in whose sight the net is so often spread in vain, even though it be baited with the priceless privilege of tea, tobacco, and the talk of a well-informed man, comes in troops and companies to see him.'

On most evenings the Dean could be found working in his rooms. You entered and a mumbled greeting made you instantly at home: 'Imperceptibly the work is laid aside, and if the hour is about 10 p.m., as it generally seems to be when that picture comes back to one, tea is made and the party steadily grows; and he, though he never seems to dominate it, is, of course, the life and soul of that party.'[12]

Those, however, who wished for intellectual challenge and an abrasive confrontation with ideas had to go elsewhere—to Nathaniel Wedd, for instance, by now an active intellectual force in King's, passionate, inspiring, and still an agnostic. Wedd disapproved of the way Monty James avoided free intellectual discussion. He tells the story of two young men discussing some philosophical problem within

Monty's hearing: 'He rapped sharply on the table with his pipe and called out: "No thinking, gentlemen, please." "Thought" in this sense really did disturb Monty throughout his life.'[13] One wonders not about the authenticity of the remark, but whether it could really have been made without a mischievous twinkle of the eye: a pronouncement like this, *ex cathedra*, seems out of character. Yet there is truth in what Wedd goes on to say, and for which the influence of Monty's father must have been partly responsible: 'The eager pursuit of truth along many paths, regardless of where the path would lead and what obstacles would be thrust aside or destroyed in blazing the trail—this, which is the hall-mark of a living college, was not to Monty's taste.'

But there were ample compensations for Monty's conservatism and his dislike of unfettered debate. Above all, he embodied the very essence of collegiate life at Oxford and Cambridge—that life-enhancing sense of corporate continuity and fellowship, the individual indissolubly bonded into a community that linked the past, the present and the future. In this respect, even someone like Wedd was deeply appreciative of Monty's presence. As he wrote when Monty finally left Cambridge in 1918:

This is a bad blow. I find it little use to tell myself that I should be glad, since you must have wanted the change. The fact remains that I feel your departure as a disaster to the College and a most dismal loss to me personally. For twenty-nine years you have been the soul of the place, the chief inspiration of the things that make King's better to live in than other places.

Goldsworthy Lowes Dickinson (elected to a King's Fellowship in the same year as Monty) provided another focal point for those who found the Dean's company too cosy and unadventurous. Lowes Dickinson was an idealist. His humanism and gentle Socratic seriousness, as well as the vigorous individualism of Wedd, made King's a richer place; but so did Monty James. Not everyone is troubled by a relentless social conscience, or even by the enigma of their own being. Monty was well aware that he stood for values that were increasingly out of step with the pace of the times; but they were part of a civilized and civilizing tradition that was of permanent significance and that could not simply be brushed aside in the name of progress. Perhaps it was not so much that Monty James was antagonistic to the new, but that the best of the old claimed him so completely.

*   *   *

The 1890s saw the beginnings of some of Monty's deepest friendships—in particular, with Walter Morley Fletcher and James McBryde.

He was introduced to Walter Fletcher in the May Term of 1893 by Gurney Lubbock, who had come up to King's from Eton the previous year. With Walter, Monty soon settled into the kind of intimacy he cherished most: an easy, uncomplicated and unsentimental companionship. Walter was elected to a Trinity Fellowship in 1897, and until he left Cambridge in 1914 he and Monty saw each other constantly. There were countless evenings spent over their favourite card game of piquet, working towards a score of a million points; bicycle rides, including an annual expedition to the source of the Cam on Walter's birthday in July; and holidays abroad, when Walter would show himself 'properly inquisitive about dates, images, painted glass and the rest'. His receptivity endeared him to Monty:

It is a vast advantage to be curious, by which I do not mean addicted to asking questions, but rather being ready to allow that what our friends take trouble to enquire into is probably worth our attention; and we very quickly find out whether or no we shall ever make anything of it ourselves; but anyhow, the process of talking it over makes for companionableness and *may* often give each a better opinion of the other's intelligence.[14]

Characteristically, there was a large element of purely boyish fun in Monty's relationship with Walter Fletcher, who would take part in a game (probably devised by Monty) played in the Fellows' Garden at King's. All round the edge of the garden was a path, thickly lined on both sides with evergreen bushes and shrubs. One person had to make his way round this path, without running or making a noise. Walter Fletcher's son has described how the others hid in the bushes 'and either made eerie noises as the victim passed, or gently clutched at his clothes and so on. It was very rare, my father said, for anyone to succeed in getting round. Monty was particularly good at making ghostly noises.'[15]

In the autumn of 1893 James McBryde came up to King's from Shrewsbury to read Natural Sciences, which Walter Fletcher was reading at Trinity. Whereas Walter Fletcher was to achieve distinction as a medical researcher, McBryde was intellectually unremarkable; but he had all the qualities Monty most prized. He was open, guileless, unassuming, keenly observant and full of humour. Radiantly good humoured and of 'angelic temper', he was an ideal companion: 'In person he was not tall, had light curly hair, and a kind smile: in short, conciliated goodwill. Before long he formed the habit, which I always encouraged, of dropping in uninvited at a late hour of the evening, and joining a congregation which was usually to be found in the inner room.'[16]

There was no companion who so completed a circle—no one who, even when he supposed himself out of spirits, brought so much enjoyment into an expedition. A smile will never be far off when his friends speak of him . . . For the accident (he always described it as an accident) which enabled him to pass into King's, the College may be very grateful. The presence in it of so much affection, truth, innocence, and humour could not but make an enormous difference to the atmosphere of the place; and how much pleasure of the best kind his companionship brought into the lives of his nearer friends it is not possible for one of them, at least, to put into words.[17]

For eleven years, until his early death in 1904, McBryde provided Monty with what was perhaps the most significant friendship of his life. Those years, as Monty wrote after McBryde's death, 'left no single act or word of his which I could wish to forget'.

There were, however, many more besides Walter Fletcher and James McBryde who gave Monty 'pleasure of the best kind'. The companionship of Eustace Talbot, a Trinity freshman of 1892, also provided 'a secure delight'. You were, said Monty, 'certain of being happy with him', whatever mood he was in: 'He was (I can summon no better phrase) a great possession.' And yet this friendship, like all his others, was, in Monty's own words, 'hedged about with reticences'. With Talbot, there were many subjects that were left to be understood in silence. 'I do not know', wrote Monty, 'whether there was more of advantage or disadvantage in this attitude; but at least it was natural to both of us . . . '[18]

Monty, indeed, had so many friends that it is difficult to avoid an extensive listing of them. Some, however, must be mentioned: A. B. Ramsay, for instance, an elegant classicist who came up to King's from Eton in 1891. 'Ram', who after teaching at Eton for many years became Master of Magdalene, was devoted to Monty, as was S. G. ('Jimbo') Lubbock, author of the *Memoir*. Lubbock's brothers Cecil ('Cis') and Percy, and their cousins Harold and Eric Lubbock, were also numbered amongst the inner circle of Monty's closest friends. There were others, less close perhaps, but still regular companions— such as Mark Sykes, a well-travelled individualist from Jesus, and

Walter Headlam, elected to a King's Fellowship in 1890 and one of the most brilliant Greek scholars of his day.

So one could go on. With such as these Monty James found what he called 'a certainty of delight'. He did not look for intensity in friendship: he neither wished to change others or be changed himself. He valued restraint, humour, security, stability and innocence, feeling most at ease with those who observed traditional decencies of thought and expression and acknowledged, as he did, that there were many areas of a person's life friendship need not comprehend. But it did not follow that these relationships existed merely on a shallow social level. On the contrary, it is clear that those special friendships that gave light to life—it is Monty's phrase—meant a very great deal to him indeed, even though he was without the capacity to give unfettered utterance to his feelings.

*   *   *

Throughout the 1890s Monty's load of official duties, for King's and for the University, increased steadily, and in spite of many compensations his responsibilities often set up a disagreeable counterpoint to his life. He gradually came to regard sitting on boards, committees and syndicates as an imposition and bore it all with a kind of grim stoicism, outwardly equable and always efficient, but inwardly deploring the inroads into his time. Even at the beginning of his deanship he gave in to exasperation:

The idiotic and fidgeting body of men who examine for the Theological Tripos want to revise the papers on the 23rd of April and they are to go to press by the 13th. Heaven knows why. But the general result is that I shall most likely not get away till after Easter. This weather too! Altogether I am in a very unpleasant frame of mind and have nothing of the theologian about me but the odium.[19]

That same year, 1891, he told Leo Maxse:

Even at King's there comes satiety of delights. There are evenings when I have to dine seated between Stearn and Nixon and it is then that I think to myself, am I going to stop here always, and can't I even have a nice little sinecure and go and work in foreign libraries . . . I am rapidly crystallizing into a don. When I hear three undergraduates singing loud in the court, my brow contracts and I look round the corner of the blind to see what they are doing, and when a lamp is put out, my high moral tone is I should think very impressive.[20]

He kept out of University politics as much as he could, though there were some issues on which he felt bound to take a stand. The question of women's degrees was one. He remained firmly opposed to allowing women to become full members of the University, prompting Cis Lubbock in May 1897 to hope that he was flourishing and 'still unhurt by the machinations of your foes, the would-be lady MAs'. He was no less determined in his resistance to abolishing Greek in the Little-go. The issue came to a head in 1904 and 1905. When Arthur Benson discussed the matter with him in January 1904 Monty seemed 'horribly Tory', his point being that Greek was a supreme literature and that 'the best education is arrived at by bringing human minds near to one great period'. Arthur, with practical teaching experience, knew that this was an excellent ideal but inapplicable to minds who were incapable of approaching either the Greek spirit or the Greek language.[21] The General Committee, formed to defend the position of the classical languages in the Little-go and of which Monty was a member, believed that the intentions of the progressives would have 'disastrous effects not only on the University, but on the higher intellectual life of the whole country'.[22] When it came to a vote in the Senate in 1905 there was a majority in favour of retaining Greek, a satisfactory outcome for Monty and for Nathaniel Wedd, who had been an unlikely ally throughout the controversy.

Though Monty claimed, no doubt truthfully, that he had less and less time to devote to his scholarly researches, the decade from 1889 to 1899 was an astonishingly productive one for him in terms of published work. In fact, it was a puzzle to some, as indicated by the following oft-quoted story, just how he achieved his immense output:

When Monty was in his early thirties, Lord Acton came here [to King's] . . . 'You know Montague James?' he asked a King's man. 'Yes, I know him.' 'Is it true that he is ready to spend every evening playing games or talking with undergraduates?' 'Yes, the evenings and more.' 'And do you know that in knowledge of MSS he is already third or fourth in Europe?' 'I am interested to hear you say so, Sir.' 'Then how does he manage it?' 'We have not yet found out.'[23]

One reason was the possession of extraordinary mental energy, as well as exceptional powers of concentration, which he could call on at a moment's notice. 'A picture of him reappears on the screen of memory,' wrote Gurney Lubbock, 'a guest in a country house, writing on odd sheets of notepaper a paper to be read at some Church

Congress, and keeping contact all the time with a youthful and noisy party surging about him. His power of concentration was such that he could switch from one thing to another, giving his whole mind to each, and entirely undistracted by the transition.' A glimpse of the physical and mental demands involved in his work on manuscripts is given in a letter to his father of June 1899:

Behold me at Oxford since Thursday morning . . . Work consists in looking at every manuscript of a certain collection known as the Bodleian MSS, being those collected I suppose in or near Thomas Bodley's own time. They consist of 800 or 900. I have at present got through 400 odd and shall not finish this time . . . This Bodleian work is very laborious and trying to the eyes. But it is good to do it, and with luck I may do almost 200 more books before I go. It is only the beginning.

It is no part of my purpose, as I have made clear, to analyse and assess the immense corpus—reviews, editions, translations, articles, catalogues, monographs—of Monty's scholarly writings. It is perhaps enough for the non-specialist to glance over S. G. Lubbock's list of writings at the end of the *Memoir*, or (better) over Dr R. W. Pfaff's more authoritative and accurate bibliography, to obtain an impression of the range and level of his achievement. However, a few points of interest from the work done during Monty's deanship may be noted.

During the Long Vacation of 1890 Monty breakfasted at Christ's with his friend J. Armitage Robinson, a Fellow there since 1881.* Robinson was a man of decided views (after becoming Dean of Westminster in 1902 he rejected a proposal that George Meredith should be buried in the Abbey on the basis of his personal literary judgement); but he and Monty shared many scholarly enthusiasms and got on well together. When Robinson left Cambridge Monty felt his departure keenly. 'There is no one left', he told his father, 'who has the faculty he had of organizing work and getting people to do it, as well as doing it himself. And certainly nobody remains who will take a rational interest in the topics which I have at heart.'[24]

With Armitage Robinson at the Long Vacation breakfast at Christ's were 'various divines', including Rendel Harris, the biblical scholar, mathematician and Orientalist. They discussed the setting up of a

---

* Monty had a small circle of friends at Christ's, including (besides Robinson) Arthur Shipley and W. Robertson Smith, a distinguished polymath who succeeded Bradshaw as University Librarian.

series of biblical and patristic studies, 'a sort of organ', as Monty described it to his parents, 'that would appear at irregular intervals and contain texts, articles and monographs too short for a book and too long for a paper'. The idea came to fruition as *Texts and Studies*, to the second volume of which (in 1892) Monty contributed his text of the Testament of Abraham (dedicated to 'H.J., M.E.J. and H.L.'—that is, to his parents and Eton tutor; Luxmoor was deeply touched by 'the incomparable compliment of putting my initials with those others'). In 1893 he also contributed a first series of *Apocrypha Anecdota*—thirteen apocryphal pieces that included the Acts of Xanthippe and Polyxena and the important Apocalypse of Paul.

In the field of manuscripts, there was occasionally a sense of drama in discovering lost material, which was drawn on, for instance, in 'Canon Alberic's Scrap-book' ('At once all Dennistoun's cherished dreams of finding priceless manuscripts in untrodden corners of France flashed up . . . '). In 1890 Monty came across a long-lost life by Thomas of Monmouth of St William of Norwich, a boy supposed to have been kidnapped and crucified by Norwich Jews in mockery of Christ's passion during Holy Week 1144. The manuscript was part of a library bequeathed about 1700 to the parish of Brent Eleigh in Suffolk. In 1887 two items were sold, but the rest, Monty learned, remained in a small dank building in the churchyard at Brent Eleigh—a promising enough setting for a ghost story. On inspecting the collection, it did not take him long to decide (somewhat like Dennistoun in 'Canon Alberic') that they should return with him to Cambridge, and eventually they were acquired—one manuscript for the Fitzwilliam, the rest for the University Library. Through the St William manuscript Monty met the well-known Norwich antiquary Augustus Jessop* and together they prepared an edition, *The Life and Miracles of St William of Norwich*, which was published by the Cambridge University Press in 1896.

At the end of the Lent Term 1893 he travelled down to the West Country to visit some King's properties—including Sampford Court-

---

* Dr Jessop, incidentally, had had a remarkable, apparently supernatural, experience in October 1879 at Mannington Hall near Norwich, the home of Lord Orford. Whilst working in the library at about one in the morning he became aware of a man in 'a kind of ecclesiastical habit' at his back, examining the pile of books on which he had been working. His account of the incident, first published in the *Athenaeum*, appeared in *Lord Halifax's Ghost Book* (1936). One would like to think that Monty was given a description of the experience by Dr Jessop himself at some point during their association.

enay, the setting of 'Martin's Close'. Before he left, he told his parents that 'Sidney Sussex College has agreed to print a catalogue of their manuscripts which I am to make, on condition that some other College will join in the scheme and have them done at the same time. I have hopes that King's and Jesus may join. This will be a step towards my cherished design of making Catalogues of the manuscripts in all or most of the College libraries here.' Though Sidney was the first Cambridge college with which Monty made formal cataloguing arrangements, he had been working on the Western manuscripts in King's since at least the autumn of 1885. It is not clear if, or to what extent, he consulted Bradshaw when he began his work (Bradshaw, it will be remembered, died in 1886); but at some point he had access to Bradshaw's notes, consisting of partial descriptions and some complete collations of eighteen of the manuscripts.

After the Cyprus excavations, Monty may have intended to make classical archaeology his main subject; but purely classical studies were soon somewhat eclipsed by his work on Apocrypha and Christian origins. And then, in the mid–1890s, came the first of the unrivalled series of manuscript catalogues, perhaps his greatest and most enduring monument as a scholar. 'Others perhaps could have done the work, or some of it, on Apocrypha,' wrote Sir Stephen Gaselee, 'but his encyclopaedic knowledge, marvellous memory, vast industry, and curious *flair* made him uniquely fitted for his great series of books cataloguing medieval manuscripts in the greater libraries of England.' 'There has never been before,' Gaselee continued, 'and probably there will never be again, a single man with the same accomplishment and combination of memory, palaeography, medieval learning, and artistic knowledge . . . I consider him in *volume* of learning the greatest scholar it has been my good fortune to know.'[25]

Monty himself modestly considered his catalogues to have been preliminary work, though he admitted they were 'on a scale that had not been tried before'. They resulted in 'the accumulation of a heap of scraps of odd miscellaneous information, scraps which often enough are found to be really threads connecting one book with another, and perhaps in the end helping to link up a whole group, and reveal a whole chapter in the history of a library'.[26] His broader aim, hinted at here, was to use the detailed examination of many thousands of manuscripts to build up a picture of individual medieval libraries and then, cumulatively, to understand the overall literary framework of medieval civilization. It was an attempt, as Dr Pfaff has put it, 'to construct a kind of *bibliothèque imaginaire* of the books of medieval England, and to a lesser extent of medieval Europe as a whole'.[27]

In 1895 Monty published four descriptive catalogues of Cambridge manuscripts: for King's (in which he paid tribute to 'the brilliance and thoroughness' of Bradshaw's work and reproduced in one description an ingenious diagram of Bradshaw's on the disarrangement of MS 3); for the Fitzwilliam; for Jesus and Sidney Sussex. His Eton catalogue also appeared that year. This first series was followed by catalogues for all the other colleges, ending with St Catharine's in 1925. Besides these there were other catalogues for the collections of Henry Yates Thompson, J. Pierpont Morgan, the John Rylands Library at Manchester, Aberdeen University Library and Lambeth Palace. By any standard, it was a stupendous achievement, and its effects have been lasting, as the following expert assessment, written nearly thirty years after Monty's death, makes clear:

The effects of James's achievement were many and far-reaching: perhaps most important, it perfected the method of description of manuscripts which had been gradually developed by Delisle, Warner and Maunde Thompson, and established it as a form of scholarship demanding the highest degree of learning, aesthetic appreciation, imagination, patience and recollection. James was blessed with a wonderful memory both for visual appearance and for fact, which enabled him to recall a book read or a manuscript seen long before. His learning enabled him to unravel the most complicated liturgical problem or the obscurest medieval text. His gift of imagination and his understanding of the development of scripts, the change of style in illumination, the construction of medieval books and the methods of medieval libraries, enabled him to link together manuscripts, by provenance and on stylistic grounds, and thus to provide a coherent map of what had been largely uncharted territory. That we now have a fairly clear picture of the activity, in different places and at different times, of the various centres which produced manuscripts in England in the Middle Ages, is largely due to M. R. James.[28]

CHAPTER 10

DR JAMES
King's 1892–1900

Of the subjects within his vast field of learning he never spoke
unless questioned, and it was difficult to believe that he could take
any interest in the gossip and badinage which formed the staple of
the talk, yet there was always a curious feeling of intimacy about
the gatherings, which made one realize why it was that Monty
James made more friends amongst the fleeting Cambridge
generations than any other of the dons and kept those friendships
longer.

Charles Tennyson, *Stars and Markets*

THE double tricycle trip to France with Hugh Childers in 1884 had,
said Monty, 'settled the question as to what was to be the holiday
country'. Year after year he returned to France with small parties of
friends. In the spring of 1892 the party included Armitage Robinson
and Arthur Shipley. From Paris they had travelled to Bordeaux and
then inland to Auch, where the cathedral with its magnificent black
stalls received Monty's full approval. At Tarbes, their next stop, the
cathedral was dismissed as being 'very stupid'. A branch line from
Montréjeau took them to Lourdes, where they fortified themselves
with Madeira and biscuits before travelling in a closed fly through a
snow-covered landscape to St Bertrand de Comminges, which Monty
had been wanting to see since at least 1887.

St Bertrand is the setting of 'Canon Alberic's Scrap-book', probably
the first of the published ghost stories to have been written. The
features of the cathedral at St Bertrand, described in the story as 'a
decayed town on the spurs of the Pyrenees', were noted and marked by
Monty on a sketch plan sent to his parents and reappear in the story:
the dusty crocodile skin that hung at the western end, the 'enormous
dilapidated organ', the stalls of Bishop Jean de Mauléon, and the
treasury, containing the ivory crozier said to have belonged to St

Bertrand himself. One of the few lyrical passages in the ghost stories describes the locality of St Bertrand:

It was time to ring the Angelus. A few pulls at the reluctant rope, and the great bell Bertrande, high in the tower, began to speak, and swung her voice up among the pines and down to the valleys, loud with mountain-streams, calling the dwellers on those lonely hills to remember and repeat the salutation of the angel to her whom he called Blessed among women.

In July Monty visited Ireland, where Ber was now stationed. He was struck by the general capacity of the people he met to consume whisky, and was also impressed by the 'horrid' vaults of St Michan's Church in Dublin, which had the property of preserving corpses in a dry and dusty state for centuries. They were, he admitted, 'a nightmare'. The memory was incorporated into 'Lost Hearts', another early ghost story (probably the second to be written): 'His description of what he saw reminds me of what I once beheld myself in the famous vaults of St Michan's Church ... A figure inexpressibly thin and pathetic, of a dusty leaden colour, enveloped in a shroud-like garment ... '[1]

Whilst in Ireland Monty also heard tales about fairies from the man who took him from Castlebar to Westport, viewed Murrisk Abbey, and admired the island-studded expanse of Clew Bay from the summit of Croagh Patrick. At Galway he noted a good deal of Parnellite enthusiasm: 'They call Parnell the murdered chief, for some reason best known to themselves.' He met some Irish politicians, of whom he considered that only John Dillon could be called a gentleman: 'The others are second or third or fifth raters. Dillon is I think an honest man but a fanatic.'[2] On the whole Ireland depressed him and he came away convinced that Home Rule was ridiculous.

In August he was thirty and received a letter from his mother expressing 'thankful remembrance of all you have been to us from the time that you were our "Baby"!' Soon afterwards he spent some time with Sir Arthur Hamilton Gordon, the father of a young Trinity friend, George Hamilton Gordon, at his home at Ascot. Monty rather took to Hamilton Gordon, who was an amateur antiquarian, a keen photographer and 'the only other man [i.e. apart from Monty] who knows all the French Bishoprics'.[3] There was friendly rivalry between them as to who would see all the French cathedrals first. They made two trips to France together, the first being in 1896.

This trip was accomplished by train and carriage; but more usually holidays abroad for Monty involved the bicycle. In the 1880s there had

been an extraordinary range of machines available for the enthusiast—
including the 'Ordinary' (i.e. the 'penny-farthing', still supreme in the
mid-1880s), 'dwarf' Ordinaries, tandem tricycles, 'sociable' tricycles
(two people sitting side by side), and quadricycles. In 1884–5 came the
rear-driven 'safety' bicycle, and in July 1888 J. B. Dunlop patented his
pneumatic tyre. Soon everyone was cycling. In 1895 and 1896 the best
of London society could be seen on safety bicycles in Rotten Row;
in 1896 H. G. Wells published *The Wheels of Chance*, in which
Hoopdriver finds freedom and adventure on a bicycle; and at Easter
1895 the Dean of King's College, Cambridge, who had been amongst
the intrepid minority of earlier cyclists, took his first holiday abroad on
a pneumatic-tyred safety bicycle.

He had needed some persuasion to adopt the new machine, being,
as Gurney Lubbock said, 'always conservative and not very adventurous in such matters'. But he was an enthusiastic convert and as far as
holidays were concerned the mode of travel was now settled. 'Who
shall duly celebrate the excellences of the push-bike tour in France,
particularly in the years before the War? Over thirty times I did it, so I
do not speak without knowledge.'[4]

In September 1895, during his second Continental trip on the new
bicycle, he embarked on the longest ride he ever made—from Dieppe
to Regensburg (Ratisbon) on the Danube, with S. G. Lubbock and
James McBryde. The French section of the tour was described to his
parents in an unusually expansive letter. Between Noyon and Coucy
they had crossed a canal and Monty had been struck by 'the great
procession of trees each side going right away into the distance with
the water between them and the sun at the other end'.[5] At Coucy the
inn was small, but owing to the good offices of the patron they were
able to take a cold bath in a wooden tub in the stable yard—'a curious
sight', remarked Monty.

From Laon their road took them through a strange country, flat and
treeless, which they crossed in gathering darkness. There was nothing
to see 'but the skyline, the white road, and the moon: we got over it
quickly, but all the time the breeze made curious moaning sounds as if
the country was full of wandering souls'. Reaching Neufchâtel, they
were led by the patron of the inn down to the river to bathe by the town
bridge in bright moonlight: 'It was about 9 o'clock, and all the available
people came to sit on the bank and see us through it.' The next day
they reached Reims, to find that their luggage had not arrived, which
was too much even for Monty's equanimity. 'What incredible,

Monty on a visit to the Cropper family in Westmorland, probably 1903

Left to right: James McBryde, Monty James, and S. G. ('Jimbo') Lubbock, Regensburg, 1895

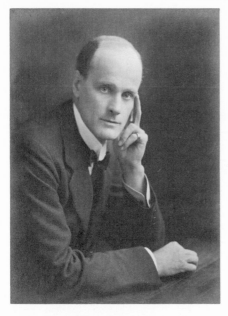

Walter Fletcher, 1920

Gordon Carey

The Cropper family at Ellergreen, August 1901. *Front row, left to right*: Eleanor, James (Jem), Maisie, Margaret, and Sibyl (Billy). *Back row, left to right*: Edith Cropper, Charles James Cropper

unimaginative, effete, inadequate, conceited, incompetent, muddle-headed, unintelligent, fussy, infernal imbeciles all and every single person in the whole of France in any way connected with railways or luggage is or are,' he fumed (the memory returned many years later when, in the generally restrained pages of *Eton and King's*, he spoke of 'the phenomenal perennial pigheadedness of French railwaymen about luggage'). But nothing could produce in McBryde anything approaching irritation, 'while the courage which enabled him to seize by its sinewy leg the largest spider I have ever seen in a derelict bath at Verdun commanded the deepest respect'.[6] But in spite of the railwaymen, France remained, as Gurney Lubbock said, Monty's greatest love and left him with a rich store of memories—of churches, cathedrals, landscapes, and a thousand incidents shared with those friends who explored with him the byways of provincial France.

The route of each holiday was more or less determined by the sites of cathedrals or former cathedrals ('The sight of a cathedral ought to do any one good, not only morally but physically,' Monty had written back in 1883). As always, Monty was able to make good use of his time, and the holiday explorations in France were important for deepening his knowledge of medieval art and architecture—in one of his notebooks, for instance, is an extraordinarily detailed plan of the nave and apse-roof of Albi Cathedral, showing the exact disposition of the paintings and inscriptions. In Gurney Lubbock's experience, travelling with Monty James was 'a liberal education in architecture and in the meaning of every bit of sculpture and painted glass'.

Besides the many French holidays, Monty also bicycled in Denmark and Sweden. He was particularly fond of Denmark:

Hans Andersen and the old ballads had already prepared me to find in Denmark what I daresay a great many people do not look for there—a land of romance. The first evening we spent there fully answered expectation, as we lay on the edge of the river in the big meadow by Ribe and watched the behaviour of the storks on the housetops over against us, with Ribe cathedral tower in the background, and a most radiant sunset.[7]

He first visited Denmark, with McBryde and Will Stone, another good friend of Monty's, in the summer of 1899 and took to the country immediately, finding the people 'very un-foreign on the whole: not German-like'. His experience of the Danes is incorporated into his story 'Number 13', in which Anderson, finding his portmanteau missing, dismisses the idea of theft at once: 'Such things rarely happen in Denmark, but some piece of stupidity had certainly been performed (which is not so uncommon) . . . '[8]

He was engrossed by Jutland folklore and savoured the magical feel of the landscape: 'We saw mirage effects twice yesterday,' runs one passage, 'appearances on the horizon of woods and water, where there may have been trees but water certainly was not.' They saw the standing stones on the wild Jutland heath, and a fresco in the cathedral at Roskilde that showed a devil writing, with the inscription (in Monty's translation), 'I take the names of those who are late and walk about talking idly.'

At Odense, Monty signalled his entrance into the town by knocking over a Danish lady on her bicycle. In Copenhagen they visited the Thorwaldsden Museum—'a most dreary show'—and the Museum of Northern Antiquities, which was much better and 'quite wonderful in gold ornaments, flint weapons, bronze war trumpets and church curiosities'. He returned to Denmark the following year (1900), again with McBryde, and stayed in Viborg, the setting of 'Number 13'.* Sweden, which they had crossed over to briefly in 1899, they visited properly in 1901. One of the highlights was at Uppsala, where Monty saw 'two contracts with the devil written (and signed in blood) in 1718 by Daniel Salthenius, who was condemned to death for writing them. He escaped that and died professor of divinity at Königsberg.'[9] Sweden furnished the background for 'Count Magnus', one of the most powerful of Monty's early ghost stories.

*   *   *

Ever since his Fellowship in 1887 Monty had continued as Assistant Director of the Fitzwilliam Museum, the post secured for him by Waldstein in October 1886. He had been appointed in the first instance for three years. The expiration of this period, in the Michaelmas Term of 1889, coincided with the departure of Waldstein for the American School at Athens and the election of a new director. Monty boldly decided to put himself up for the post. He did not want to break his connection with the Museum, but he knew he had little chance of success if, as seemed probable, J. H. Middleton, the colourful Slade Professor of Fine Art, also stood. Middleton is described with affection and amusement in *Eton and King's*: 'Clad in a

---

* According to the Preface of the *Collected Ghost Stories* (1931), however, 'Number 13' was written in 1899, i.e. after the first trip to Denmark.

dressing-gown or a velveteen coat, and a skull-cap, and smoking a kind of shag (as I should call it) named "Golden Returns", he sat and retailed in a level voice, with frequent slight dramatic pauses, the most startling personal experiences.' But in spite of his liking for Middleton, Monty was not convinced that he was a wise choice for the directorship of the Museum. As he wrote frankly to Francis Jenkinson, a distinguished bibliographical scholar and Fellow of Trinity who became University Librarian in the autumn of 1889:

To tell you true, I am a little frightened at the prospect of Middleton in his relation to the staff and I think it a mistake that he should succeed Waldstein. Now I suppose it is impossible to suggest that Middleton should be appointed a deputy during the term that Waldstein is away: but if in that way or some way like it, a complete change could be obviated, I believe it would be a good thing.[10]

But Middleton was elected and he immediately asked that Monty's appointment as Assistant Director be renewed for a further three years. In 1893, when Middleton left Cambridge for the South Kensington Museum (now the Victoria and Albert), it was inevitable that Monty would succeed him. The only objection raised against him, according to Middleton, was that he was already fully occupied with College and University work; but he was elected unanimously (there were no other candidates). He received a note of congratulation from Edmund Gosse, then a lecturer in English Literature at Trinity whom Monty had met at a Savile Club lunch in 1888.* 'The Fitzwilliam will be a capital field for the exercise of some of those talents which everyone who knows you (except yourself) recognizes and admires,' wrote Gosse. 'I suppose it will still leave your evenings free for those poor old doggrell-mongers of the third century on whom you expend (notice! I don't say *waste*) what was meant for mankind?' Two years later, in 1895, Monty received the degree of Doctor of Letters, at the early age of thirty-three—a recognition of his already impressive academic achievements, as well as of his work at the Fitzwilliam.

One consequence of the directorship was that he had to give up one of his college offices. A. H. Cooke was about to vacate the position of Senior Dean, and though A. E. Brooke, Monty's Eton contemporary, could fill the junior post, Monty could not see who would take over as Senior Dean if he resigned. His lectureship should go, then—with few

---

* He had met Thomas Hardy on the same occasion.

regrets. In spite of its association with the Chapel and the Choir School, there were also times when he wished he could give up the deanship as well. During the summer of 1896, Cooke wrote to dissuade him from taking such a step: 'Banish such a thought from your mind. It doesn't come within the range of practical politics at all. There is nobody here who could take it. We may (here and there) reform you—we couldn't replace you.'

Throughout these years, Monty kept up a connection with Eton, going there often on purely social visits, but also on official business. In 1895 he examined for the Newcastle for the second time, and while he was there he looked in on Arthur Benson, now a housemaster. Arthur's boys acted two plays that they had written, one a tragedy, the other a farce. Monty remarked that they were both extremely funny. The following year he was with Arthur briefly at Tan-yr-allt, the house near Portmadoc once occupied by Shelley and now joint-leased by A. C. Ainger and Howard Sturgis, two close friends of Arthur's, as a bachelor retreat. From Tan, Monty bicycled to Caernarvon, where he was met by James McBryde and taken to his home in Beaumaris to meet James's father and two sisters.

Cycling offered him frequent escape from the dull round of Cambridge business, and even provided an occasional welcome break from manuscript cataloguing. There would also be days in London, as in January 1898, when he did some work at the British Museum, saw a pantomime (a favourite outing of his for Christmas and the New Year) and went to 'the Aquarium and saw the cinematograph of the great fight between Corbett and Fitzsimmons. Contrary to my expectations it interested me very much, and I could not see any brutality in it.'*

Part at least of the Christmas holidays was usually spent at Livermere, but as early as 1891 Monty felt that the break-up of the home circle was not far distant. Leaving after the family gathering that year had been 'rather gloomy work; though nobody makes the remark, I feel always that everybody is thinking "This is the last time": especially when one's parents are sixty-nine and seventy-three.'[11] Ber left to serve in China in 1892, and Sydney seemed settled as a bachelor housemaster at Eton. Then in 1897 Sydney announced his engagement to Linda Hoare, whose uncle owned Ampton Hall, just a mile or

---

* The fight between Jim Corbett and Bob Fitzsimmons, one of the classic contests of early heavyweight boxing, took place in Carson City, USA, in 1897.

so from Livermere. Monty, faced with writing to his prospective sister-in-law, was not sure what he should say; but his mother, who perhaps hoped that it would not be long before Monty found a suitable wife, was elated. She wrote to him from Livermere in a cold January, heading her letter 'Arctic Regions': 'Only a line of congratulation! for I am sure you are glad of Sydney's engagement . . . I think it is as nice as possible! (only I wish she were not so delicate!).'

Sydney and Linda were married in April 1897 and returned to Eton for what was to be Sydney's last half. On hearing that the headmastership of Malvern was vacant, Sydney decided to offer himself as a candidate, describing himself in his application as 'an attached Churchman, without belonging to any ecclesiastical party or section'. 'I shall be pretty sick at leaving this place,' he told Monty.

A spark of ambition and the possibility of moving from here before settling quite down into married life and the bracing air for Linda and the fact that I have got to the end of my tether here in several ways, combined to start me on the idea.

Sydney's application was successful and he was elected Headmaster at the end of June. Malvern meant an interesting new locality for Monty to visit, and in time there was a flock of nieces and nephews. One interesting consequence of Sydney's new post was that Monty drew up a scheme for the glass in the new chapel at Malvern, which was used for the first time in March 1899.

In February 1898 Monty's mother celebrated what was to be her last birthday. She died peacefully at Livermere, aged eighty, that September and was buried in the churchyard. Early the following year, when James McBryde's father died, Monty looked back to the loss of his mother in a letter of sympathy to his friend. 'It changes the world a good deal and makes you feel older,' he wrote, 'and all things look for a time less certain than they did . . . To us who have been for years accustomed to being long away from home it is not quite so shocking and terrible.' 'And yet', he went on, 'there are other things to be thought of. I like to think—indeed it is more than thinking—that people when they go into the next world lose all the weakness and bodily trouble in which we have known them, and are young again, and see the others whom they have been missing for a long time here, and are at their best, growing to be more perfect instead of weaker.'[12] Mary Emily's life, he is supposed to have said, was the most perfect he had ever known.[13] His father, now seventy-six, at last agreed to share his

parochial work with a resident curate, the Revd J. E. Woodhouse, an
Oxford man some six years older than Monty.

*   *   *

Soon after his mother's death, in October 1898, Monty had to read
a paper at a Church Congress in York and found time to inspect 'two
charming churches'—Skelton and Nun Monkton. 'At Nun Monkton',
he told his father, 'a beautiful house adjoins the church—Queen Anne
with a sweet garden and leaden statues and a summerhouse—
panelled, with a lead roof and cupola. You may have it for £30 a
year—it is haunted.' That was exactly the kind of house—with or
without a ghost—that Monty dreamed of owning, preferably in East
Anglia. The opening paragraph of his story 'The Ash-tree' describes
just such a house:

Everyone who has travelled over Eastern England knows the smaller
country-houses with which it is studded—the rather dank little buildings,
usually in the Italian style, surrounded with parks of some eighty to a hundred
acres. For me they have always had a very strong attraction: with the grey
paling of split oak, the noble trees, the meres with their reed-beds, and the line
of distant woods. Then, I like the pillared portico—perhaps stuck on to a
red-brick Queen Anne house which as been faced with stucco to bring it into
line with the 'Grecian' taste of the end of the eighteenth century . . . and
perhaps most of all I like fancying what life in such a house was when it was
first built . . . I wish to have one of these houses, and enough money to keep it
together and entertain my friends in it modestly.[14]

But if that was his dream, there seemed little chance that it would
come true without the means to break away into independence.

March 1899 found him battling with the Fitzwilliam accounts ('It is
extraordinary what figures will do if you add them up a few times'),
working on 'a *stratum* of nasty paper books at Trinity which yield very
little satisfaction', and cycling to Bartlow with Marcus Dimsdale and
Percy Lubbock. Snow then kept him indoors for a week and restricted
his exercise to a little battledore and shuttlecock in Hall. McBryde's
father died that month, and James talked of giving up the idea of a
medical career and trying to make a living as an artist instead: 'I hardly
know what to advise him. He never liked medicine, and I don't know
that it suited him: one thing is fortunate, that if he decides not to go on,
he will not be in want. But at present he is in great trouble. He was a
very great friend of his father's.'

By the early part of the summer work began to pile up: manuscripts at Christ's and Trinity (he had also 'made overtures to Clare'), a trip to Sotheby's, chorister trials, three lectures on non-canonical Revelations to write for the Church Congress in Leeds towards the end of June, Tripos work, and 'forty thousand other things'.

In November he alerted his father to developments that seemed to bear directly on his position at King's. A. H. Cooke, then Tutor, had decided to stand for the headmastership of Aldenham: 'It will then probably become a question of whether the undersigned takes part of the Tutorial work . . . Therefore if you see that Cooke is appointed to Aldenham you will know that the fat is in the Fire.' 'Cooke has been made Headmaster of Aldenham,' his next letter begins, 'so the fat is where I said it would be . . . ' It now seemed likely that he would be made Tutor: 'Among my frenzied supporters I reckon Cooke and O.B. and the Provost and the Vice-Provost. I should of course be immensely relieved if [W. H.] Macaulay—say—were made Tutor instead. But if I am wanted, I must not say No.'

In January 1900, Monty told his father that he had been appointed Tutor: 'I do not propose—as at present advised—to lecture nor continue to be Dean . . . The new trade will take me some time to master.' Luxmoore was doubtful if the appointment was a wise one either for King's or for Monty:

Of course it's a compliment to elect him and shews due honour from his College . . . But either it might stir him out of his somewhat unproductive groove, for he does 'produce' too little for his powers! Or it might just take him from what suits him to more office work, which he might not exert himself enough to fulfil. One can't fancy him answering letters, and while he exercises the old charm on his own circle he may fail to exert himself to reach the less congenial undergraduates. It is a doubtful prospect.[15]

CHAPTER 11

CHANGES
King's 1900–1904

Still are thy pleasant voices, thy nightingales, awake;
For Death, he taketh all away, but them he cannot take.

William (Johnson) Cory, *Heraclitus*

THE 'new trade' was largely, and uncongenially, administrative: hiring lodgings, assigning rooms, dealing with admissions, and overseeing undergraduate studies. Added to his other obligations, the tutorship reduced Monty's free time still further. He wrote to his father in May 1900:

The busy end of the term is creeping on. I am this week occupied with assignment of rooms: then will come hiring of lodgings, then a Council: then a Fitzwilliam Syndicate, and Library ditto, a Congregation, an Entrance Examination, an Election to Scholarships and Exhibitions, award of prizes and general mess lasting until about June 20, and then I hope for a short holiday. I am proposing to bicycle towards Malvern. But it seems years ahead. I shall be most thankful when the Long Vacation has really begun . . . The country is, as they say, looking its best. Would that I could see more of it.

In October things were no better: 'Interview of one hour with a distressed parent being over, I snatch a few moments before port time to give you no news . . . I have had no visitors from outside, and have been trying to make acquaintance with freshmen and get through work of different kinds. No travels, exercise . . . ' It was not long before he began to look for a way out. 'I am sorry you are overburdened with the Tutorship,' wrote Arthur Benson from Eton. 'I always thought you self-sacrificing to take it. Similar functions here are a good deal too much for me very often . . . We are getting old, sir!'[1]

Some relief was provided by a controversy over the windows of Malvern Priory, which contained fifteenth-century glass in a generally defective state and in which Monty had been interested since the 1880s. He had visited Malvern, staying with Sydney, in June 1899, 'to confer with those in authority on the possibility of rearranging the Priory Church windows. This would be a job after my own heart.' But his proposals ran counter to those of a Mrs McClure, a member of the local restoration committee, whom Monty described as 'a lady resident at Malvern who thinks we ought to restore the mutilated pictures in the glass or else do nothing: how completely I disagree with her I can hardly express in polite language.'[2]

The following year (1901) he involved himself in another antiquarian controversy, this time concerning the bones of St Edmund. Monty's interest in the Abbey at Bury and in St Edmund himself was of course of long standing (he had already written a monograph on the library and the interior of the Abbey Church in 1895).* In 1901, as he later described in *Suffolk and Norfolk*, 'certain relics were obtained from the Canons of St Sernin's Church at Toulouse to be deposited in the Westminster Cathedral, then newly built. They were said to be the relics of St Edmund.' He dismissed the claims of the Toulouse bones to be genuine and wrote a letter to *The Times* 'about the bones of St Edmund which the Papists are foisting upon us. I don't believe in them.'[3]

By the end of November 1900 the main question in Monty's mind was how soon he could decently leave off being Tutor. 'There will be many protestations and declamations,' he said, 'but the prospect of an indefinite period of arranging for examinations, taking lodgings, arranging rooms, deciding about payments, which with other like duties are seven-eighths of the work, is one which I cannot face with equanimity.'

But he pressed on for the time being, accommodating his other commitments as best he could. He had already mentioned to the Provost that he was considering resignation. Austen Leigh wrote to him offering to take on the most troublesome part of the work himself and enclosing part of a letter he had received from A. H. Cooke 'in which he speaks his mind about the consequences of your retiring. I do not think he expresses them too strongly.'[4]

I hear [wrote Cooke] what seem more than rumours that James contemplates giving up the tutorship at an early date. I trust he may at least be induced to hold on until some acceptable person has qualified to succeed him. It would be a terrible calamity to the College to put one of the ungodly party—like Wedd

---

* In 1902, Monty supervised excavations at the Abbey in conjunction with Sir Ernest Clarke, during which the remains of six abbots were found.

or Berry [a mathematics don at King's], or even Macaulay—in his place. I would move heaven and earth to prevent the scandal of the College, which possesses King's Chapel, having a tutor who never entered it.[5]

In a long letter Austen Leigh elaborated upon the reasons why he was anxious Monty should not give up the tutorship. His letter is of considerable importance, not only because of its bearing on Monty's career, but also because of the light it throws on a crucial phase of the College's development. It clearly shows the split between the Churchmen and the agnostics—a transmutation of the old division between the Exclusives and the Excluded—that was, to some extent, responsible for confirming Monty's inclination to leave Cambridge at the end of the First World War, by which time the 'ungodly' element was well and truly in the ascendant. Austen Leigh listed three points in which Monty's ceasing to be Tutor would be, in his opinion, a great loss to the College:

(1) We should have a less distinguished man.
(2) We should probably have a Tutor who would be less human, less able to understand and be understood by undergraduates.
(3) We should have one whose religious influence and example would be at best nil, and therefore mischievous.

The central problem from Austen Leigh's point of view was the lack of sound Christian types amongst the likely candidates for the tutorship. 'If our Assistant Tutors and Lecturers were all men who set an example of Christian faith and practice, it would be of less importance if the Tutor himself happened to be an exception. But you know what our staff are.' He finished his letter with a direct appeal to Monty's conscience: 'Except in the case of such literary work as really influences our deepest convictions and consequently our character, it is not so important as the conduct and character of several generations of undergraduates. And I feel that, in *the particular circumstances of the College*, it may be right for you to choose the more distasteful course.'[6] Put like that, there was little Monty could do but continue as Tutor, though unwillingly. He bore it all for another eighteen months, but by May 1902 it was over and W. H. Macaulay, an able if rather formidable mathematician, was appointed Tutor in his place. Monty told Henry Babington Smith: 'The correspondence and routine have no terrors for one who has been a bursar so long, and the work doesn't keep him from other pursuits.' Monty's relief at getting rid of the tutorship was considerable, and as he explained to his father: 'It was never my job really this dealing with organization, and I am only too thankful to have got through my period of office without making such a hash as might have been expected.'[7]

He was now without a College post, though he still complained of too little free time: 'I have had too much to do and too many people to see to allow me to go on very far with my literary work. I really must find means to get more time to myself.' To comply with the 1882 Statutes, the College made him a lecturer (in Palaeography) in order to continue his Fellowship. It was 'a mere name', noted Arthur Benson, 'no lectures—not even a syllabus. I suggested that one should be founded of Neography and conferred on me. I could discourse critically about Fred's [his brother's] novels.'[8]

The flavour and vigour of turn-of-the-century King's are caught in the pages of *Basileona* (later called *Basileon*), a college magazine started in the summer of 1900 by Charles Tennyson and R. H. Malden, two Old Etonian undergraduates who were associated with Monty's circle. It nevertheless attracted contributions from all sections of King's society and from 1900 to 1914 its contributors included E. M. Forster, Stephen Gaselee, J. T. Sheppard, C. R. Fay, Gilbert Cannan, A. D. (Dilwyn) Knox, J. R. (Shane) Leslie, A. F. Scholfield, Hugh Dalton, Arthur (Waley) Schloss, and Rupert Brooke. The last of Brooke's contributions, in June 1912, was the serio-comic 'Fragments from a poem to be entitled "The Sentimental Exile"', which the world now knows as 'The Old Vicarage, Grantchester'. From amongst Monty's friends, Percy Lubbock supplied poems, and James McBryde some sets of his comic drawings. Monty himself never wrote for *Basileon* or its successors, except for a short eulogistic piece when Fred Whitting retired as Vice-Provost in 1910; but he is referred to in 'The Fresher's Guide to College Clubs and Societies', written by Gerald Shove for the magazine in June 1909. After dealing with three College societies, the piece concludes:

The remainder of the College affect one of these three groups:
  1. The Sheppard's flock.
  2. The Dicken's sons.
  3. They who keep Montem.*

Amongst new friends made at this period who contributed to

---

* The allusions are to J. T Sheppard, a future Provost, G. L. Dickinson, and Monty. Montem was an Etonian ceremony (abolished in 1847) in which money was collected to help pay for the Captain of the School's expenses at University.

Basileon were Stephen Gaselee and Alwyn Scholfield, two Etonians who came up to King's in 1901 and 1903 respectively. Gaselee, described by a contemporary as 'a first-class classical scholar, a bibliophile, a bibliographer, a liturgiologist . . . a lay Prince of the Church, Ecclesiastic Militant and Gastronomer Royal',[9] was a celebrated Cambridge character. Though never one of Monty's closest friends, his tastes and background ensured him a welcome. 'Conversation was general,' he wrote of the evening gatherings in Monty's rooms,

but he was pleased above all to resolve questions on learned subjects; which he would either answer from his own great store of knowledge, or by that faculty particularly ascribed to lawyers, of knowing exactly where the required information was to be found. I think, from descriptions given me by my father, this was much in the tradition of Henry Bradshaw . . . He was a devoted son of the Church of England and would describe himself as protestant, though he liked a grave and dignified ceremonial: he had some sympathy with the tractarians, but none with 'the ritualists'; in politics, uninterested, but faintly conservative.[10]

Alwyn Scholfield was also a bibliophile, as well as being prominent in University drama. He taught briefly at Eton and in 1923 became both a Fellow of King's and University Librarian. 'Scho' was much closer than Gaselee to Monty, whose letters to Scholfield are an important source of information for the latter half of his life.

On 22 January 1901 the Victorian age came to an end with the death of the Queen. 'We had a huge crowd yesterday afternoon in Chapel,' Monty reported. 'Their appetite for the Dead March is always keen and they flock whenever there is a chance of it, but on this occasion they are to be credited with better motives.' In February came a more personal loss: the death from pneumonia of Will Stone, who had shared two recent Scandinavian holidays with Monty and McBryde. It was a great blow, 'not to be realized all in a moment, but the gap is a large one . . . For myself, it is the first time I have lost a companion of that age and those associations and I do not at all know what to make of it.'[11] Monty's father was 'sorry, very sorry, for your sorrow' and tried to encourage a recognition of God's deeper purpose: 'You will feel, I know, that He is speaking to you in the removal of your friend with the loving purpose that you may come nearer to Him, and make Him to be the very Life of your life.' Luxmoore saw clearly that Monty had been wounded by Will Stone's death; but as he told Herbert James, there was something in the thought that King's 'and especially as I believe

Monty's friendship were what gave the boy his "lift" and enabled him to find himself'.

In November the following year, Monty learned over tea with Walter Fletcher of his engagement to Maisie Cropper, the sister of a younger Trinity man, James ('Jem') Cropper. Monty was delighted for him and immediately sent off a letter to Maisie, whom he had never met. Maisie responded appreciatively to the kindness he had evidently shown in his letter: 'I'm so glad you do feel that I'm not in any way taking away from Walter's friendship only, if I may, adding mine to his . . . I know how much your friendship has meant and means to Walter and will mean. I trust to both of us in the time that's coming: and it's very generous of you to welcome me like this.' A few days later Monty dashed in for tea with Walter to show him Maisie's reply, 'which he wears next to his heart to make me feel jealous'.[12]

When Maisie eventually came down to Cambridge from her home in Westmorland she was taken 'almost trembling' to meet Monty over lunch; but he put her completely at her ease, and in fact reduced her to tears of laughter with his imitation of Fred Whitting, who suddenly walked in to deliver his congratulations to Walter while Monty was in full flight. The following evening, over a late-night game of piquet, Monty told Walter that Maisie was 'perfectly right in every possible direction—he gives you full marks and says I couldn't conceivably have been luckier in being loved, and he says he is almost homesick to see you again and make proper friends.'[13] It was unusual for Monty to be so enthusiastic at the prospect of a friend's marriage. For one thing, as he had written to Leo Maxse in 1891, when those around him began to succumb to matrimony, 'I begin to think my time is approaching, but only in my wilder moments.' For another, the marriage of friends had an obvious effect on their social lives. As he told Henry Babington Smith in 1903, 'Most of the people I know best here are beginning to get married. Marcus Dimsdale, who did so last year, has become completely invisible.'[14]

The Croppers were of old Quaker stock. Charles and Edith Cropper had five children: Eleanor, Jem, Maisie, Margaret, and Sibyl. Margaret and Sibyl, the two youngest daughters, were known as 'the Billies', after Sibyl's nickname, 'Billy'. Monty paid the first of many visits to the Croppers' home, Ellergreen, near Cowan Bridge over Christmas 1902, the first of Walter's friends to be introduced to his fiancée's family. Monty's arrival was described by Sibyl in 1939, in a short introduction to a selection of Monty's letters to her:

When I was a little girl of twelve—the rather precocious youngest of a largish family—Dr James first came to stay at my home in Westmorland. On his arrival we somehow failed to meet his train and he made his way from the station, a quarter of a mile or so, on foot. My first encounter with him was then, when I found him wandering round the house in the early winter dusk, trying to find the front door, and murmuring to himself: 'I don't see no red carpet laid down, I don't see no flags a-flying.'

From that day onwards we became friends. On holiday visits in winter there was reading of ghost stories by candlelight, in summer there were long games of croquet and garden golf, and between whiles, in term-time, a nonsense correspondence . . . about such absorbing topics as college cats, importunate rooks and inebriate owls.[15]

In these letters, Monty would address Sibyl as 'Dear Fellow-Scientist', and she would reply to 'Dear Dr Apple Pie'. When she invited Monty to see Buffalo Bill's Wild West Show in London, he accepted, to the complete amazement of Walter Fletcher, who wrote: 'I pretended not to be surprised when he admitted it, but internally I gasped.' When Sibyl came to Cambridge, Monty took her on the roof of King's Chapel and provided fresh flowers for the luncheon table—'a unique performance, absolutely', said Walter.[16] Maisie also continued to be warmly received in Dr James's bachelor domain, as she described to Sibyl:

We had such a jolly time in Monty's rooms yesterday. When I say he was hardly himself at all, I don't mean there was anything wrong with him, only that he was impersonating first one person and then another in a continual stream, jumping from character to character. I never saw his room quite so gloriously chaotic before. To begin with all the floor was covered with waste paper in his dining-room—I don't think he keeps a waste paper basket but it would need six. It was great fun to walk about on. It was like walking on dried leaves.[17]

The whole Cropper family took to Dr James, who when staying at Ellergreen joined in with Mr Cropper's Westmorland songs, gave his own rendition of 'I'm a man wot's done wrong to me parents', and told ghost stories. 'Even in such an unghostly house as Ellergreen', recalled Maisie, 'it wasn't easy to go along a dark corridor to bed after hearing "Whistle and I'll come to you" [sic].' 'Dear Monty,' wrote Mrs Cropper, 'Billy is commissioned to tell you how very glad we shall be if anything brings you here. It can't happen too often.'

By 1902 James McBryde, also a friend of Walter Fletcher's, had finally abandoned the idea of a medical career, though he had completed his training at St Bartholomew's, and had decided to try and fulfil his ambition of becoming a professional artist. He started studying at the Slade in the autumn of 1902 and sent Monty a report of his progress in November:

I like it far better than doing medicine and work very hard . . . I have never had such contempt for any class of thing created as for the female art students. I think Berry and Wedd should be sent there to see them apropos of their women's degree ideas for Cambridge . . . I don't think they ever wash, they never do their hair properly, they wear pinafores unbuttoned and dirty . . . They are fat and hideous . . . But that is not why I dislike them so much but because they giggle continuously and come and sit by each other to whisper hysterically some stupid trash that could not be caricatured for foolishness and emptiness.

Monty's relationship with McBryde had deepened considerably in the six years or so they had known each other, and it was probably around this time that he wrote the following draft of a testimonial to McBryde:

I shall, if you will permit me, write quite freely. He is—as I think you must have seen—entirely unspoilt. He has passed through school (he was a Shrewsbury boy) and University and hospital practice without picking up any of the common vices: he is childlike, modest, amusing to the last degree, good in every way. I have seen him at home when he had a home . . . and I have spent a great part of my vacations in his company at different times. There are not many people with whom I am more familiar, and hardly any for whom I have a warmer affection.[18]

In the summer of 1903 McBryde was married to Gwendolen Grotrian, to whom he had been engaged for some time. Monty went up to Yorkshire for the wedding but found the whole function 'most oppressive . . . I fled as soon as I decently could and slept at York . . . I have had a letter from the victim since . . . He seemed quite happy.'

The following month, August, he was in Kent, bicycling with Percy Lubbock, and visited his birthplace, Goodnestone. In Rye they met Henry James, a friend of Lubbock's. 'A very pleasant man, he is,' was Monty's verdict, 'talking just as he writes, with punctilious effort to use exactly the word he wants: looks like a respectable butler.'[19] Then it was up to Ellergreen before accompanying his King's friend Oliffe Richmond, an Etonian scholar of the year 1900, to Germany. Richmond, who was working on the text of Propertius for his Fellowship dissertation, wished to consult a manuscript at Wolfenbüttel, and Monty hoped he could locate another containing Walter Map's

Latin poems. But he disliked Germany and told his father that he would be glad when he was out of it. To Sibyl Cropper he wrote: 'I don't believe in this nation a bit. I wish I'd stopped at home.'[20] At least there had been one new and generally enjoyable experience: *Tannhaüser*, the first Wagner opera Monty had seen. He told Sibyl Cropper: 'The story interests me very much, and the music a great deal less.' According to Oliffe Richmond, he sat bolt upright on the edge of his seat, 'keenly watching', throughout the performance. Once back in Cambridge, he was approached by Corpus Christi to catalogue their important manuscript collection, a long job that could only be done *in situ*, whereas Monty usually worked on batches of the Cambridge manuscripts in his rooms in King's. In his unpublished reminiscences Oliffe Richmond recounted an incident arising out of the work at Corpus: 'One winter evening . . . Monty was locked into the library by the porter. He broke a pane of a lattice window, but it was a long time before his cries were heard. Surely a situation for a ghost story.'

The year 1903 was Arthur Benson's last as an Eton master. He had been contemplating resignation for some time, but he finally broke away after being commissioned to edit Queen Victoria's letters. In August 1901 he had been in Cambridge on a short visit, his first for thirteen years. Monty had been on holiday in Sweden with James McBryde, but he had lent Benson his rooms, in which a new volume of Arthur's compulsively kept diary was begun on the 4th: '[Monty's] Litt.D. gown and velvet hat hang on the door—incredible dust and confusion on the shelves and in all places where letters can be put down. It would kill me!' The following autumn, when he and Monty dined at Eton with Luxmoore, Benson was very glad to find that his friendship with Monty was being revived. He thought Monty carried his learning lightly and noted that he seemed not to have aged: 'his complexion still very youthful'. They spoke of painted glass, and it was a surprise to find Monty professing 'very republican principles', even though in a subsequent conversation, on the glass in King's Chapel, Benson found him 'rather pedantic'.

Benson's response to Monty combined almost starry-eyed admiration with frank and sometimes tetchy criticism. Into the care of his extraordinary diary he committed numerous observations, impatient, shrewd, barbed, and admiring by turn, that provide an invaluable perspective on Monty's later career at Cambridge.

In September 1903 Benson was in Cambridge and bumped into

Monty, 'in grey flannel, white-hatted'. They returned to King's and soon started on Nixon imitations. Benson left 'shattered with laughter; head aching behind the ears; after a thoroughly irresponsible evening'. Monty was an odd fellow, he reflected, 'with rather a romantic capacity for friendship. I was touched by his getting out an envelope containing a large bunch of my old letters to him.' (Monty had sorted through his old correspondence at the beginning of the year. 'You should be flattered to hear', he had told Henry Babington Smith, 'that I have recently arranged and digested all my old letters and that you fill a fat envelope of the largest size.')

Benson took a house in Cambridge and now, with leisure and opportunity to scrutinize Monty at close quarters, began to write down regular reflections on his old friend in his diary. In October, for instance, he took a walk with A. B. Ramsay:

He [Ramsay] talked with profound admiration of Monty James and his mind. Now I don't think Monty James is in the palace at all—he seems to me to be nothing but a servant in the antechamber, handing things to those who go in. MRJ has an immense and accurate memory for details (which Ramsay seems to admire) but not the least constructive or poetical power. He is *very* humorous too—but after that his mind is the mind of a nice child—he hates and fears all problems, all speculation; all originality or novelty of view. His spirit is both timid and unadventurous. He is *much* abler than I am, much better, much more effective—yet I feel that he is a kind of child.[21]

These were to form the substance of Benson's reservations about Monty for the next twenty years or so, although behind all his criticisms were genuine fondness and admiration, and even sometimes a kind of envy for Monty's assurance and self-reliance. Another typical analysis appears in the diary in February 1910:

What a strange creature Monty is! So absolutely the same, so stubbornly Tory, so inaccessible to all ideas, so hating discussion and speculation, yet so affectionate (though I don't think he would ever miss anyone) and so full of humour that he is delightful. But if it were not for his humour he would be frozen, dull, inaccessible; the very worst kind of Don. He does carry his erudition very lightly, too—I don't suppose anyone alive knows so much or so little worth knowing! He is very dear to me—but he seems to me like a person in a pleasant dream. Or is it only that he is reticent?[22]

The more Benson saw of Monty the more he felt 'what a funny comfortable little paddock' his friend's mind was: 'Every year the hedge grows a little higher. I suppose it is the same with all of us—but

I had seen your dear friend only four times I think, and had been singularly
attracted by him, as indeed every one would be who saw his charm and knew
his power and skill—to me he had the added interest of being your friend.
Those who have not a wife and home circle of their own give hostages to
fortune perhaps in greater dependence on and closeness to their friends, and
to you this loss means a very deep and painful wound.[27]

The funeral was on the afternoon of 8 June, at St Helen's in
Lancashire; a memorial service was held at St Barnabas's, Kensington,
at the same time. Monty travelled up to Lancashire by train with
Walter Fletcher, taking with him roses, syringa and honeysuckle from
the Fellows' Garden at King's, which he threw into the grave after the
other mourners had gone. A few days later he wrote to Arthur Benson,
who was much moved by the letter. He had not known that McBryde
had been ill: 'It was the other day only that I was looking at his picture
in your rooms and asking Percy Lubbock about him . . . ' Monty,
apparently (his letter does not survive), had implicitly raised the
question of how a naturally reticent nature found expression in the face
of a deep personal loss without giving in to 'sentiment'. 'I wonder if
what you say about sentiment is quite true?' replied Arthur. 'If you
mean sentimentality, it is of course entirely so; but I sometimes wonder
if in steering clear of that, which one instinctively dislikes, and grows to
dislike more and more, we don't perhaps err by over-suppression, and
keep our feelings so close and dissemble them so completely that they
tend to die of inanition.' Gentlemanly reserve, Arthur seemed to be
saying, was all very well, but 'One wants to know that people *care*. That
is one of the few things that endures—companionship over champagne
and cigars, and even over ruined abbeys, is not very sustaining.'[28]

In his diary, Arthur reflected on Monty's reaction to McBryde's
death in more detail:

A sad and moving letter from MRJ telling me of McBryde's death . . . Monty's
letter touched me very much; for he called me his oldest friend. But there
seemed a curious effort in the letter not to let himself go, not to dive deep; to
take the thing as lightly as was consistent with feeling it very much—not to let
it be a sad remembrance. He spoke strongly of McB as being a friend who
didn't want sentimentality. But here I believe Monty a little deceives himself.
He likes beautiful graceful people and what is that but a refined sentimentality?
He is not demonstrative and thinks that is unsentimental.[29]

As a public memorial to McBryde and his talent for comic drawing
Monty decided to put in hand the publication of *The Story of a*

Troll-hunt, a tale written and illustrated by McBryde which had been inspired by their first holiday in Denmark in 1899. He began to make enquiries about a private printing in October, telling Gwendolen that 'A good many friends I am sure would like to have copies, and I find on consulting an expert that the drawings and text can be well and easily reproduced.' He subsequently provided a warm and appreciative Preface:

The issuing of these pictures affords an opportunity—which comes also in the aspect of a duty—of writing a few prefatory lines about him who drew them . . . I speak as one who first came to know James McBryde when he entered Cambridge eleven years ago, and who, ever since our first meeting, have found in his friendship an unfailing source of content. No one whom I have known could enlist the warmest affection more easily or retain it more surely . . .

The idea of the *Troll-hunt* seems to have been Monty's: 'It was eagerly adopted, because we had all been much engrossed by the folklore of Jutland, which peoples its wide and lonely heaths with many strange beings. The working-out is entirely due to McBryde, and gives as characteristic a specimen of his particular humour, both in the pictures and in the text, as it is now possible to procure.'

At the end of 1904 Gwendolen McBryde gave birth to a daughter, christened Jane. 'I rather regret its sex,' admitted Monty, 'but it must be as it may.' He told Gwendolen on 13 December: 'I am very glad to hear from you in person, and rejoice that the infant is so thriving. I wonder when I shall find a moment to look in and make its (her, I beg pardon) acquaintance.'

Walter Fletcher stood godfather to Jane and Monty agreed to act as her guardian. Gwendolen felt that

She will need someone to look up to as much as a boy would have so you will forgive my having troubled you. I had no choice in the matter for I did not want anyone else. If I tell you she weighs 9 lbs I suppose you will feel it your duty to take an armful of books down to the kitchen and weigh them in the cook's scales to gain a correct impression. You need not see baby until I get her well on her feet and able to tell you stories.[30]

After receiving a letter from Gwendolen's brother, Harold Grotrian, about a Trust that was to be set up for Jane, Monty, while admitting that he was 'not very conversant with these matters', expressed himself willing and anxious to be and do whatever Gwendolen considered most useful. Like Gwendolen, he had no choice. His feelings for James made him ever aware that 'it doesn't end here'.

A few weeks after McBryde's death Walter Fletcher married Maisie Cropper at Ellergreen. Like most things connected with the delightful Cropper family, Monty found no cause for complaint, telling his father: 'These weddings are fearful strains on the emotions, but nothing could have been better done than this one. All the same, the bridegroom was a sad sight between one and two o'clock just before the ceremony.' Afterwards, he went to stay with the newly married Lionel Ford, now Headmaster of Repton, while Walter and Maisie set off on a bicyling honeymoon, the final part of which was spent with Sydney and Linda James at Malvern, before settling into their new home in Cambridge, 18 Brookside. At Malvern, Maisie had been delighted by Linda's natural malapropisms and her way of mixing metaphors (Linda's eccentricity was to increase with age)—such as 'It's only four miles as the cock crows', or 'Mr D. is a man who likes to have a voice in every pie'. Sydney would recount the latest examples with relish. 'Before I forget them, ' he told Monty in 1913, 'there are two priceless sayings of Linda's, one old and one new, which you ought to know. (1) Some time ago I was going to preach at Eton and she asked me what my text was to be and I said "Citizens of no mean city". "Oh" said she "Sodom and Gomorrah, I suppose." (2) Tonight at dinner she was complaining that I hadn't told her something and said, "You old secretion".'

In the autumn Monty found himself in the awkward position of being nominated by the classics faction at Eton to stand for the position of masters' representative on the Governing Body against Arthur Benson, who desperately wanted the post. Benson was a reformer and a modernist. As he said later in a printed circular, 'No one would I think deny that the selection of M. R. James and myself as candidates was, to a certain extent, influenced by the fact that we were known to be in general sympathy, respectively, with divergent views of education.' In the end, he and Monty discussed the matter frankly, both of them disapproving intensely of the party element in it all, and decided that the best course was for them both to withdraw.

Benson, who was mortified and humiliated by the whole business, was also agonizing over the possibility that he might be offered the Head Mastership of Eton. In September Warre had signified his intention of resigning in July 1905. Soon after the announcement Sydney told Monty that he would be standing for the post, even though he admitted that he had little chance. Commented Benson: 'Sydney James *does* want to stand—God help us!'

Benson was a front-runner for the headmastership: Warre had actually said that he regarded Benson as his natural successor. Against him stood Edward Lyttelton, the forthright, dogmatic and rather cranky Headmaster of Haileybury, described by Benson (at his most acute) as 'a man of no literary sense, and with a really fundamentally unbalanced mind . . . He is so easily converted to any point of view that is strikingly put; and his own convictions are both fluid in essence and definite in form. That is always a dangerous thing.'[31] After much soul-searching, during which he consulted with Monty, Benson told the Governing Body at Eton that he would refuse an offer of the headmastership and the post went to Lyttelton, whose appointment coincided with Monty's own increasing involvement in Eton affairs.

CHAPTER 12

A PEEP INTO PANDEMONIUM
The Ghost Stories

'I wants to make your flesh creep,' replied the boy.

Dickens, The Pickwick Papers

Through the smallest aperture, for a moment, I had had a peep into Pandemonium.

Maud Ruthyn in J. S. Le Fanu, Uncle Silas

'I KEEP Christmas at King's,' wrote Luxmoore in 1903. 'The charm of social life is so best mingled with the independence gained by a set of rooms given me and one's own fire and table and oak. But O how the time goes in talk, talk, talk and overmuch eating.'[1]

The previous year, Luxmoore had observed the informal annual gathering of Monty's Eton and Cambridge friends with mildly puzzled censure:

I am spending Christmas in this wonderful place with great enjoyment of grounds and chapel. It is like a most splendidly appointed club in which each member has also a suite of noble rooms to himself and is paid an income instead of subscribing . . . Last night Monty James read us a new Christmas story of most blood curdling character, after which those played animal grab who did not mind having their clothes torn to pieces and their hands nailscored. The cleverness and gaiety of them all is wonderful and yet if it goes on like this in term time—and it does—where is the strenuous life, and search for truth and for knowledge that one looks for at College? Chaff and extravagant fancy and mimicry and camaraderie and groups that gather and dissolve first in this room and then in that, like the midges that dance their rings in the sunshine, ought to be only the fringe of life and I doubt if here it does not cover the whole, or nearly so.

As for his former pupil, now a scholar of undisputed eminence, Luxmoore was forced to conclude: 'Monty James, with his amazing knowledge and power of absorbing learning without seeming to work, with his boyish and untidy humour and his unruffled goodness, is a dangerous model for young men who have to make their own way in the world.'[2]

Luxmoore was a regular member of the Christmas parties at King's until 1917, when his conscience would not allow him to travel from Eton during that 'grim time' for the non-essential purpose of enjoying himself. 'What?' he wrote to Monty, 'shall I pass a Christmas without "in dulci jubilo" . . . ? Without that madeira? Without animal grab? And the walk in the Backs and the talk with ghosts and the sense of friendship and old days and above all the mystery of the beauty of Chapel and the fellowship of Christmas Communion?'

Monty looked back wistfully at the pre-war Christmases at King's in his recollections:

It would be Christmas Eve: we of the College surpliced ourselves and repaired to Chapel. Choir and ante-chapel were full, and dark. Just before the clock struck five the boys would issue from their vestry on the north side, the men from the Hacombleyn chantry on the south; last, the officers came from the Brassie chantry, and, led by Walter Littlechild with his silver verge, proceeded westwards and took their stand near the south door. A faint musical hum was heard, of the choir taking up the note, and then——it seemed to give the very spirit of Christmas—the boys broke quite softly into 'Once in Royal David's City', and began moving eastward. With the second verse the men joined in. I declare I do not know what has moved me more than this did, and still does when I recall it.

Dinner in Hall followed; hot spiced beer, in the College's largest silver tankard, was served (earlier there had been a tea for the choristers). Towards the end of the meal, the choral scholars might slip out, 'and suddenly we would hear from the western gallery their quartet, led, we will say, by the delicious alto of Horace Wyndham Thomas. "When the crimson sun was set" is music that lingers in memory still.' After Combination Room* there might be cards, and then usually an adjournment to Monty's rooms, where his guests would probably hear a new ghost story 'composed at fever heat, but not always able to ward off sleep from some listener's eye (this rankles a little still)'. Oliffe Richmond described a typical reading:

Monty disappeared into his bedroom. We sat and waited in the candlelight. Perhaps someone played a few bars on the piano, and desisted, for good reason . . . The people in the room varied from year to year, but some of the following were sure to be present: Luxmoore himself, [A. E.] Conybeare

* The common-room for senior members of the College.

(whose home was in Cambridge), Gurney Lubbock, author of the Memoir, and Ramsay, from Eton: Walter Morley Fletcher from Trinity: Owen Hugh Smith from London (he almost always): the Revd Swain, or his successor, F. E. Hutchinson, our Chaplain: McBryde, the artist of the 'Troll Hunt'. Someone I have not named may have been lurking beyond the fire. Perhaps Percy Lubbock or Arthur Benson had slipped in from Magdalene . . . Monty emerged from the bedroom, manuscript in hand, at last, and blew out all the candles but one, by which he seated himself. He then began to read, with more confidence than anyone else could have mustered, his well-nigh illegible script in the dim light.[3]

'All very pedestrian and Anglican and Victorian and everything else that it ought not to be,' wrote Monty of this Christmas ritual, 'but I should like well enough to have it over again.'

Other members of the party would also try their hand at writing and reading stories. In 1903, Arthur Benson followed Monty with one called 'The House at Trehele', which lasted two nights, and Percy Lubbock read a fragment concerning a school inspector, which 'drew up the curtain on a lurid scene only to drop it again hastily'.[4] Benson recorded that 'MRJ read us one of his medieval ghost stories—this is a pleasant habit of his—the local colouring is excellent, and the stories grim—but there is a certain want of depth about them. The people are like elderly dons.'[5] As time went on, stories were repeated and on one occasion at least, in 1913, Monty was unable to finish the story in time to read to his guests.[6]

Once embarked on the custom of writing Christmas ghost stories, Monty had little choice but to go on satisfying the demand. But why did he start writing them in the first place? Of course he had always had a penchant for the supernatural and the macabre, as his family well knew. In 1884 his father had written to say that he had been to 'a large old roomy Queen Anny kind of house, with any amount of closets. Just the place for a Psychical Researcher.'* And his cousin Freda Loraine had written in 1892: 'Monty! We have got a most superb ghost at Markyate—we'll tell you all about her another time. We want to keep it from the children if possible—so don't ask me before them ever. I mean to take notes and will tell you my experiences, *when* I have any.'

J. A. Venn, in *Alumni Cantabrigienses*, implies that the early stories were written for the King's choristers. Monty nowhere confirms or

---

* The Society for Psychical Research had been founded two years earlier, in 1882, with a strong Cambridge contingent among the founding fathers. 'Queen Anny' houses figure frequently in Monty's ghost stories.

denies this. Certainly the two earliest stories were written during his deanship, when he was actively involved with the Choir School, and only two or three years before the Ali Baba and Bluebeard plays. It may also be significant that he presented a copy of his first collection, *Ghost Stories of an Antiquary*, to the Choir School, though this may just have been a characteristically considerate act. The only story he definitely states was composed for the choristers is 'A School Story', the first tale in his second collection, *More Ghost Stories of an Antiquary*, which was not published until 1911.

Whatever the original impetus, by March 1904 he had written seven stories that he considered were fit to be read by other people, and some more, one gathers, that he did not feel were up to the mark, including 'Lost Hearts'. (James McBryde, early in 1904, seemed to recall he had written one about troglodytes.) The earliest of those seven was 'Canon Alberic's Scrap-book', written before 28 October 1893 (when it was read at the 601st meeting of the Chitchat) and after April 1892, when he had visited St Bertrand de Comminges, the setting and inspiration of the story.* Early in 1894 Monty sent two stories, of which 'Canon Alberic' was one, to Leo Maxse, who then owned and edited the *National Review*. 'I hope you will at some time set yourself to the task of a story for the *National Review*,' Maxse replied. 'The one I return would not suit but I should like to have another look at the other, if I may keep it a little longer.' The story Maxse kept was 'Canon Alberic', then called 'A Curious Book'. He wrote again later the same day: 'On carefully thinking over your second story, "A Curious Book", I should like to have it for the *National Review* provided you will give me the benefit of your name by signing it and will not mind a delay of two or three months in its appearance ... I am sorry to say the *National Review* is only able at present to offer you 10s a page for stories; perhaps you will think this too mean.'[7] The story, retitled 'The Scrap-book of Canon Alberic', duly appeared in the *National Review*, though not until March 1895, and was signed 'M.R. James'. Arthur Machen, author of supernatural stories such as *The Great God Pan* (1894), read it and immediately wrote to Monty to congratulate him on 'a marvellous piece of work': 'I am myself somewhat curious and critical in horrors and mysteries, and know how immensely difficult is

---

* The statement in the Preface to the *Collected Ghost Stories* (1931) that 'Canon Alberic' was written in 1894 is incorrect.

the concoction of the genuine article; but I have seen nothing for a very long time that is half as good as the "Scrapbook".[8]

'Lost Hearts' must have been written at much the same time as 'Canon Alberic'. The reference in it to the preserved corpses in St Michan's, Dublin, places its composition some time after July 1892, when Monty was in Ireland, and before October 1893, when, with 'Canon Alberic', it was read to the Chitchat. 'Lost Hearts' was first published in the *Pall Mall Magazine*, which had only been launched in May 1893, for December 1895. It was signed 'Montague James' and was accompanied by five rather feeble illustrations by Simon Harmon Vedder.

Of the other stories that were to make up Monty's first published collection, 'Number 13', set in Viborg, was written, according to Monty's own statement, in 1899—that is, after returning from the first trip to Denmark with McBryde and Will Stone. (There is, however, no mention of Viborg in the itinerary for this trip that Monty wrote down in the interleaved Greek Testament that served as a diary. They stayed in Viborg the following year, 1900.) 'Number 13' was one of the stories Luxmoore heard at Christmas 1903, but it may have been read before that. Luxmoore also heard what he called 'Fur flebis' (i.e. ' "Oh, Whistle, and I'll Come to You, My Lad" ') that Christmas. 'Count Magnus', set mainly in Sweden, dates probably from late 1901 or early 1902.

During McBryde's second attack of appendicitis in March 1904, L. F. Giblin, a friend who had entered King's in the same year as McBryde, called on him to suggest that he should illustrate Monty's ghost stories with a view to their publication. 'What do you think?' McBryde asked Monty. 'I should like to do it very much, especially as I have some time now.' Giblin had been Monty's guest at the Founder's Day dinner on 6 December (1903) and had spent Christmas at King's with Arthur Benson, Luxmoore, and the others. There had been talk then of publishing the stories, and after seeing McBryde in March Giblin wrote to Monty to encourage him in the idea: 'Don't let it drop, and this is a favourable time for beginning. McB has a fortnight's convalescence before him with no regular work and is keen to try his hand on the illustrations during it. So be good and send him the manuscript to work on.'[9]

Monty wrote to his 'dear boy' on the 13th, welcoming the idea that McBryde should illustrate the stories: 'It would be capital. They are at present in a very rough manuscript. Shall I have them typewritten or bring or send them as they are? Or do you remember any of them well enough to sketch out any ideas?'

At this point, as he went on to tell McBryde, there were six stories he thought would be suitable for publication:

1. One that came out in the *National Review* of '94 [*sic*]. A man goes to S. Bertrand de Comminges, spends a day in the church sketching and so on and buys a book from the sacristan in the evening. There is a very odd picture in the book of Solomon on his throne and a demon strangling one of his bodyguard. When my man is in his room looking over the book at night he sees a hairy hand on the table by him and finds the demon in question standing behind him and just going to pounce. Of course he is rescued.
2. The Mezzotint.
3. The Spiders [i.e. 'The Ash-tree'].
4. The No. 13 story.
5. The Swedish story about Count Magnus.
6. The one about the whistle.

I don't think I have any others that will do. There was one in the *Pall Mall Magazine* for 1895—called 'Lost Hearts'—but I don't much care about it.[10]

By the beginning of May 1904 McBryde had made good progress with drawings for ' "Oh, Whistle" ' and 'Count Magnus' and he wrote enthusiastically to Monty:

I don't think I have ever done anything I liked better than illustrating your stories. To begin with I sat down and learned advanced perspective and the laws of shadows, etc, etc . . . You see it is difficult to do an octagonal mausoleum with oval windows and to put the right thickness of wall through each.

I have finished the Whistle ghost . . . I covered yards of paper to put in the moon shadows correctly and it is certainly the best thing I have ever drawn.

I am doing them large so that they can be reduced ad lib. I have drawn the tombs in Count Magnus . . . I think the best picture will be Mr Wraxall seeing two figures standing in the moonlight by the cross roads while arriving in his closed fly . . . Much trouble about inclined plane of trap and shadows. I mean to get them quite correct.[11]

But the illustrations for 'Count Magnus'—one of the interior of the eight-sided de la Gardie mausoleum and another of Mr Wraxall's meeting with his pursuers at the crossroads near Belchamp St Paul*—were never finished. McBryde died a month after writing this letter, having completed only four pictures, two for ' "Oh, Whistle" '

* A village in Essex, not far from Sudbury.

and two for 'Canon Alberic'. The first for 'Canon Alberic', drawn from a photograph of the interior of St Bertrand de Comminges, was used as the frontispiece of the first published collection; Gurney Lubbock says that it contains 'an easily recognizable sketch of Monty himself; the bend of the knee alone would identify it'. The second picture for 'Canon Alberic' shows Dennistoun, having just taken off the crucifix given to him by the sacristan's daughter, seated at his table and about to take stock of Canon Alberic's scrap-book full of manuscript treasures, while at his elbow the demon crouches, its appalling hand already on the table, its eyes burning in the darkness. The intended resemblance of Dennistoun, with his round glasses, square jaw and pipe, to Monty is clear in this picture.

The first of the pictures for ' "Oh, Whistle" ' is of the man in Professor Parkins's dream fleeing along a beach, intersected with black groynes, pursued by a figure in pale fluttering draperies. 'I like the distance in the groins picture,' wrote Gwendolen McBryde. 'It looks endless.'[12] The last drawing showed the famous 'Whistle ghost' itself, with its 'intensely horrible' face of crumpled linen.

Four day after James died, Gwendolen sent these four drawings to Monty: 'I have an idea there is another ghost story,' she said, 'and a few more sketches for the illustrations. If you will describe to me the appearance of anything I have not discovered I will have it found.' This was, presumably, the first time that Monty had seen the four finished pictures, which he thought 'more than good'. Gwendolen wrote again on 11 June, three days after the funeral:

I have found the notebook and the Count Magnus illustrations. The perspective was the lengthy part. In the 'Whistle' one all the moonlight patches and shadows are worked out correctly as they would have fallen on the various objects in the room.

There is a first rough sketch in some book that I have not found of the two figures at the crossroads. It was waiting for a model of the carriage back. The spider tree [i.e 'The Ash-tree'] was to be done from an Ingmanthorpe* ash.[13]

There seems no particular reason why Monty chose Edward Arnold to publish the ghost stories, other than the fact that he had been corresponding with Arnold in February/March 1903 about writing what Arnold called 'a volume of "Chapters on Learning in England" during the Renaissance'. This never materialized; but soon after McBryde's death, Monty sent Arnold some, probably six, of the

* Ingmanthorpe Hall was Gwendolen's family home in Yorkshire.

stories, and perhaps the illustrations as well. Arnold replied on 22 June and asked if there were any more: 'Please let me know as soon as you can, for we have greatly enjoyed the stories and must manage to make a book of them somehow, whatever happens: but if they could be eked out by more material it would be much easier.'[14] (Arnold's letter also contained the, to me, puzzling remark: 'Mumm thinks he remembers having once read a very good story by your brother, and it occurred to us whether it might be possible to work a joint volume.' On the face of things, it seems unlikely that Sydney or Ber were writers of ghost stories. Could 'Mumm' have mistaken Henry James for Monty's brother? 'The Turn of the Screw' was first published in *Collier's Weekly* in 1898.)

Towards the end of June Arnold again asked Monty, who was in Westmorland for Walter Fletcher's wedding, to torture his brains 'and extract some more horrors so as to make up the volume to 6/– length':

We are thinking whom we can suggest as illustrator, but it is not easy to find anyone whose style would match those you sent us. H. J. Ford might do, but he is expensive; probably he would charge £4.4.0. a drawing. Should you feel disposed to pay for them? We do not as a rule do more than incur the cost of reproduction, but we might contribute something if desired.

The new matter ought to be in our hands by the end of July if possible.

We hear no more of Ford,* or of anyone else. Arnold seems not to have realized that Monty wanted no other illustrations than the ones he had provided, for the publication of *Ghost Stories of an Antiquary* was to be an act of homage to the memory of James McBryde. The first paragraph of Monty's Preface to the collection made that clear:

I wrote these stories at long intervals, and most of them were read to patient friends, usually at the season of Christmas. One of those friends offered to illustrate them, and it was agreed that, if he would do that, I would consider the question of publishing them. Four pictures he completed, which will be found in this volume, and then, very quickly and unexpectedly, he was taken away. This is the reason why the greater part of the stories are not provided with illustrations. Those who knew the artist will understand how much I wished to give a permanent form even to a fragment of his work; others will appreciate the fact that here a remembrance is made of one in whom many friendships centred.

* Ford was, however, to be the illustrator of Monty's *Old Testament Legends* (1913), a book intended for young readers.

The title of the book was fixed by 25 July, when Monty signed his agreement with Arnold, and the date for the delivery of the final copy was set for the 31st of that month. To fill up the volume, Monty decided to include 'Lost Hearts' and managed to write one new story, 'The Treasure of Abbot Thomas'. Early in the month he had gone to inspect the glass in the private chapel at Ashridge Park, the Hertfordshire home of Lord Brownlow (a relative of Harry Cust's), where the ECRV had camped in the summer of 1882. A privately printed pamphlet, 'Notes of Glass in Ashridge Chapel', appeared two years later in 1906. The sixteenth-century glass in the chapel came from Steinfeld, a Premonstratensian abbey in the Eifel region of Germany. It was at Steinfeld that Monty set the main part of the action of 'Abbot Thomas', and it was in the windows of a private chapel that Mr Somerton found the clues that finally led him to the Abbot's treasure and its loathsome guardian.

The proofs of the book began to come in towards the end of October. Monty told his father: 'I shall be rather amused at correcting proofs of so different a character to my catalogues.' *Ghost Stories of an Antiquary* was published in time for the Christmas trade and was dedicated

TO ALL THOSE WHO AT VARIOUS TIMES
HAVE LISTENED TO THEM

'The stories themselves', Monty wrote in his Preface, 'do not make any very exalted claim. If any of them succeed in causing their readers to feel pleasantly uncomfortable when walking along a solitary road at nightfall, or sitting over a dying fire in the small hours, my purpose in writing them will have been attained.'

*   *   *

So began the ghost stories of M. R. James, which made his name known to a wide reading public that was, and has remained, largely unaware of the extent and distinction of his other activities. The *Collected Ghost Stories* of 1931 remains in print; individual stories are regularly anthologized and have also formed the basis of adaptations, some extremely fanciful, ranging from the 1957 film *Night of the Demon*, based very loosely on 'Casting the Runes', to Jonathan Miller's 1967 version of '"Oh, Whistle"' for BBC Television.

Critically, the stories have always been awarded a high place, often the highest, in the English ghost story tradition, and this estimation

Gwendolen and James McBryde

Above and below, two drawings by James McBryde
for 'Canon Alberic's Scrap-book' in *Ghost Stories of
an Antiquary* (1904)

King's from the Bene't Street corner, *c.* 1890. The railings have since been removed

M. R. James during his provostship of King's

shows no sign of falling off.* Probably the first 'critical' essay on them appeared in the *London Mercury* in February 1934, an article by Mary Butts called 'The Art of Montagu [*sic*] James'. Monty dismissed it as 'a fulsome article on *my* art—save the mark. I knew not that I had any.'[15]

His friends reacted with delighted appreciation to the publication of *Ghost Stories of an Antiquary*. Gwendolen McBryde's artistic eye judged the book to be 'beautifully got up'; Arthur Benson, on the other hand, rather regretted that it was 'bound in sackcloth', but thought the inside of the book charming, 'both the type and the reading. I haven't done much of the latter yet, but my blood freezes pleasantly as I peep.' The Croppers were also delighted. 'I have shivered over "Lost Hearts",' wrote Edith Cropper, 'but it is not easy to find the book. I came in yesterday evening to have a quiet hour with it and traced it with some trouble to Eleanor's room, where she was reading it with much expression to the horrified Billies ... We all like the pictures— especially the man tumbling over the breakwater.' Sibyl herself wrote just before Christmas and put her finger squarely on one of Monty's favourite and most successful techniques: 'I do like your ghost stories. I think the best of them as one reads them, and the worst of them, when one [has] blown out the candle, is that they begin with such trifling little things. Anything might make a beginning. If the bed squeaks louder than usual or the cistern outside my door, it may be an incident in a blood-curdling story.' As Monty himself said, 'There may be possibilities, too, in the Christmas cracker, if the right people pull it, and if the motto which they find inside has the right message on it.'[16] Like the Billies, Eustace Talbot responded to the stories in exactly the right way: 'You have succeeded in giving me two bad nights and one jumpy walk on a dark foggy evening in the country when every tree became possessed of horrible long arms and every step was dogged by hideous echoes about ten yards behind.' One perceptive comment came from Ronald Norman, whom Monty had taught at Eton when he was a temporary master in 1886: 'I hear you have published a book of ghost stories which I must procure. They must be a pleasant change from apocryphal gospels, and both alike are children of your fantasy.'

Although the book was not extensively reviewed, it sold well enough

---

* And yet no completely satisfactory book has been written on the ghost stories, about which (debarring psycho-critical speculation) there is much to be said. There are chapters in Peter Penzoldt's oft-quoted but sterile study *The Supernatural in Fiction* (1952), in Julia Briggs' *Night Visitors* (1977), and, the best of recent commentaries, in Jack Sullivan's *Elegant Nightmares* (1978).

for Arnold to issue a second impression the following year. Inevitably, there were letters and queries from readers. S. M. Ellis* wrote appreciatively in March 1905: 'Although a stranger I hope you will permit me to say how much I have enjoyed reading your "Ghost Stories of an Antiquary". I am very interested in "supernatural literature", and can truthfully say I have never read more effective ghost stories than yours.'[17] Some weeks before, Monty had received the following testimony to the plausibility of his backgrounds:

Dear Sir,

Please pardon me for writing to ask you a question. We have been reading your book *Ghost Stories of an Antiquary*.

I live in Lincolnshire—not so very far from Aswarby Hall [the setting of 'Lost Hearts']—but my question has nothing to do with that at all.

It is—are these stories *real?* gathered from antiquarian research, or are they your own manufacture and imagination on antiquarian lines?

Please assure me, if it is possible to [*sic*] you to do so. I have a real reason for asking.[18]

Another query came from a native of Steinfeld who was gathering material for a history of the abbey there and who wished to examine the glass at Ashridge, while a reader from near Dorchester wrote to ask Monty about the local belief that the appearance of molehills near a home portended death: 'Can you throw any light on this curious superstition?'

What is so remarkable about *Ghost Stories of an Antiquary* is the level of originality, ingenuity, and sheer artistic accomplishment apparent in most of the stories. This is in no sense a novice volume but a collection of exceptional maturity. Monty's techniques are already highly developed and confidently applied: here are the antiquarian details and the scholarly background material that lend authenticity to the narrative and that are fundamental to the maintenance of Monty's characteristically urbane and learned tone, which counterbalances a mood of detachment against the mounting horror of the stories. The plots are cleverly manipulated, and even a stock, almost pantomimic element such as the sheeted ghost in ' "Oh, Whistle" ' is given a new intensity and impact.

Perhaps the most innovatory technique used in this first collection is the creation of spurious documentation, which draws on the ability he

---

* The author of *Mainly Victorian* (1925), which includes 'The Ghost Story and its Exponents' (pp.322–31), and *Wilkie Collins, Le Fanu and Others* (1931).

had had even as an Eton schoolboy to absorb the essence of period language and idiom and reproduce its *timbre* exactly in a totally convincing pastiche. This mimetic brilliance is seen in 'The Ash-tree':

'And what is as yet unexplain'd, and to myself the Argument of some Horrid and Artfull Designe in the Perpetrators of this Barbarous Murther, was this, that the Women which were entrusted with the laying-out of the Corpse and washing it, being both sad Persons and very well Respected in their Mournfull Profession, came to me in a great Pain and Distress both of Mind and Body, saying, what was indeed confirmed upon the first View, that they had no sooner touch'd the Breast of the Corpse with their naked Hands than they were sensible of a more than ordinary violent Smart and Acheing in their Palms, which, with their whole Forearms, in no long time swell'd so immoderately, the Pain still continuing, that, as afterwards proved, during many weeks they were forc'd to lay by the exercise of their Calling; and yet no mark seen on the Skin . . . '

More Ghost Stories of an Antiquary was published by Edward Arnold in 1911.* There were seven stories: 'A School Story' (written, as previously noted, for the King's choristers), 'The Rose Garden', 'The Tractate Middoth' (set in the old University Library at Cambridge), 'Casting the Runes', 'The Stalls of Barchester Cathedral' (which first appeared in the *Contemporary Review* in 1910), 'Martin's Close', and 'Mr Humphreys and his Inheritance', which contains one of Monty's best parodies: his pseudo-seventeenth-century meditation on mazes, as a 'Parable of this Unhappy Condition'.

In 1919 Arnold published a third volume of only five stories: *A Thin Ghost*. This contained 'The Residence at Whitminster', 'The Diary of Mr Poynter', 'An Episode of Cathedral History', and 'The Story of a Disappearance and an Appearance' (the last two were first published in the *Cambridge Review*), and one of Monty's least successful stories, 'Two Doctors'. Luxmoore read 'An Episode of Cathedral History' from the *Cambridge Review* 'to a dear old lady in the sunshine among the roses . . . I thought the humour of Mr Worby and the setting of the story came out in reading even better than I had remembered.'[19] On the occasion of the first reading of 'A Story of a Disappearance and an Appearance' (which Gurney Lubbock called 'the Punch and Judy story' in his *Memoir*), 'the silence which fell when the grim story ended was broken by the voice of Luxmoore: "Were there envelopes in those days?"' Monty, says Lubbock, was easily able to prove that there were.

* Arnold was confident enough to offer Monty improved terms and an advance against royalties of £30.

Finally, in 1925, came *A Warning to the Curious*, again published by Edward Arnold. This did well, appearing in October 1925 and reprinting in November and December of that year; there was another impression in February 1926, and another in June 1927. Five of the six stories in the collection had appeared in print before. The first, 'The Haunted Doll's House' (a variation on the theme of 'The Mezzotint'), was written for the library of Queen Mary's Doll's House at Windsor and was subsequently published in the *Empire Review* in February 1923; 'The Uncommon Prayer-book' (based on the fanatical royalism of Dame Anne Sadleir, the donor of the Trinity Apocalypse at Trinity College, Cambridge)* appeared in the *Atlantic Monthly* for June 1921; 'A View From a Hill' and the title story, 'A Warning to the Curious', were both published in the *London Mercury* in 1925 (in May and August respectively); 'A Neighbour's Landmark' first saw the light in an Eton ephemeral, the *Eton Chronic*.

'Martin's Close', in *More Ghost Stories*, had already used the language of the State Trials, which Monty always delighted to read, to describe the trial of George Martin before Judge Jeffreys (spelt thus, correctly, in the *Collected Ghost Stories* and, incorrectly, Jeffries in *More Ghost Stories*). He drew on them again for the motive of 'A Neighbour's Landmark' in *A Warning to the Curious*, in which the concluding explanation for the haunting of Betton Wood is connected with the Lady Ivy, formerly Theodosia Bryan, who was actually tried before Lord Chief Justice Jeffreys for her claim to a valuable portion of land in Shadwell. In the *Collected Ghost Stories*, the following paragraph is appended to the story: 'Thanks to the researches of Sir John Fox, in his book on *The Lady Ivie's Trial* (Oxford, 1929), we now know that my heroine died in her bed in 1695, having—heaven knows how—been acquitted of the forgery [sc. of the deeds on which her claims were based], for which she had undoubtedly been responsible.'

The point here is that for once this is not a piece of invented documentation. Monty had suggested to Sir John Fox that the trial of the Lady Ivy should be reissued, which it was—by the Clarendon Press in 1929. What is more, Monty supplied a Preface, in which he described the appeal of the State Trials, which first began to be issued in 1809:

---

* Monty had edited a facsimile edition of the Trinity Apocalypse for the Roxburghe Club in 1909, returned to it again in his Schweich Lectures to the British Academy in 1927 (subsequently published in 1931 as *The Apocalypse in Art*), and of course had dealt with it in his Descriptive Catalogue of the Trinity MSS (Volume II, 1901).

It is not until 1649 that we begin to get really lively reports. From that date till the end of the century the volumes contain the cream of the collection . . . those of the period of the Popish Plot,* the reign of James II, and the years immediately following the Revolution are undoubtedly the richest; and, I should say, among them, the trials in which the figure of Jeffreys appears. Things are never dull when he is at the bar or on the bench . . . Some of his cases, such as those of Alice Lisle and Sir Thomas Armstrong, one cannot read with equanimity, but when no life is in peril, one can afford to enjoy and even admire.

Of this class is *The Lady Ivie's Trial for a great part of Shadwell*. It has long been one of my favourites, and often have I wished that some one would tell us all about its context and its results, and would explain the topography of the region discussed in it, and trace the careers of the protagonists, especially that of Lady Ivie herself, who does seem to answer very completely to the French designation of a *triste personnage*.

Here, then, is Monty's source for the idea behind 'A Neighbour's Landmark'. He also valued the State Trials because 'in them alone, as far as I can see, do we find the unadorned common speech of Englishmen; the plays of the time do not afford it—they are sophisticated; still less do the novels. In the trials alone can the style of dialogue or narrative be rightly studied.'

A couplet in 'A Neighbour's Landmark'† ('Than that which walks in Betton Wood/Knows why it walks or why it cries') was praised by A. E. Housman for being 'good poetry'. Housman also told Monty that there was 'something wrong with the optics' in 'A View from a Hill', the plot of which turns on a pair of remarkable binoculars. 'Well, there may be,' was Monty's comment to Alwyn Scholfield, 'but if these things happen, what are you going to do about it?'[20] Besides Housman, other distinguished readers of his ghost stories included Theodore Roosevelt and Thomas Hardy. Hardy, as Florence Hardy told Monty, sent him a Christmas card 'in a fit of enthusiasm after reading some of your stories'.[21]

The twenty-six stories in the four separate volumes were collected together in 1931 as *The Collected Ghost Stories of M. R. James*, and to them were appended four pieces: 'There Was a Man Dwelt By a Churchyard', 'Rats', 'After Dark in the Playing Fields', and 'Wailing

---

* Jeffreys' predecessor as Lord Chief Justice, Sir William Scroggs, who displayed brutal zeal for the Protestant cause during the Popish Plot, is the source of the unpleasant experiences in 'The Rose Garden'.

† The reference in the title is to the Book of Common Prayer: 'Cursed is he that removeth a neighbour's landmark.'

Well', of which the first three appeared in Eton ephemerals. The fourth, 'Wailing Well', was written especially for the Eton Boy Scouts and read to them by Monty round their camp fire at Worbarrow Bay in Dorset in the summer of 1927. 'Rats' is the only one of these pieces that recalls M. R. James at his best.

To finish off the Collected Edition Monty supplied some desultory remarks on 'Stories I Have Tried to Write', which began with the disclaimer: 'I have neither much experience nor much perseverance in the writing of stories—I am thinking exclusively of ghost stories, for I never cared to try any other kind.' In the Preface he wrote for this edition he rejected the need to describe how the stories had come about, identified a few of the original locations (places, he said, had been 'prolific in suggestion'), added some 'bibliographical' notes, and completely avoided two important questions: Did he have any theories as to the writing of ghost stories? and Did he believe in ghosts? To the first question he answered, 'None that are worthy of the name or need to be repeated here'; to the second, 'I am prepared to consider evidence and accept it if it satisfies me.'

Subsequent critics have bemoaned this reticence, but in fact Monty had already said a good deal (more, say, than Le Fanu) on his approach to writing ghost stories. The Preface to *More Ghost Stories*, for instance, contained some general comments on his practice:

The ghost should be malevolent or odious: amiable and helpful apparitions are all very well in fairy tales or in local legends, but I have no use for them in a fictitious ghost story. Again, I feel that the technical terms of 'occultism', if they are not very carefully handled, tend to put the mere ghost story (which is all that I am attempting) upon a quasi-scientific plane, and to call into play faculties quite other than the imaginative. I am well aware that mine is a nineteenth- (and not a twentieth-) century conception of this class of tale; but were not the prototypes of all the best ghost stories written in the sixties and seventies?

He gave more pointers in his Introduction to *Ghosts and Marvels*, an anthology of stories (including 'Casting the Runes') selected by V. H. Collins and published in 'The World's Classics' series in 1924. The Introduction contains a clear account of his technical approach to composition:

Let us, then, be introduced to the actors in a placid way; let us see them going about their ordinary business, undisturbed by forebodings, pleased with their surroundings; and into this calm environment, let the ominous thing put out its head, unobtrusively at first, and then more insistently, until it holds the stage. It is not amiss sometimes to leave a loophole for a natural explanation: but, I would say, let the loophole be so narrow as not to be quite practicable. Then, for the setting. The detective story cannot be too much up-to-date: the motor, the telephone, the aeroplane, the newest slang, are all in place there. For the ghost story, a slight haze of distance is desirable. 'Thirty years ago', 'Not long before the war', are very proper openings . . . For some degree of actuality is the charm of the best ghost stories; not a very insistent actuality, but one strong enough to allow the reader to identify with the patient.

The longest critical essay Monty wrote on the ghost story genre was published as 'Some Remarks on Ghost Stories' in *The Bookman* for December 1929 and consists of a concise historical survey inter-spersed with some general observations on technique. The tradition of the literary ghost story began for Monty with inferior progenitors. Horace Walpole's *The Castle of Otranto* (1764) was 'merely amusing in the modern sense'; Mrs Ann Radcliffe, thirty years later, was better, but her ghosts were all explained away 'with exasperating timidity', whilst M. G. Lewis (*The Monk*, 1796) was 'odious and horrible without being impressive'.

It was in Scott that Monty identified the real beginnings of 'the short prose ghost story'—in those 'two classic specimens', 'Wandering Willie's Tale' (from *Redgauntlet*, 1824) and 'The Tapestried Cham-ber'. Then came the stories in the magazines, annuals and periodicals of the 1830s and 1840s; and so on to Dickens, whose moralistic *A Christmas Carol* Monty did not consider to be a ghost story proper, though other of Dickens's stories did qualify.

But it was Joseph Sheridan Le Fanu (1814–73) who held the palm: 'Is it the blend of French and Irish in Le Fanu's descent and surroundings that gives him the knack of infusing ominousness into his atmosphere? He is anyhow an artist in words . . . Upon mature consideration, I do not think that there are better ghost stories anywhere than the best of Le Fanu's.' Le Fanu had been part of Monty's literary upbringing. He had recommended *Uncle Silas* to Leo Maxse in the mid-1880s; he himself had read Le Fanu as a child. He recalled seeing a magazine illustration for 'Mr Justice Harbottle' and in 1923 could still remember 'being alarmed by it'.[22] At some point after the end of the First World War he began to hunt out the first appearances of Le Fanu's stories, and for the fiftieth anniversary of the author's death he gave a lecture at the Royal Institution (16 March 1923) on 'The Novels and Stories of J. Sheridan Le Fanu'. An abstract of the lecture was published in the *Proceedings of the Royal Institution*.[23] 'Without claiming for him the status of a great novelist,' part of it ran, 'the lecturer pleaded for his recognition as one of the best story-tellers of the nineteenth century.' Later that same year he provided a Prologue and an Epilogue for a collection of Le Fanu's stories, *Madame Crowl's Ghost and Other Tales of Mystery*. In the Prologue, Monty wrote of Le Fanu:

He stands absolutely in the first rank as a writer of ghost stories. That is my deliberate verdict, after reading all the supernatural tales I have been able to get hold of. Nobody sets the scene better than he, nobody touches in the effective detail more deftly. I do not think it is merely the fact of my being past middle age that leads me to regard the leisureliness of his style as a merit; for I am by no means inappreciative of the more modern efforts in this branch of fiction. No, it has to be recognised, I am sure, that the ghost story is in itself a slightly old-fashioned form; it needs some deliberateness in the telling . . . .

The Prologue is a brief one; the Epilogue runs to some thirteen pages and contains the fruits of Monty's bibliographical searchings. (He acknowledges the help given him by S. M. Ellis, who had contributed a bibliography of Le Fanu to the *Irish Book Lover* in 1916.) Three years later, in 1926, Oxford published *Uncle Silas* in 'The World's Classics' series with an introduction by Monty, in which, as he told Gwendolen McBryde, 'I exposed Conan Doyle's cribbing of the plot,* and also a London firm which issues an abridged edition without warning'.

Amongst modern ghost story writers he read widely, but rarely gave unqualified approval. H. Russell Wakefield's first volume of stories, *They Return at Evening* (1928), which he thought was a good title, 'gives us a mixed bag, from which I should remove one or two that leave a nasty taste'; Algernon Blackwood's John Silence stories were 'rather over-technically "occult"'; and as for the many volumes by Elliott O'Donnell, Monty did not know whether to class them as 'narratives of fact or exercises in fiction. I hope they be of the latter sort, for life in a world managed by his gods and infested by his demons seems a risky business.'[24] The partnership of Erckmann-Chatrian, however, was warmly recommended, especially for the shorter stories, which 'have for years delighted and alarmed me. It is high time that they were made more accessible than they are.'

Monty's own stories, in spite of many unique qualities, were

* In *The Firm of Girdlestone* (1890).

self-consciously part of this nineteenth-century literary tradition.
From a critical point of view, it is this aspect of them, together with
their being rooted in Monty's Cambridge and Eton world, that needs
to be grasped. When Monty first began to write them, with the
intention of inducing a pleasing terror in his listeners, he did so as an
avid and discerning reader and connoisseur of the genre, keenly aware
of his precedents and of the characteristics, objectives, and limitations
of the ghost story as he understood the term.*

Seen as representatives of a specific literary form (which is how
Monty himself viewed them), the stories assume their true importance.
Their lineage goes no further back than the first half of the nineteenth
century (though, as he said, he tried to make his ghosts act in ways not
inconsistent with the rules of folklore), in particular to Le Fanu, but
also, in a more general way, to the magazine stories that were intended
'to amuse the family circle'.²⁵ Monty initially had just such an
environment in which to develop his stories, in the gathering of friends
at King's over Christmas, that most appropriate of seasons for
supernatural stories; so, in a broad sense, he was also working in a
much older *oral* tradition of seasonal tale-telling. The passage, he said,
that justified all ghost stories and put them in their proper place could
be found in *The Winter's Tale* (II.i):

Mamillius.	A sad tale's best for winter: I have one
	Of sprites and goblins.
Hermione.	Let's have that, good sir.
	Come on, sit down, come on, and do your best
	To fright me with your sprites: you're powerful at it.
Mam.	There was a man—
Her.	Nay, come sit down; then on.
Mam.	Dwelt by a churchyard: I will tell it softly,
	Yond crickets shall not hear it.
Her.	Come on then,
	And giv't me in mine ear.

---

* It is misguided to approach the ghost stories as if they were examples of the highest
artistic and literary endeavour. They are amongst the very best of their kind; but it is easy
to claim too much for them, and even easier to impose on them a weight of critical
analysis and speculation that they can hardly bear. A clever professional psychoanalyst,
with some justice, or a foolish amateur one, with none, may discern significance in
certain images, names or situations for, as Algernon Blackwood once remarked, 'the
subconscious always dramatizes'. But this is to miss the point and character of Monty's
stories: to dwell on them as vehicles of unconscious psychological revelation, to the
exclusion of all other considerations, is to view them though a distorting glass.

Monty's stories provided both general and direct inspiration to several members of his circle. The three Benson brothers, Arthur, Edward Frederic, and Robert Hugh, all published collections of supernatural tales. Arthur's 'medieval' tales, told to Eton boys when he was a housemaster, were written at about the same time as Monty's early stories and are typically overlaid with pensiveness and archaic romanticism. There were two collections: *The Hill of Trouble* (published in 1903, thus predating *Ghost Stories of an Antiquary*) and *The Isles of Sunset* (1904).

Monty thought that E. F. Benson's stories ranked high. However, Monty criticized him for 'stepping over the line of legitimate horridness'. It was very easy, he observed, to be nauseating: 'I, *moi qui vous parle*, could undertake to make a reader physically sick, if I chose to think and write in terms of the Grand Guignol.' Warming to his theme, he went on:

Reticence may be an elderly doctrine to preach, yet from the artistic point of view I am sure it is a sound one. Reticence conduces to effect, blatancy ruins it, and there is much blatancy in a lot of recent stories [he was writing in 1929]. They drag in sex too, which is a fatal mistake; sex is tiresome enough in the novels; in a ghost story, or as the backbone of a ghost story, I have no patience with it.[26]

Hugh Benson's fervid stories found less favour with Monty, who thought them 'too ecclesiastical'.

More directly inspired by Monty's stories—indeed they may be said to have initiated something of an M. R. Jamesian school—were E. G. Swain, Chaplain of King's until 1905, and R. H. Malden, sometime Dean of Wells—both friends of Monty. Swain's *The Stoneground Ghost Tales* were published in 1912, 'Compiled from the recollections of the Reverend Roland Batchell, Vicar of the Parish'. It contained nine stories and was dedicated to Monty, 'FOR TWENTY PLEASANT YEARS MR BATCHELL'S FRIEND,/AND THE INDULGENT PARENT OF SUCH TASTES/AS THESE PAGES INDICATE.'

Malden's *Nine Ghosts* did not appear until 1943, though the first story, 'A Collector's Company', was written in 1909. The publisher was Edward Arnold and the flap copy asked: 'How many readers have regretted that there were no more of M. R. James's ghost stories to come? Yet Dr James has found his successor in the Dean of Wells. No more need be said than that the connoisseur will find in these stories a

draught of the genuine vintage with its own subtle flavour.' Malden,
understandably, did not claim so much for his stories:

Anyone familiar with *Ghost Stories of an Antiquary* will have no difficulty in
recognising their *provenance*. It was my good fortune to know Dr James for
more than thirty years. Among my many debts to him is an introduction to the
work of Joseph Sheridan Le Fanu, whom he always regarded as The Master.

Sufficient time has now elapsed since Dr James's death to make some
attempt to continue the tradition admissible or even welcome to his friends and
readers. It is as such that these stories have been collected and revised now.
They are in some sort a tribute to his memory, if not comparable to his work.*

Three ghost stories appeared after the collected edition was
published in April 1931. The first, 'The Experiment: A New Year's
Eve Ghost Story', appeared in the *Morning Post* on 31 December 1931.
The second, 'The Malice of Inanimate Objects', was contributed to
the first number of *The Masquerade*, an Eton ephemeral, in June 1933.
It is a slight affair, though it contains the chilling phrase, 'the angry
dead'. The third story, 'A Vignette', was published soon after Monty's
death in the *London Mercury*. He sent it to the editor on 12 December
1935, at the request of Owen Hugh Smith, accompanied by a letter: 'I
am ill satisfied with what I enclose. It comes late and is short and ill
written. There have been a good many events conspiring to keep it
back, besides a growing inability. So pray don't use it unless it has
some quality I do not see in it.'[27] The lack of a plot, the childhood
memories of Livermere and the first-person narrative all lend an
autobiographical flavour to 'A Vignette'.

One afternoon—the day being neither overcast nor threatening—I was at my
window in the upper floor of the house. All the family were out. From some
obscure shelf in a disused room I had worried out a book, not very recondite: it
was, in fact, a bound volume of a magazine in which were contained parts of a
novel. I know now what novel it was, but I did not then, and a sentence struck
and arrested me. Someone was walking at dusk up a solitary lane by an old
mansion in Ireland, and being a man of imagination he was suddenly forcibly
impressed by what he calls 'the aerial image of the old house, with its peculiar
malign, sacred, and skulking aspect' peering out of the shade of its neglected

---

* Two more volumes that continued Monty's style should be briefly noted: Arthur
Gray's *Tedious Brief Tales of Granta and Gramarye* (1919), and A. N. L. Munby's
accomplished collection *The Alabaster Hand* (1949), with its dedication to Monty: 'Dis
Manibus/Montague Rhodes James/Collegii Nostri Olim Praepositi/Huiusce Generis
Fabularum/Sine Aemulo Creatoris.'

old trees.* The words were quite enough to set my own fancy on a bleak track. Inevitably I looked and looked with apprehension, to the Plantation gate. As was but right it was shut, and nobody was upon the path that led to it or from it. But as I said a while ago, there was in it a square hole giving access to the fastening: and through that hole, I could see—and it struck like a blow on the diaphragm—something white or partly white. Now this I could not bear, and with an access of something like courage—only it was more like desperation, like determining that I must know the worst—I did steal down and, quite uselessly, of course, taking cover behind bushes as I went, I made progress until I was within range of the gate and the hole. Things were, alas!, worse than I had feared. Through that hole a face was looking my way. It was not monstrous, not pale, fleshless, spectral. Malevolent I thought and think it was; at any rate the eyes were large and open and fixed. It was pink and, I thought, hot, and just above the eyes the border of a white linen drapery hung down from the brows . . . Do not press me with questions as to how I bore myself when it became necessary to face my family again. That I was upset by something I had seen must have been pretty clear, but I am very sure that I fought off all attempts to describe it. Why I make a lame effort to do it now I cannot very well explain: it undoubtedly has had some formidable power of clinging through many years to my imagination. I feel that even now I should be circumspect in passing that Plantation gate; and every now and again the query haunts me: Are there here and there sequestered places which some curious creatures still frequent, whom once on a time anybody could see and speak to as they went about on their daily occasions, whereas now only at rare intervals in a series of years does one cross their paths and become aware of them; and perhaps that is just as well for the peace of mind of simple people.

* The story was by Le Fanu. Cf. 'Some Remarks on Ghost Stories', p. 170.

CHAPTER 13

THE LODGE
King's 1905

> And when, after the feast, the choir are singing their sweet
> Elizabethan madrigals, the lights are turned down in the Hall, all
> except those above the portraits, and you see only the faces and
> forms of that goodly company, with some of whom you used to sit
> at meat night after night in this same building, while the others
> looked down from the walls just as they do now. Lowes Dickinson,
> O.B., Walter Durnford, Monty James—here they are in Hall as
> visibly and vividly as ever.
>
> Esmé Wingfield-Stratford, *Before the Lamps Went Out*

ON 28 January 1905 Augustus Austen Leigh died quietly and
suddenly. He was sixty-four years old, but looked ten years younger.
Monty was not in Cambridge that day, but he received a letter from
Walter Durnford telling him the news: ' . . . he died in a moment about
4.30. We are knocked flat as you may suppose: it is impossible to
realize.' Durnford, in tears, had also broken the news to Arthur
Benson, who wrote in his diary: '[Austen Leigh] was not a man of great
distinction or ability: but he was kind, amiable, sensible, and very
modest. No shadow of pomposity ever touched him . . . '[1]

For the moment, Monty's thoughts were distracted by his sister
Grace, who had suffered a seizure while running for a train; but it soon
appeared that there was no danger and Monty returned to a table
'more than usually horrescent with papers' and to the events in King's.
The Provost's funeral was on 1 February, a bright, cold, windy day that
ruffled hair and buffeted the gowns of the procession as it moved along
the river front of Gibbs' Building. In the Chapel, a large wreath of
lilies was placed in the Provost's stall. 'The music was sweet and soft,'
noted Arthur Benson. 'But [Herbert] Ryle read the lesson in a voice
like the quacking of a gigantic duck—that horrid guttural twang he has
lately caught.'[2]

With the Provost laid to rest, the question of his successor became a matter for open debate. Monty told his father that the provostship was said to be between himself and Walter Durnford, 'but I don't see myself in that chair. The man I want is Arthur Benson.' Arthur had been astounded and delighted to learn that he was being considered as a possible candidate, and Monty, not wishing for the post himself, had urged him to put his name forward.

Meanwhile, Monty was being encouraged by J. W. Clark to think of himself as the only possible candidate, which amused but did not convince him. Then in March the provostship was offered first to George Prothero,* who refused it, and then to Lord Rayleigh, a distinguished physicist and Fellow of Trinity, who also turned it down. It was then offered to Monty, who wrote in some perplexity to Arthur Benson to tell him that *his* candidature would not now be considered. Arthur could not advise Monty to accept the offer, writing in his diary: 'He would hate it; he wouldn't do it well. If he felt sure that King's would *suffer* if he didn't, it might be a duty—but he can't feel that.'[3] He expressed his reservations openly to Monty on the 23rd:

The principal use of the Head of a House is to manage a lot of rather opinionated men—well, I think you would do it with great skill, but I don't think you would like doing it. Then comes the ceaseless *business*, letters, meetings, reception of big persons, official hospitality, the nightmare of the Vice-Chancellorship etc, etc. This could be minimized by a Secretary, I think, to some extent; but not wholly. It would be an end to liberty, to going and coming as one wishes, to leisurely ways. Of course it may be argued that one had better become a buffer with a bound, in a dignified way, for to bufferdom we must all come . . . It seems to me that your *ideal* place is to be Vice-Provost; just as the summit of *my* ambitions is the Vice-Provostship of Eton!

The next day Monty received a letter from Prothero, who felt that King's would have good cause to congratulate itself 'if it gets for its Provost one on whom I always think the mantle of dear old Bradshaw has fallen, both in regard to scholarship and his power of annexing the young. You will still be able to wear that mantle in the Lodge.' He had also received a frank letter from Walter Headlam urging him to accept the provostship.

Doubts have been suggested, you won't be altogether surprised to know, whether you wouldn't find the business part of it too irksome. But it would be a

* Prothero had left King's in 1894 to become Professor of History at Edinburgh. He subsequently edited the *Quarterly Review*.

good deal less troublesome than the Tutor's business, which you managed in a way to surprise some expectations . . . What people want is not so much a business manager as a scholar with the right ideals for the College; and all things equal, wouldn't you prefer a Kingsman and an Etonian?[4]

One of the most forceful letters of encouragement, and perhaps one of the ones that carried most weight for Monty, was from William Austen Leigh, a former Second Bursar and an influential benefactor of the College:

I know the prospect is in many ways not pleasant for you: and I should not say what I do if there seemed any chance that either Walter Durnford or Arthur Benson would be selected . . . My sister-in-law [i.e. the former Provost's widow] and all of us would certainly feel great satisfaction in thinking of you as occupying my brother's place—this is of course a private consideration. But the *public* one is that you have an extraordinary combination of qualifications. You are very well known and much loved in the College—the 'distinction' clause has no terrors for you—you are an Etonian—and (last but not least) you love the Chapel and its services, and would do your best to foster that side of College life—I want you to consider whether it is not a sacrifice due to the institution which we both love so much. I feel that any probable alternatives— such as the election of Sir R. Ball (Lowndean Professor of Astronomy and Geometry]—would (much as one likes him) make a serious and dangerous break in the continuity of College history.[5]

The next day Monty made up his mind to accept and went round to tell Arthur: 'Monty said plainly that if they would have taken Walter Durnford or me, he would have declined. But W.D. has no qualification of eminence, and I am not sufficiently connected with the place (nor, I gather, academically distinguished enough). He is evidently very reluctant, and it is a *real* sacrifice to duty.' Monty then went off to the doctor's, 'to be overhauled, to see that his health was all right'.[6]

Herbert James was told of Monty's decision on the 26th. 'The balance of duty seemed to verge that way, certainly not that of inclination,' wrote Monty. His father thought he had taken the right step, 'though it is one which called for no small self-denial. But the potentialities of usefulness abound . . . One great gain will be the having a very definite object in life with every opportunity for exercising a most helpful influence in various ways.' Sydney agreed, telling his father that '[Monty's] own particular work will, I fancy, not suffer as much as he imagines, and it is a huge benefit to the College to be under a man whom all look up to.'

Luxmoore, however, had misgivings, having received a candid letter from Monty disclaiming his fitness for the post. Monty had also taken the extraordinary step of sending an analysis of his unsuitability to the King's Fellows, which, by its honesty and the self-knowledge it displayed, as Nathaniel Wedd recorded, 'only made his supporters more anxious to have him as Provost'.[7] Luxmoore knew that there was little prospect of personal happiness in the provostship for Monty, but he recognized that it must be embraced as a duty, 'for the sake of so good a place and so benignant a nursing mother, who cannot be let fall into the hands of the philistine and agnostic'.

All seemed settled, then, and the election of Monty James as Provost of King's looked like a mere formality. The news even crossed the Empire. From Lahore, Malcolm Darling, an Old Etonian friend of E. M. Forster now in the Indian Civil Service, wrote:

My dear Dr James,

I should say Mr Provost, as I learn on quite unimpeachable authority . . . that you are for the Lodge. I hardly know whether to congratulate you, as I suspect you are attached to those rooms a-top of 'D' [staircase], but I do feel that King's is to be most honestly congratulated on their choice, and I can hardly say more . . . Were we more numerous here, we should have had a dinner to celebrate the event, but in this province I think we are only three.[8]

At the end of April, Monty was engaged to dine with Arthur Benson, Stephen Gaselee, and Arthur Shipley, but for some reason did not turn up. In his absence, the other guests naturally began to talk about him. 'The odd thing is', said Arthur, 'that both Shipley and Gaselee put Monty, as a man of genius, among the four greatest of Cambridge men. Monty's knowledge is extraordinarily accurate and minute; but mainly concerned with unimportant matters—and his mind has *nothing* constructive in it. He seems to me to be an almost perfect instance of high talent; a perfect second-rate man.' Arthur suspected that, at bottom, Monty was beginning mildly to enjoy the prospect of his new position, but 'I wish he wouldn't fall back *quite* so much on its being done from a sense of duty'.[9]

And then, five days later, on 3 May, Marcus Dimsdale called on Arthur 'in some anxiety' with dramatic news from King's. Prothero, having definitely refused the provostship on account of his wife's health, had now, at the last moment, announced that Mrs Prothero took a more cheerful view of things and that he could therefore take on the responsibility. Arthur was highly indignant: 'Dickinson and his men now want to bring Prothero in after all. This would be an intolerable humiliation and mortification for Monty. And besides, it is easy to see that *having* accepted, having made up his mind, the pomp and circumstance have begun to tell on Monty's mind; and though he still thinks he regrets his liberty, he would regret the loss of his dignity more.'[10]

There are indications in Arthur's diary that the strain of these events was beginning to tell on Monty. The entry for 6 May records that Arthur went round to King's to find him playing 'some ugly old song on his cracked piano', and a little pompous in his attitude: 'He seemed to think that I was to make all the arrangements—"Where are you going to take me?" Hang it, he is younger than me!' Afterwards, Arthur decided that Monty had been 'pettish and out of temper'. They had discussed the prolongation of personal identity after death. Monty showed, as Arthur thought, 'a petulant and childish mind, confusing a scientific certainty with an inherited prejudice. He showed himself to be of the school described by M'Taggart who when they say that they *believe* that a thing will happen only mean that they will be much annoyed if it does not.' Looking back over the day, Arthur concluded that Monty had been 'a little self-conscious and inconsiderate—things I had never seen in him before'.

On the 8th there was another development in what had now turned into a contest for the provostship. Monty told his father: 'Hope springs eternal in the human heart and I hear tonight that some at least are likely to vote for Walter Durnford . . . As I have told him, it seems the first ray of sunlight that has crossed my path for some weeks: but it may be delusive.' He also heard from Prothero himself, who wrote: 'I feel I owe an apology to you, above all others, for the inconvenience I have caused. I trust you will forgive me.' Still, Monty was 'just a little annoyed with Prothero for not making up his mind to more purpose at an earlier date, for he would have spared me a good deal of commotion by so doing. But he was always a little inclined to wobble.'[11] As a point of honour he wrote to those who had previously pledged their support to Prothero and begged them not to consider themselves bound in any way by their subsequent pledge to himself.

Arthur Benson was still angry and incredulous at Prothero's decision, as he told Monty: 'I simply cannot understand a man of delicate perceptions and high-minded character acting as he has done . . . I know of course that you will take the affront, for it is that, with engaging amiability and enviable tranquillity; but it does not prevent my feeling, as I said, *deeply* indignant about it all.'*

In the upper levels of Cambridge society, the election was being followed with keen interest. Arthur Benson heard one prominent Cambridge lady speak with vexation of Monty—' "doesn't like women; will close the Lodge to them".'[12] On the 12th, the day before the election, Arthur went to see Monty to tell him that he had decided to be nominated, but Monty was out and so Arthur sat reading a book on French cathedrals until he returned, 'rather flushed with wine'. Monty was happy for Arthur to enter the contest, though he felt that Prothero would probably win. On the same day, Luxmoore wrote from Eton, disturbed at the 'strange rumours' coming to him from King's: 'I am full of angry sympathy, and am now of course a partisan, which I was not before.'

Herbert James, eagerly awaiting the outcome of the election at Livermere, had been advised by his son to be prudent and to view the matter in what he called its true dimensions, 'which are not very enormous':

I'm afraid I must repeat that I shall not be at all sorry—really profoundly pleased—if not elected and I shall have the proud consciousness of not having refused to stand. I shall then be elected Master of Corpus or Cats [St Catharine's] or some nice tranquil foundation and spend a dignified maturity in the pursuit of literature and the cultivation of the neglected undergraduates of those regions. But I realize that you would like to see me Provost, and my only regret will be for you.

For himself, he went off to enjoy a gathering of the Family, a select Cambridge dining club, at J. W. Clark's, whilst the 'vultures', in the shape of the non-resident Fellows, began to assemble in King's.

The next day, the 13th, though he had expected two votings, the election was settled decisively in one.

*   *   *

From where the Provost sits in King's College Chapel the eye sweeps eastwards beyond dark stalls crowned with soaring stone and coloured glass towards the altar and the image of Christ crucified glowing in the

---

* Undoubtedly, though, Prothero—supported by his wife—would have made a fine Provost. Nathaniel Wedd, for one, knowing Prothero's liberal and wide-ranging intellectual sympathies, dreamed of what the Lodge at King's might have been like if Mrs Prothero had not been taken ill.

great east window. The Provost's stall is to the right of the archway of the massive rood screen as you move towards the eastern end of the choir; and on the pavement before it stands a modest but irresistible focus: a diminutive statue of the Founder surmounting the lectern given by Provost Hacomblen.

Into this stall, after being formerly admitted at Lincoln by the Visitor, Bishop King, Dr M. R. James was bowed as Provost of King's College. His new office was one of dignity and long historical associations, which he had not, in truth, desired for himself, but which circumstances, looking strangely like destiny, had forced upon him. The Provost did not feel inclined to inquire into figures: he knew at least that no one would resent his election;* and if he claimed not to take much personal pleasure in his triumph, he was glad, at least, for his father's sake.

The letters of congratulation poured in. 'I know of no-one in this world', wrote Florence Austen Leigh, the late Provost's widow, 'so well qualified to rule over our dear King's.' Amongst the Heads of Houses, the Master of Trinity, Dr Butler, claimed to have foreseen Monty's eventual succession to the provostship as far back as 1887: 'As to Trinity,' he wrote, 'you have long known, and you know by recent confidence, how dear your name is to us and how warmly we have appreciated the many important services which you have rendered to us. Your appointment now is the surest of guarantees that the happy relations between the two "Royal Colleges" will continue unimpaired . . . My Ted will indeed rejoice.'

The new Provost was also popular with the younger generation. The Headmaster of Uppingham, E. C. Selwyn, heard from his son (an Etonian Scholar) that the undergraduates were delighted and Selwyn wrote to Herbert James to say that, 'A man more greatly beloved, in quality and quantity, of those whose love is most worth having, has seldom been elected by a college.'

Some, though, could not help wondering if things could ever be the same: would the Provost in his Lodge be as approachable as the Dean? A more personal sense of regret was apparent in Percy Lubbock's letter:

I simply can't bear to think of your rooms becoming Another's, and of you retreating behind a locked front door. You must know partly, but very likely

---

* The figures, according to Arthur Benson, were: Monty, 25 votes; Prothero, 16; Walter Durnford, 3; and Arthur himself, 2.

you don't know entirely, what your rooms have meant for me—or what I have learnt there—or what your everlasting kindness and goodness has [sic] been. But I should just like to tell you this once that I have some knowledge of what I owe you.

Arthur Benson, with the dream of ruling over King's now probably gone forever, rejoiced in the honour that Monty had been given, but wished that the Provost's duties were more to his liking. 'I hope that you will be rewarded,' he wrote, 'and that the duties will prove an easy burden; so God bless you, mon vieux!' In private, Arthur was worried that Monty's simple charm might become submerged beneath the prestige of the provostship. In June he sat alone in Monty's rooms—amidst the debris of the Provost's 'odd' lunch: cherries, cheese, strawberry cream, and whisky, set on a cloth laid at the end of a table covered in papers—and pondered this possibility:

A saturnine man in the inner room said that he [Monty] had gone to the Varsity Sermon. God help him! I fear that the going-in, in his red gown, in the slow, blear-eyed, panting procession of Heads, is a positive joy to him! . . . The stupid conventionality and stuffiness of the whole thing. But it will really be *awful* if God, so to speak, does give Monty another heart on his being crowned King, and if he dances naked with the sons of the prophet. The horror will be if the heavy respectability, the complacent security, the dull consciousness of rectitude and worth and success, flows in over Monty's very simple and cheerful soul. Yet I cannot say that I do not think there is a danger of this.[13]

Typically, this was Arthur Benson picturing the worst to himself, although, as so often, there was a hint of the truth in what he said. But to Monty's father there seemed few drawbacks to the provostship; for him it was a moment of quite legitimate pride:

You secure a post of influence. You have the proof of your friends' appreciation of you. You can carry on much of your past work. You can help largely towards maintaining the fair name of the College.
All this, I think, calls for thankfulness and congratulation. And so, where you may feel cause for rejoicing, I joy with you, as a not un-proud father.

From Ellergreen, Sibyl Cropper wrote after seeing Monty's photograph in a newspaper: 'This pen can't restrain its joy at finding its old friend Provost of King's. That's why it's smudging.' But Monty had already sent off a letter to Sibyl, from whom he had not heard for some time:

Dear Master of Clare,
    I am sorry that you had—
    I had got so far when I thought I would alter the destination of this letter and write to you instead. I am quite sure you are preparing to send me a very charming congratulatory note and think I will anticipate it by saying how much pleasure it gives me. But indeed it is a little serious that no letter, friendly or otherwise, has passed between us for some months: it seems as if there must be a coolness somewhere. Assure me, dear William, that I am mistaken ... Before me lies a pile of letters newly written—the third such pile I have despatched today ... Let me advise you to be very careful how you allow yourself to be elected Provost of your College. It entails a great deal of wear and tear of plant and rolling stock as the income tax paper truly says.[14]

By 20 May the pile of letters to be answered had been materially reduced, but there were a hundred other things to be done. He called on Mrs Austen Leigh to discuss the domestic arrangements of the Lodge and agreed to buy some of the Austen Leighs' furniture. He also had to put his mind to the job (a new one for him) of procuring linen, china, and staff; he was helped in his search for the latter by Lady Albinia Donaldson, Stuart Donaldson's wife, who drew up an advertisement for a cook-housekeeper and an upper housemaid. He took Arthur Benson over the Lodge towards the end of June. It struck Arthur as being 'a horrible, dreary house' and that Monty was 'rather conscious of possession, and inclined to resent suggestions ... How [he] will live in that vast house, like a Bishop's palace, on £1200 a year, I can't see.'[15] The question of the Fitzwilliam also had to be settled. It would have been an appropriate moment for Monty to resign the directorship, but he was willing to carry on for another two years (slightly longer, as it turned out) and to use his discretion as to the amount of attendance he could give. On this basis he remained Director until March 1908.

His first Council as Provost was on 20 May. Part of the business concerned the resignations of the Chaplain, E. G. Swain, and of the Headmaster of the Choir School, Benjamin Benham. The departure of Swain, a delightful and much-loved figure, was a real loss for Monty. Benham was a considerably less attractive character, although Monty seems to have liked him. After the Council meeting he went round to see Benham and suggested that he might like to act as his secretary, an idea that Benham embraced eagerly. As Head of the Choir School, Benham had often employed highly intimidating behaviour to assert his authority over the boys; but he idolized Monty and mellowed with the years. 'To me', wrote Gordon Carey, who had suffered as a chorister under Benham, 'the *vultus instantis tyranni* of my young days bore only the faintest resemblance to the 1913 vintage Benham of the cheerful smile and abundant store of University gossip.'[16]

Strange to say, one of Monty's supporters in the provostship election had been Oscar Browning. Monty never wholly conquered his early dislike of him, although he conceded that his abilities 'sometimes reminded one of genius'. He continued to deplore Browning's egoism, his belligerence towards Eton, and his volatility; for his part, Browning criticized Monty's blind loyalty to Eton, which he felt hindered King's from stepping boldly into an independent future. 'I have lost my interest in the College,' Browning wrote in 1912. 'I laboured hard to emancipate it both from Eton and Trinity, and succeeded for some time in doing so. But now by the influence of Monty James and Walter Durnford it has fallen into the bondage of both, and God help it!'[17]

Soon after Monty become Provost it fell to him to tell Browning that the Council had reappointed him as History Tutor for only three years instead of the usual seven, and that at the end of that time, since he would then be over seventy, he would be superannuated. Monty broke the news to Browning informally one morning coming out of Chapel. He was understandably indignant; but it was due to Monty that he was later voted a pension only slightly less than his previous stipend. Indeed, Monty felt so strongly about the matter that he told Arthur Benson that if Browning were turned out penniless, he would resign.[18] Those who came to see Monty James as something of a trimmer incapable of taking a firm stand on an issue were presumably either ignorant of or deliberately ignored his exemplary conduct in the Browning affair, which caused a considerable stir in the College at the time. As Arthur Berry told Monty, things would have been a great deal worse 'if we had had a less tactful and amiable man to guide our controversies'.

And what of Oscar Browning? After being ousted, as he saw it, from the principalship of the Day Training College (a move he attributed to the machinations of Walter Durnford, who succeeded him) he finally left Cambridge in 1909, angry and resentful, and eventually retired to Rome. He seemed to feel no gratitude for what Monty had been able to do for him during his last years at King's; in fact he numbered the Provost amongst his enemies. 'Monty James,' he wrote airily some years later, 'for whom I have little respect, was as bad as any of them.'[19]

The pensioning off of Oscar Browning had showed that Monty had both principles and the ability to acquit himself honourably and effectively in a controversy. The odd thing was that he seemed to take no pleasure or pride in his manifest talents as a chairman and arbitrator. Esmé Wingfield-Stratford, a Fellow, knew of no one 'who could preside with a more unruffled urbanity over those interminable meetings of the College Council'.[20] This ability to direct and quietly dominate proceedings did not make his preposital duties more palatable for Monty. He had barely been in office six months before he was returning to his official work 'with bewilderment and shrinking'. As well as the, to him, distasteful responsibility of pronouncing on personal destinies (as in the case of Oscar Browning), and his dislike of factional unpleasantness, there was the deadening burden of administrative minutiae. He wrote: 'The consciousness that you are directing the destinies of a great institution, which should always be present to your mind, is, except on rare occasions, too apt to disappear, veiled in a mist of smallnesses, financial, agricultural, educational—lecture fees, pigsties, servants' wages, plans for the new bathroom at the Manor Farm.'[21]

But he let little or none of this show and few felt that his election had been anything but a good thing for King's. One critical voice belonged to W. F. Reddaway, who was for many years on the College's history staff. He strongly disapproved of Monty's lack of policy and educational principles and thought his election had been '*purely emollient*'. Arthur Benson recorded Reddaway's opinion that ' "under *no* circumstance was it conceivable that Monty should make even a tolerable Provost—it is this hateful prestige that attaches to the post: so many people would like it that a compromise is necessary, and it falls to the most inoffensive man" '.[22] But this was an extreme reaction. Generally, even amongst those who were unsympathetic to Monty's patrician conservatism, his suitability and his genial efficiency were acknowledged. Nathaniel Wedd, though a stout defender of the Classics, was numbered amongst the liberal agnostics in King's; but in November 1905 he told Arthur Benson that Monty was 'an admirable Provost, a first-rate chairman, keeping business straight, even stopping the Vice-Provost [Fred Whitting] from gossiping by a gentle pressure of hand on arm . . . Everyone feels that they have a *friend* at the head of things—not a mere kindly man, like the late Provost, but a sympathetic friend.'[23]

The Provost tried to encourage the kind of informal association with undergraduates that had been possible during his deanship. He made it easy for visitors to come and go from the Lodge and placed syphons, decanters, tobacco, and cards out ready in the hall. This accessibility was not only a reflection of a naturally sociable disposition; it had always had an element of grateful obligation about it, for, as he said later in his memorial tribute to Walter Durnford, it was possible to serve an institution like King's in several ways—in teaching, for instance, or in administrative work, or by pure research: 'And to any or all of these another way is open, which is not less valuable to the Society. It is to look upon the College as a family of which the more part consists of the young.'[24]

It was felt in some quarters that Monty James would now be better off with a wife, someone to share the social duties of a Head of House and to take charge of running the Lodge. 'Obviously you will now have to marry,' Edward Austen Leigh had written bluntly. With equal emphasis, Henry Yates Thompson* told him, 'You will have to get a Provostess. That's flat.' The defeated Prothero also urged him to find someone 'who will be as kind as you are to the young men—and then the College will have reason doubly to congratulate itself'. But Monty maintained a dignified—or perhaps stubborn—silence in the face of these promptings, except that he apparently suggested to Prothero that an actress he had seen in the 1905 production of *Peter Pan* might make a suitable consort. 'She is fascinating,' agreed Prothero.

As a young man, Monty had occasionally affected the misogynist. At Eton in April 1886, for instance, at a dinner at the Lodge in honour of the Bishop of Oxford, he had taken in a lady 'who had been to every part of the globe and revelled in every kind of athletic pursuit except dancing. I contrived I hope to appear thoroughly contemptible to her.' The result was that, when Maisie Fletcher first knew Monty, he had 'quite wrongly achieved the reputation of being a woman hater'.[25] But in fact Monty got on well with a number of women, including Adie Browne (Lady Donaldson's companion), Gwendolen McBryde, and of course the Cropper ladies. He also found certain women physically beautiful—Stella Duckworth, for example, or Monica Sanderson, Ted Sanderson's sister, or the sisters of Leo Maxse, whom he described in 1889 as 'very taking'; and back in the 1880s he had aroused the, probably unwelcome, advances of a friend of Grace's, Annie Walker,

---

* The pre-eminent English collector of manuscripts, many of which were catalogued by Monty.

who wrote to him in November 1886: 'I hope you haven't forgotten who I am; if you have Gracie can tell you. You see I haven't forgotten the compliment you paid me when I was at Livermere.'

But Monty never seriously considered marriage as a practical, or desirable, possibility. To the modern mind, this reluctance raises questions on the nature of his sexuality that would have been deeply distasteful to Monty himself. We can talk glibly of his being a 'repressed homosexual', but this seems a hopelessly inadequate summation of the complex cultural and personal factors behind his resistance to marriage. Further, in the context of his life this resistance was a good deal less significant than, say, his decision not to take Holy Orders, which produced discernible tensions in a way the marriage question never did.

No 'woman hater', then, but one of nature's bachelors, jealous of his independence and a connoisseur of the pleasures generated by the predominantly male society in which he moved. In 1903 he wrote: 'Arthur Benson has taken a house in Cambridge . . . I don't think he contemplates matrimony. Nor does George Duckworth . . . Nor does yours truly.'[26] But if Monty James was not what Arthur Benson called 'a marriageable man', the demands of his position as Provost of King's probably brought him nearer to contemplating marriage than any other period of his life.

According to Oliffe Richmond, who told Arthur Benson in 1916, Monty had been on the brink of marriage twice: first to Norah Lyttelton (the granddaughter by marriage of Lady Sybella Lyttelton, second wife of the 4th Baron Lyttelton) and then to Sibyl Cropper. There seems no other evidence to support Richmond's assertion, so it must stand on its own—except that in February 1907 Arthur Benson dined in King's with Monty and wrote in his diary:

This was an interesting party, Owen Hugh Smith, Caryl Lyttelton, [Clive] Carey, Neville Lyttelton, Lady Lyttelton, Miss Lyttelton. I took in the latter, a pretty and charming girl to whom I rather lost my heart. . . . But there was a sense of dim relations about that puzzled me. Is Monty going to marry the charming girl? I can't make out. Lady Lyttelton is an inveterate match-maker, and Monty has been often there of late. He is a very confirmed bachelor, but I think he feels he wants a wife, and I think Lady Lyttelton feels so too. Well, he will be very lucky—she is a pretty, simple, lively creature. I wish it were going to be my good fortune to deserve her.[27]

There was one woman who saw a good deal of Monty during his later years: Gwendolen McBryde. Gwendolen occupied a special place in his life, as James McBryde's widow to begin with, but then on her own account; and to her, and later to her daughter Jane, Monty directed a regular flow of letters—especially after his father's death in 1909.

In Gwendolen's rambling introduction to *Letters to a Friend* (1956), she describes, in prose that is faintly flushed with romance, how she had first seen Monty, 'a misty, if not fabulous being, the precious possession of those undergraduates at Cambridge then known to me', during a May Week service in King's Chapel. Her eye had ranged over the surpliced figures, on past the choir, 'and was arrested—I did not need to be told that I was looking on Dr James. For the first time I wished that I had been born a boy, with the chance of living quite differently, even if I could not have arrived inside the charmed circle.'

It is easy to imagine Gwendolen becoming attached beyond simple friendship to Monty, a distinguished and not unattractive older man who had shown her much kindness during a difficult period in her life—though there is no evidence to show that this was the case. It is less easy to picture Monty James seriously considering marriage to Gwendolen; and yet she clearly meant *something* to him. Their relationship was conducted with the utmost propriety (he went on calling her 'Mrs McBryde' in his letters for some time), and even though he perhaps endured much for James's sake that he might otherwise have found tiresome, Gwendolen was welcoming, lively, and affectionate—a 'chirrupy' sort of person, as she has been described. And yet Walter Fletcher's son Charles, who saw them together, could not recall anything approaching endearment in Monty's conversation with Gwendolen, although he was often teasing.[28]

Monty took his duties towards Jane extremely seriously, and he extended his care and oversight to Gwendolen also, as he told her: 'I am sure that it will always be a first charge to me to do anything that can be of any gratification to you: and I look to you to let me know how I can serve you.'[29] In 1906 Gwendolen and Jane moved from Ingmanthorpe to a new house—Woodlands, in Herefordshire. It was there that Monty first met Jane, with Walter Fletcher, in June of that year—'a pleasant and interesting meeting'. From Woodlands he went to Eton, and then on to Ramsbury in Wiltshire, where Owen Hugh Smith part-owned a cottage used as a base for fishing in the Kennet. From Ramsbury Monty wrote, in part regretfully, to Gwendolen about his visit: 'It was a real pleasure to see you and Jane . . . and as for the surroundings, I think them ideal. The only thing which I repented of was that I never did what I was always on the point of doing and that was to talk about James, who is continually in my mind. It was only an unreasoning shyness which kept me from it but I did and do regret it very much.'[30]

Jane inherited both her parents' talent for drawing, which she later employed to create pictures very much to her guardian's taste, showing witches, vampires and 'gaping square tombs with creatures crawling out of them by moonlight'.[31] With Jane, as with Sibyl Cropper, Monty showed an aptitude for entering the world of the young and his friendship with these lively and intelligent girls seem to have been both emancipating for him and, in a way, therapeutic. With them he could briefly repossess that inner country of childhood, which many people lose sense of but which in him stood intact and unviolated by cynicism. The boy was never far below the surface of the man, and it must have been a pleasure occasionally to let him have his head.

He visited Woodlands nearly every year until 1929, when Gwendolen and Jane moved to another house, Dippersmoor, a few miles away. Woodlands seems to have become a substitute for Livermere after Herbert James's death. It was a place where Monty could relax in congenial surroundings, where he was free to do as he wished, and where he was treated with affectionate and admiring indulgence. Gwendolen was also good at providing creature comforts, which Monty appreciated. He could play patience, write, walk, lie under the trees or by the stream, read or work, as he chose. 'We all carried on with our own jobs,' wrote Gwendolen, 'and I think I never discussed anything in particular with MRJ. He would know what you meant by your fragmentary utterances and you knew just what he liked. There really was nothing you could supply. He did the entertaining, and oddly enough he would say "You know I am bad at expressing myself", and would murmur remarks more to himself than to you, such as "I call you my gracious silence".' On one perfect summer evening he read aloud from *A Midsummer Night's Dream* to a background of nightjars. Gwendolen recalled 'his beautiful voice' and remembered how when Monty read aloud he 'lent you his own understanding'.

There would be impersonations—Monty as a country yokel (Barker, doubtless), or a cockney; Jane as Miss Smith, 'a highly imaginary governess'. Sometimes over lunch he would give an imitation of a speech or sermon 'which said nothing at all, but went on endlessly until we roused ourselves from the apathy into which we had sunk, as one does on real occasions when this happens, and we would rebel and shout him down'. On Sundays he would go to church (he said he felt a worm otherwise) and on one occasion he was invited to read the lesson at nearby Abbey Dore, one of his favourite churches. 'It was strange', wrote Gwendolen, 'in the small church to hear his fine slightly plaintive voice: he seemed to be so much too large for the place. It always gave me an unreal feeling, as if some saint held forth to lesser creatures and birds.'[32]

* * *

After the busy end of the Summer Term 1905 Monty snatched a few days' bicycling in Lincolnshire with Walter Fletcher and paid visits to Ellergreen and to the Lytteltons at Hagley. The Lodge was not ready for him until after Christmas, and even then some work remained to be done. He found the idea of managing a household alarming but hoped that 'when the new staff has made acquaintance with itself and its duties, wheels may turn easily enough'.

Only a few weeks after becoming Provost the news came that his friend Eustace Talbot had died—almost exactly a year after McBryde's death, and, like him, following an operation. Eustace, Monty told Herbert James, had been 'one of the ones I prized most'. He remembered walking with Eustace in the garden at Ellergreen the night before Walter Fletcher's wedding. They had spoken of James McBryde, recently dead, and Eustace had told Monty what he thought and had seen of death as a medical student—'how easy it seemed was the process of dying: how evident it was to him that death was not the end: and how sure he had come to be that love was at the back of it all'.[33] Now Eustace himself was dead, and perhaps Monty recalled his friend's words written to him after receiving a copy of *The Story of a Troll-hunt*: 'There is nothing harder to believe than that the mysterious relation between those who are left and those who are chosen is in the hands of love. It so often seems that all that is fairest in promise is cut off and it is difficult not to resent the apparently haphazard choice.'[34]

Both Monty and Walter Fletcher contributed to a privately printed memoir of Eustace. Monty's piece concluded: 'But an end must be made, and the most fitting is the thought, which is present whenever we think of Eustace, of thanks to the faithful Creator who gave us this friend and promises us a continuance of his friendship.'

CHAPTER 14

A PROVOST'S LIFE
King's 1905–1914

'Remember, if you please,' said my friend, looking at me over his
spectacles, 'that I am a Victorian by birth and education, and that
the Victorian tree may not unreasonably be expected to bear
Victorian fruit.'

M. R. James, 'A Neighbour's Landmark'

THE first Fellow of King's to be admitted by Monty James as Provost
was Oliffe Richmond, elected on the strength of his Propertius
dissertation in 1905. The next Etonian Fellow (in 1909) was John
Maynard Keynes, who beat Stephen Gaselee to the only vacant
Fellowship after an all-day debate by the electors. 'Gaselee's thesis',
wrote Oliffe Richmond, 'was an outspoken and immensely learned
commentary on Petronius, which scared old Whitting and perhaps
some others. Perhaps Monty was no less scared by Keynes; but if he
had to give a casting vote, it was for Keynes, and Gaselee was quickly
absorbed by Magdalene.'[1]

Keynes's tutor at Eton had been Gurney Lubbock, and it is nicely
ironic that Keynes, who seemed to stand for much that was
antipathetic to Monty, was watched over and guided at school by a
thorough-going Montyite. Arriving in King's, Keynes enjoyed the
Provost's hospitality and resorted to him for information on books
(Keynes was already a discerning collector) and medieval Latin. Yet,
even as a freshman, Keynes exhibited the kind of intellectual
aggressiveness and analytical brilliance that Monty was distrustful of.
'I've had a good look round this place,' was Keynes's famous remark,
made soon after he went up to King's, 'and come to the conclusion that
it's pretty inefficient'.[2] Though this was not arrogance, merely the
application of an extraordinary intellect, it might very well have seemed
like it. The same applies to the explosion in 1912, when Keynes moved
three motions, the third of which was an implicit attack on the financial
management of the College.

This kind of behaviour disturbed Monty James: it shook foundations and threatened collegiate unity. One can easily see why Keynes, standing for a vigorous moral and intellectual reassessment of the society in which he found himself, rather than for a reverent acceptance of inherited imperatives, was not someone the Provost could take to his heart.

On the other hand, there was a party amongst the Fellows of King's, including Keynes, that thought Monty lacked moral decisiveness as Provost; that he hedged when he should have stood firm for progressive attitudes; that he acquiesced when he should have taken a lead; that he avoided confrontation when he should have sought it out for the sake of fruitful innovation. Monty's reaction to Keynes was of course a complex amalgamation of dislikes. He was unsettled by Keynes's agnosticism, certainly, but also probably by his potential for disrupting tradition. Perhaps, finally, it was simply the twentieth century (for all that Keynes was an establishment figure) drawing away once and for all from the settled bulk of the Victorian shoreline that put distance between Keynes and Monty James.

Rooted in another age, and in the evangelical culture of his childhood, Monty perhaps could not help but see Keynes as a threatening *enfant terrible*, a symbol of the ungodly. When Walter Durnford, who succeeded Monty as Provost, died in 1926, Monty considered it 'An anxious question whom they will elect. As long as it is not one Maynard Keynes I think all may be well.'[3] It was, in fact, only after Monty left Cambridge in 1918 that Keynes really began to rise to power, supervising the College's finances and transforming them with characteristic brilliance as Second Bursar (1919–24) and then Bursar.

Keynes, however, never became Provost. After Walter Durnford's death, Keynes and J. H. Clapham, a conscientious Wesleyan who had been Tutor since 1913, were the two main candidates to succeed to the provostship. Clapham was the choice of the cautious senior conservatives; Keynes appealed mainly to the younger Fellows. To avoid an open rift in the College, a compromise candidate—A. E. Brooke—was found and duly elected. But though Brooke administered College business conscientiously, real power in King's lay elsewhere, with such as Keynes and J. T. Sheppard: 'Though the preposital contest had been aborted by compromise, the ultimate inclination of the scales was to the side of Keynes.'[4]

Monty seemed to foresee this shift of power away from the old

Eton-dominated ethos. Speaking at Walter Durnford's memorial service in King's Chapel, he took the opportunity to lay a clear charge on those who now had the care of King's:

This is a new King's. No one is now resident who became a Fellow under the Founder's Statutes ... But ... however new King's may be, statutes and newcomers must not be allowed so to change it that it shall cease to be a family and become a machine. Men like Walter Durnford ... have worked to preserve the kind of family spirit that has room for normality as well as for genius—for the stupid as well as the clever, and it is your business to see that that spirit does not die.[5]

On the first Sunday of the Michaelmas Term 1906, Rupert Brooke appeared at the Lodge to pay the customary courtesy visit of freshmen to the Provost. Much of Brooke's undergraduate energy went into Cambridge theatricals, and it was through these that he would have come into more informal contact with Monty. As a member of the Greek Play Committee in 1906, Monty was involved with *Eumenides*, in which Brooke played the Herald. Arthur Benson watched the play, which he found 'very impressive, the music beautiful ... A herald made a pretty figure, spoilt by a glassy stare.' In 1907 Brooke played Mephistopheles in Marlowe's *Dr Faustus* (a set book for the Pass degree that year), which was put on by the specially formed Marlowe (Dramatic) Society, whose committee included Monty. It was an austere production: no scenery, except for some ominous green hangings, no music, and very little lighting. J. W. Clark, who viewed the play rather unwillingly, had asked Monty to go with him, needing, Monty supposed, 'moral support in his Philistine attitude':

He engaged me to be there on the same night, and sit near him. So I did: in the row immediately in front of him ... Much of the opening scenes was enacted in a subdued light: a practice which J. could never tolerate, but used to describe as 'pottering about in the dark'. When Rupert Brooke, as Mephistopheles, entered carrying—well, I really don't know what it was—a casket of some kind, J., who was by this time very rebellious, bent over to me and said in a dreadfully audible half-whisper, 'What's he bringing in a biscuit tin for?'[6]

Monty was later induced to write a burlesque of the play for an ADC smoking concert—'a modernized *Faustus* adapted to the University conditions of the time'. In some of the blank verse passages Monty liked to think he had caught 'a faint echo of the Marlowe line'. *Auditor and Impresario* (the latter character, 'a senior official of the University', is clearly intended for J. W. Clark) was performed soon after the Marlowe Society's production but was not published until 1927, when it appeared in the *Cambridge Review*. One of the great speeches of the original was transformed as follows:

> F. (*miserably*)
> Is *this* the nose that fired a thousand ships
> To entertain divine Zenocrate
> And—and—(*wildly*) emulate the cinematograph
> Or epicarbonate of benzolene . . .
> Is that enough? Do tell me. Is she gone?

> M. Yes, she *is* gone, and very much annoyed
> At your ill-timed allusion to her nose.
> If her complexion is not what it was,
> No gentleman, at least, should mention it.[7]

Rupert Brooke was next involved with a production of Milton's *Comus* in 1908. The masque (with the original music by Henry Lawes and dances arranged by E. J. Dent, the musicologist and a Fellow of King's) was put on to celebrate the tercentenary of Milton's birth.* On 10 July Monty attended a banquet in Christ's (Milton's college) prior to the first performance, in the audience for which were Alfred Austin (the Poet Laureate), Edmund Gosse, Robert Bridges (who left before the end, distressed at offences against Miltonic prosody), and Thomas Hardy. At the end, a pavane and a galliard were danced by four cavaliers and four ladies—'a pretty thing indeed', Monty told Gwendolen McBryde. Arthur Benson was also there, captivated by the music, but less enthusiastic about the play itself. Brooke, however, was 'very delightful to look at—he has beautiful arms and a radiant figure'. Monty was in his scarlet robes: 'J. W. [Clark], passing, said to him "Well, Provost, how are you after your dinner?" M. gave a short intoxicated laugh, and in the voice of a drunken rustic began "Well, I'm all right, in myself, you know"—and so on, in the old manner.'[8]

*   *   *

To the world of King's and Cambridge, at the end of 1905, Dr M. R. James seemed as assured, as amusing, and as confident as ever. He

---

* In the middle of the preparations for *Comus*, Walter Headlam died suddenly and unexpectedly in London—a grievous loss for King's and classical scholarship. Monty wrote an obituary for *The Times* and later supplied the article on Headlam for the *DNB*.

Eton, Fourth of June 1923. *Left to right*: Anne Fletcher, Anthony Cropper,
Walter Fletcher, Maisie Fletcher, Monty, Gwendolen and Jane McBryde

Eton: School Yard, Armistice Day 1931. Monty is walking
towards Chapel, in cap and gown, with the Vice-Provost Henry
Marten and Miss Marten

M. R. James as Provost of Eton, *c.*1925

was amiable, sociable, and sympathetic; a distinguished and widely respected man in a privileged position. But did he not feel, in spite of what he called 'incidental satisfactions' and continuing pleasure in his scholarly work, a nagging discontent at the prospect of an indefinite period as Provost of King's?

This is the impression left by a number of entries in Arthur Benson's diary, many of which are also frankly critical of Monty's performance as Provost. Of course Monty had not expected happiness in the position: 'even a Committee meeting was enough to damp my spirits in anticipation: it damps them now. I have never had the least satisfaction in what is called "dealing with men", or in the "sense of power". My highest hopes when I take the chair are that I shall not make any dreadful mistake and that no personal question will arise.' The 'personal question' brought 'moments that bead the brow with perspiration and shorten and darken the life of him who has, if he can, to guide and control the discussion and cannot possibly avoid listening to it. These are sad but sincere confessions.'[9] But the first few years of his provostship seem to have been even more of a burden than he had imagined. He confessed some of his unease and his frustrations to Arthur Benson, whose records of his conversations with Monty and the thoughts they drew from him supply a view of Monty James as Provost of King's that we do not get elsewhere.

Early in June 1905 Arthur went into King's Chapel to see 'the beloved Monty in state, at the head of his College'; but the sight disappointed him. The Provost looked pale and self-conscious and Arthur, with somewhat unreasonable expectations, felt a lack of 'mysterious awe'. The next day the Duchess of Albany attended a service in King's and Arthur (who had been housemaster to the Duchess's son, Prince Leopold) arrived at the main gate to find Monty looking 'pinched and frightened'. He was amused to see that the Provost's expression was 'hardly human' and that his eyes were fixed on the Duchess 'with strange wrinkles in his cheek. He had no smiles for me.' After the service the Duchess walked out with Monty, but at the gate he suddenly left her without a word, causing Arthur to note sternly: 'This was not well done.'[10]

The next month he was lunching with Hugh Childers at the Athenaeum and met Prothero, looking old and grey, who told Arthur that what had attracted him to the provostship had been the chance of expansion. That was true, thought Arthur, but a similar policy would be the last thing the College could expect from Monty James:

He will simply be a Head on the old lines—reactionary, against novelty and progress. He will initiate nothing, move nothing. Monty has *no* intellectual, religious, or philosophical interests really. He just has some aesthetic perceptions, antiquarian tastes, and a wonderful memory. But there has never been any stress or wrestling. He has just gone peacefully on, in his natural and simple instincts. It is a beautiful sort of life, in a way, but a superficial one when all is said.[11]

This succinctly puts the case 'against' Monty James's provostship of King's and voices sentiments that are still held in Cambridge.[12] His intellectual timidity (if that is what it was) is referred to also in Wedd's memoirs and echoed in the oft-heard *mot* (ascribed by J. H. Clapham to Oscar Browning), 'James hates thought'.

But in what sense was Monty a 'Head on the old lines'? Did Benson mean like Dr Okes and his predecessors, or like Augustus Austen Leigh? Certainly, as an orthodox Churchman and a loyal Etonian, he stood firm in the old ways; but to those undergraduates who cared to take advantage of his accessibility he was what no other Provost of King's had ever been. Of course it is easy to over-emphasize his geniality (he could be formidable, too) and forget that duty as well as temperament made him approachable. It had always been part of the job for him to encourage the corporate sense by allowing his juniors to seek him out freely and by making every effort to welcome newcomers. Not that the duty was always an enjoyable one. 'Expecting three freshmen to supper shortly,' he writes to Gwendolen McBryde. 'I believe one at least to be artistic: send he may not be "precious". It is a considerable lottery, and later on in the evening there is always a chance that of the various people who come in some will regard some of the others with acute disfavour which they hide but indifferently.'[13]

Yet the fact remains that, in this respect, though his accessibility was impaired to some degree by his new position, Monty's provostship was innovative. His impact on the intellectual life of King's, on the other hand, was negligible: his scholarly interests were too specialized to make much appeal to the generality of young men who came under his influence. People admired his academic accomplishments, but were not inspired to emulate them. He was never an educator in the sense that Wedd and Lowes Dickinson were. But did it really matter that he cared nothing for philosophy or politics, and had no taste for speculative argument? Was it not of the utmost value to King's to have at its head a man whose values anchored the present and its fleeting generations of young men to the best traditions of the past, and whose sympathy, modesty and dedication to humane learning could educate, by example, in the widest sense—not by the imposition of a specific intellectual or moral system, but by providing a living instance of the greatness of simplicity, and of the simplicity of true greatness?

It is true, none the less, that Monty's heart was not in the provostship of King's, and this must have impaired his effectiveness and prevented him from making the most of his position. By January 1906 he had been Provost long enough to know what the post entailed. At the end of that month he walked from the Barton Road to the Pitt Press with Arthur Benson and confessed sadly that there was nothing he did *qua* Provost that he did not hate, though he had managed to face the fact. Arthur thought that this was a hopeless way to go on and asked how long it could continue. ' "Who knows?" he said and went in smiling. This rather depressed me.'

In May, Monty reflected on his first year in office in a letter to his father, concluding rather half-heartedly that 'the provision of a house in which people can be put up is a great advantage'. To Arthur Benson later that year he admitted what he probably would not have done to his father: that he faced his work with terror and apprehension. Six days later he was still lamenting, saying he had 'no policy, desired freedom, hated business'. He contemplated resigning with a Fellowship, and though a bad cold may have made him unusually depressed and pessimistic, he was clearly unhappy. Even writing to Gwendolen McBryde that November there was a detectable note of weariness as he catalogued the deadening trivialities he was called upon to deal with:

Till today I have not been able to sit down at leisure with pen in hand and write as the fancy takes me—your letter is so welcome that it deserves even if it deprecates an answer (Johnsonian).

This last week has been occupied with audit of College accounts, entailing hospitality to tenants and land agents and—on Friday—a whole day sitting at a process called inspection of accounts, which means that the Provost, Vice-Provost and three Fellows appointed for that purpose go through the accounts for the year as signed by the auditors and get problems out of them to heckle the Bursars about. Why is so and so's rent in arrear, why gas costs more this year than last and so forth.[14]

The following January he was still telling Arthur Benson that he was tired of his work at King's. He said he was only happy in bed, or looking at manuscripts. When they dined alone together in King's that April, Monty said to Arthur: ' "I ask myself day after day, how long I *can* go on with it. I have no time and no peace—I would give anything to be a Fellow again." '[15]

The fact of Monty's dissatisfaction and unhappiness during these years seems clear; but he was not a man to brood and these, probably brief, periods of depression did not incapacitate him for work or sour his relationships in any way, and he continued, outwardly the same, for a further eight years. In any case, cheerfulness would keep breaking through—even in the midst of College business. At a Family dinner in May 1907 he sat next to Arthur Benson and told him with relish that there were moves in King's to cut down two pine trees in the Fellows' Garden, 'one because it spoilt the other, and then the other because it looked so odd alone'.

At the end of 1907, as formerly agreed with the Syndics, Monty prepared to give up the directorship of the Fitzwilliam. He had been giving less and less time to the Museum since being elected Provost; in fact in October 1907 there was a fuss about his lack of attendance. 'Ridgeway,* that firebrand, says it is a scandal,' noted Arthur Benson, 'and he will expose it all. I am *very* sorry for Monty.' But this blew over and at the end of May 1908 Sydney Cockerell was named as Monty's successor. Cockerell had given up a partnership in the family business to catalogue manuscripts for William Morris at Kelmscott, and it was in this capacity that he came to know Monty, with whom Morris had often consulted concerning his manuscript purchases. Later, Cockerell collaborated with Monty on the last three catalogues of the Henry Yates Thompson collection. He called Monty 'one of the finest, kindest, nicest, as well as the most learned of men'.[16] Monty was pleased that it was Cockerell who was taking over from him at the Fitzwilliam and generously offered to carry on any correspondence that needed attending to while Cockerell was transferring from London to Cambridge. 'The business of the place is simple enough,' he said, 'and I can within a very few hours put you up to it, and the faithful Chapman† will do the rest.'[17]

But when he arrived at the Museum Cockerell found a great deal to be done. He thought the arrangement of the exhibits was 'utterly barbarous': 'Good and bad pictures, all schools and countries mixed, were packed together on the walls to a ridiculous height and the Greek

---

* William Ridgeway of Caius, the irascible Disney Professor of Archaeology.

† H. A. Chapman, a long-serving member of the staff at the Fitzwilliam, had been Monty's principal assistant.

and Egyptian departments were a complete and repellent muddle, such little oriental china as there was being housed with other irrelevant objects in the main Greek room and the cases in the Egyptian rooms being mostly deplorable improvisations.' It was a pigsty, said Cockerell. 'I turned it into a palace.'[18] Monty would have been the first to admit that his grasp of museum science was weak, to say the least, and he completely lacked Cockerell's entrepreneurial flair and aggression; but then Cockerell was able to devote all his time to the Museum, whereas Monty had had a great many other commitments. 'Beyond the acquisition of a few good MSS (and cataloguing the MS collection)', he wrote modestly in *Eton and King's*, 'I don't think I can claim to have rendered any lasting service.'

'He had an enormous knowledge of medieval Latin,' Cockerell said of Monty. 'He'd smell a page of a manuscript and say, "St Augustine"—and it *was* St Augustine! But he had absolutely *no* taste whatever (you only had to look at his house to see that), and he hadn't the least idea how to run a museum. He just looked in occasionally to see if there were any letters.'[19]

As far as acquisitions went, Monty's record was by no means unimpressive; he had added classical antiquities, medals, gems, some paintings and miscellaneous items such as the sketch-book of B. R. Haydon (acquired for thirty-eight shillings) to the Museum's holdings. The manuscript collection, of course, derived most benefit from his directorship. Even as Assistant Director, in 1889, he had secured two notable items from the sale of Lord Hamilton's manuscripts; and throughout his time as Director, as well as continuing to purchase examples, he did what he could to attract benefactors. In his Preface to the Fitzwilliam Manuscript Catalogue he wrote:

I will freely confess, that during the compilation of this book I have more than once been stimulated by the hope that some collector who should make use of my work might be led to think of the Fitzwilliam Museum as a place where his manuscripts would be choicely valued, religiously preserved, and minutely investigated . . . The task of writing this Catalogue has been very laborious; but nothing could better repay me for my trouble than the arrival of so many new manuscripts as to entail the immediate preparation of a new edition.

This appeal seems to have worked, and it was probably due to Monty's reputation that the Fitzwilliam secured two highly important benefactions. The first was the outstanding bequest of Frank McClean, a civil engineer and amateur astronomer, who died in 1904.

McClean's 203 medieval manuscripts 'immeasurably extended both the scope and the quality' of the Museum's collection.[20] It naturally fell to Monty to catalogue this portion of the bequest, the result being the *Descriptive Catalogue of the McClean Collection* (1912).

The second benefactor was Charles Fairfax Murray, 'a great collector of pictures and manuscripts', as Monty told his father, and 'a man of extraordinary and self-effacing generosity', according to Arthur Benson, who knew him. Towards the end of 1904 Fairfax Murray asked Arthur if he knew Monty James, as he was thinking of donating a Spanish manuscript to the Fitzwilliam. A meeting was arranged at Fairfax Murray's house in West Kensington in December, during which Arthur looked on as Monty was shown 'things which possess not the *faintest* interest for me'.[21]

Monty came away with 'the best Spanish manuscript', and in February the following year Fairfax Murray visited him in King's, bringing with him three more manuscripts—'one a very good Breviary which belonged to Ruskin. He is to send a fine large fourteenth-century Italian choral book immediately, and talks in a way to make one's mouth water of the various manuscripts he intends to give as time goes on.' Monty approvingly noted that Fairfax Murray was friendly and simple, 'with none of the affectation of the art critic'. In all, he gave the Fitzwilliam thirty manuscripts. As Sydney Cockerell told Monty: 'I congratulate you very heartily on the *personal* triumph of having received that splendid legacy from F. McClean, as well as the useful additions given by Fairfax Murray. In both cases I believe the chief credit must be given to your memorable first catalogue.'[22]

Throughout his provostship of King's, Monty continued to publish steadily: manuscript catalogues, articles, reviews, monographs, and editions, on an immense range of subjects in his field—from *The Sculptured Bosses in the Roof of the Bauchun Chapel . . . In Norwich Cathedral* (1908) to a translation of *The Biblical Antiquities of Philo* (1917) for the Society for Promoting Christian Knowledge. For the *Journal of Theological Studies* (found in 1900) he contributed some fifty items between 1901 and 1934, and he also wrote for numerous other journals, including the *Classical Review*, *Cambridge Review*, *English Historical Review* and *Notes and Queries*.

It was to the *Cambridge Review* in November 1905 that Monty sent 'a lengthy document about Edwin Drood, mainly taking the form of a Report of an imaginary Syndicate', adding by way of a postscript: 'I should think I had better not sign the article if you print it.' The challenge of solving the puzzle of Dickens's unfinished mystery must have been an especially appealing one for Monty, whose enthusiasm for Dickens never waned. The piece sent to the *Review* was actually incomplete, but the editor, Walter Lamb, still felt it to be rather lengthy. 'I don't really think I could do much by way of shortening,' Monty replied. 'It is a process that takes time, of which I have little: and I feel that to be like a real Report the document should be rather long winded. I don't think I mind my initials,' he added, 'but should a little prefer to be anonymous.'[23]

The first instalment of 'The Edwin Drood Syndicate' appeared in the *Review* on 30 November; the second was published a week later and was signed 'MRJ'. The Report of the imaginary Syndicate on the Edwin Drood case is couched in the language of real Syndicate reports, which Monty knew only too well. In the second part of the article there is a discussion of the Report, a clever and delightful imitation of Senate debates as set out in the *Cambridge University Reporter*:

Mr E said he should like to ask the Syndics one plain question. Had they taken the elementary step, as he might call it, of consulting Mr Dickens himself as to the solution of this so-called mystery? He could not gather from the Report that they had. If they had not, he thought most emphatically that the Report should be referred back to them.

The Vice-Chancellor interposed with a word of explanation. Mr Dickens was dead.

Mr E said that of course that might be taken in some measure as a reply to his question. He was sorry to hear of Mr Dickens's death, but was glad that he had not lived to read the Report of the Syndicate.

In the summer of 1909, something like an 'Edwin Drood Syndicate' was actually formed, including Monty, Henry Jackson (who went on to investigate the Drood problem in depth, publishing a monograph, *About Edwin Drood*, in 1911), and a grandson of Dickens from Trinity Hall. The party went down to Rochester (Dickens's 'Cloisterham') in July that year to examine the feasibility of the various theories: 'We attained clearness on some points, but did not hit on any illuminating facts.'

Another, more curious, diversion from the day-to-day duties of the provostship came in 1910, when the Chapter of St George's at Windsor obtained permission from the King to open what was thought to be the tomb of Henry VI in order to put an end (it was hoped) to doubt as to the monarch's resting place. 'I need hardly say', wrote J. N. Dalton, Prince Eddy's old tutor and now a Canon of Windsor, to Monty, 'that this will be done quietly and privately, but we hope that you and the Provost of Eton [Edmond Warre] will be able to be present at the time.'

The coffin thought to contain Henry's remains was exhumed early in November. The contents were reverently taken out and examined by Professor Macalister, Professor of Anatomy at Cambridge. His report concluded that the bones were those 'of a fairly strong man, aged between forty-five and fifty-five [Henry was fifty when he died], who was at least 5ft. 9in. in height':

From the relative positions occupied by the bones, as they lay in the leaden casket when opened, it was certain that the body had been dismembered when it was put in. If the body had been buried in the earth for some time and then exhumed, it would account for their being in the condition in which we found them. It might also account for the absence of the bones of the right arm, as well as for the accidental enclosure of the left humerus of a small pig within the casket.[24]

To one of the pieces of skull there was still some hair attached, brown in colour, except in one place where it was darker and apparently matted with blood. 'Opinions unanimous', Warre noted in his diary, 'that the remains were those of Henry VI. Disinterment ordered for some reason of State, otherwise ought not to have been done to satisfy curiosity.'[25] After Macalister had examined the bones they were placed with great reverence on a large piece of new white silk and carefully wrapped up by Monty before being consigned once more to the grave.

*　　*　　*

Herbert James was nearly eighty-three when his son became Provost of King's, but he was still mentally alert and comparatively active, and he remained so to the end of his life. Arthur Benson, calling on Monty at the Lodge in October 1907, met Grace and 'the dear old father James, 88 [sic] years old, much bowed—looking like a Blake design of God—and with such a sweet and beautiful manner, like a courtier and a saint. It is years since I saw him—I don't think I ever saw the charm of age so graciously exhibited.' Another impression of Herbert is given by Francis Warre Cornish, who visited him at Livermere the following January and came away feeling rebuked 'by his keenness and contemporaneity with all that is going on'. Luxmoore saw him at the Lodge in December 1908: 'Wonderful he is in his power of going outside himself and knowing all about the pursuits, interests and history of the person he talks to—while I find that with age my horizon narrows and includes little but myself.'

Herbert lived on until the summer of 1909, passing away quietly at Livermere on 12 June. Monty was with him at the end. The next day he told Gwendolen McBryde:

The fears I spoke of in writing to you have been realized. My father died late last night. The thing has been very gradually broken to us by previous attacks, and we have recognized that we could not expect to have him with us very much longer: and, as in all these cases, it is not obvious to the mind that he is really dead, even though we sat by him and saw the end. His has been an extraordinarily happy and good life of eighty-six years—nearly eighty-seven— forty-four passed in this place.

All this means a break-up, and I do not know what amount of business, of staying to keep my sister company and so on, may fall to me.[26]

Luxmoore had known Herbert James for over thirty years. He wrote to Monty:

Your father's kindness to me was extraordinary from the first, and the picture of that quiet Rectory with the venerable life in it, of your father and mother, your sister's care, and the band of remarkable brothers, is quite one of the most helpful and reassuring memories that I take with me as a great privilege.

Thank you for letting me share it so much as you have.

A generous letter of sympathy also came from Nathaniel Wedd: 'It must be a comfort to you to know how your success crowned his last years: it was a joy to see him in the court, his pride and happiness was so clear.'[27]

Arthur Benson saw Monty soon after he returned to Cambridge from his father's funeral. He seemed tired, but not depressed. They dined together that evening, with Oliffe Richmond. Afterwards, when he and Arthur were alone, Monty spoke of his father's death, showing 'no sign of grief or anxiety'; he talked kindly of his sister, but was resolved that she should not live permanently with him in the Lodge. In sum, Arthur thought him 'in rather particularly good spirits, the sad days over, and grateful for that'.

Grace was approaching fifty in 1909. The years of looking after her father had doubtless been a strain. Arthur Benson provides a rare sketch of her, when he met her in March 1910 after a Family dinner in King's:

The horror of the evening was that Miss James was present, shrieking out the absurdest sentiments, the wildest indiscretions, and telling stories at the top of her voice about Monty's boyhood. I don't know how he can suffer such a silly old girl in the house. She must be fifty but behaves—and I am bound to say *looks*—like 22. Yet I rather like her, dimly, if one could but get behind the hysterical wild foolish exterior, which she seems to regret as much as anyone.[28]

That month Grace married J. E. Woodhouse, who had taken over from her father as Rector of Livermere. They lived in the rectory until August 1914, when Woodhouse died. Thereafter, Livermere ceased to be associated with the James family and in September 1916 Grace moved to a small house, quaintly called the 'Cat and Fiddle', near Presteigne in Radnorshire.

In October 1910, Cambridge lost J. W. Clark. Monty composed a memorial inscription that was placed in the University Library (now the Old Schools), and another memorial by him was set up in Trinity Chapel. He also supplied an article on Clark for the *DNB*. The following January, another link with the past was broken when Fred Whitting died suddenly (he had been succeeded as Vice-Provost in 1909 by Walter Durnford).

But Monty formed several new friendships during his last dozen years or so at Cambridge. In 1906, Gordon Carey, whom we have formerly met as a King's chorister, came up to Cambridge from Eastbourne College as a Scholar of Caius. 'I might have been too diffident to make a move', wrote Carey, 'had not my brother [Clive] already, during his recent residence at Clare, received as warm a welcome at the Lodge as now awaited me. In consequence I very soon found myself literally at home there, increasingly at ease in the company of the Provost himself and of those whom I met with him.'

This was to be the start of one of the closest friendships of Monty's later years. Carey recalled that

The Provost's Lodge was open to all comers at almost all times—at any rate of an evening, when he was usually to be found playing patience, and one would then be lured into competing (unsuccessfully as a rule) in one of the 'double' varieties thereof. Or occasionally he would be rather tentatively experimenting on the piano—it might be a Handel or Purcell air or, just as likely, a popular song. Once when I knocked on his sitting-room door he was strumming and crooning to himself in the cockney that he would so readily assume, a music-hall ditty of the moment:

"Ow are yer, 'ow are yer?'
'Very well. 'Ow's yerself?'

. . . Apart from all else, the growing insight into this great scholar's personality . . . was in itself a wonderful experience. By the time I went down I had approached the border of friendship, having crossed that of hero-worship.[29]

During his provostship, Monty also came to know Thomas Anstey Guthrie ('F. Anstey'), whose comic fantasy *Vice Versa* had brought him celebrity in 1882, and his nephew Eric Millar. Monty helped Millar secure a position in the Department of Manuscripts at the British Museum in 1912 and they corresponded regularly, usually on manuscript matters, although Monty's letters are often punctuated with the kind of humour his friends delighted in. In 1933, for instance, he sent Millar a cheque for a book with the following note:

Sir,

I have received your blackmailing letter and since circumstances have placed me in your power to the extent of one pound one, I enclose a cheque for that amount.

But let me warn you that any repetition of your demand will result in my placing the whole series of documents (if I can find them) in the hands of the police.

I am
Yours, with what feelings
you may conjecture
M. R. James.[30]

In August 1912 Monty was fifty years old. Just over a year later, in October 1913, ill health forced Stuart Donaldson to retire as Vice-Chancellor of the University and Monty was elected in his place, involving him in yet more administrative and ceremonial duties. 'Everyone is at liberty to interview me on all subjects at all times,' he told Gwendolen McBryde. 'I have two or three meetings a day and go to all University services. The Cambridge ladies are agog to be asked here and see what I actually do with my drawing-room. I have no doubt that before long I shall be asked to preside at a Sale of Work . . . It is all very shattering.'[31] But he was helped 'through the steps of the quadrille' by a number of permanent officials, including J. N. Keynes, Maynard's father, who had taken over from J. W. Clark as Registrary, and the faithful Benham was always on hand.

The summer of 1914 was much like any other for Monty, except that there was no trip to France. Harold Lubbock's wedding was in June; in July he was at Lord's for the Eton and Harrow match (which Eton won); and then he was off to Roehampton for the 'usual Sunday' at Owen Hugh Smith's. He chaired a meeting at Eton when Warre was taken ill, explored some Norfolk churches with Walter Fletcher, and did some work in Essex for the Commission on Historical Monuments.

His letters give no indication of his reaction to the worsening international crisis; but on Sunday 2 August he was in a country church in Kent praying for peace. On the Monday he returned to Cambridge. The next day the country, and King's College, were at war.

CHAPTER 15

VALE
King's 1914–1918

Tomorrow at an uncertain hour—towards tea-time, I believe—
fifty-five years will have passed over my head. Unlike most people
I am not sure that I would not have them again up to 1914.

M. R. James to Gordon Carey, 31 July 1917

Where King's is, there too are you, and will be; just as the good
father is twined about the being of his boy . . .

Eric Milner White to M. R. James, 2 October 1918

THE palmy days were over. For M. R. James, as for millions of others, life began to take on strange new aspects; the Cambridge he had known since 1882 was never to be quite the same again. He wrote to Gwendolen McBryde on 7 August:

I suppose and somewhat hope that you may be with others of the family. One wants company these times I find.

We are full enough of arrangements here: it is quite likely that Cambridge may be wanted for hospital use, and Colleges handed over: Halls turned into wards and so on.

I will not waste time upon the ordinary reflections that are in everyone's mouth. But I hope we may meet again happily.

As Provost of King's and Vice-Chancellor there was a flurry of emergency business to attend to as the University began to adjust itself to unprecedented conditions. At the beginning of October, in his official 'resignation' speech to mark the end of his first year as Vice-Chancellor, Monty expressed his strong opinion that Cambridge's peacetime functions should be maintained as an act of duty: 'The University meets in such circumstances as it has never known. We shall be few in number, and perpetually under the strain of a great anxiety . . . Yet there is no doubt that we are bound to carry on our work; for by it we can render definite service to the nation.' The task of those who remained in Cambridge, he said, was 'to keep alive that fire of "education, religion, learning and research" which will in God's good time outburn the flame of war'. He asked that controversies be confined within the narrowest limits, or postponed altogether, and that advanced research—and here the note was clearly personal—be 'unremittingly and faithfully pursued', no matter how irrelevant it might seem to the needs of the moment.[1]

A selection board for the issue of commissions, under the chairmanship of Walter Durnford, was set up in the Hall of Corpus; there were camps on Midsummer Common and Coldham's Common, regimental messes in College halls, soldiers and military vehicles everywhere. As early as 9 August the Hall at Pembroke was taken over by the Red Cross, and it was at Pembroke, too, that the first officers' school in the country was established. In September, the First Eastern Hospital temporarily took over Nevile's Court in Trinity; the men wounded in the early battles of the war were simply placed in beds round the stately cloisters (the weather was luckily mild). Later, the hospital moved to the King's and Clare playing field (the site of the present University Library), where a large hut hospital quickly sprang up. Some ninety nurses attached to the hospital occupied Bodley's Building next to the Lodge in King's.

Apart from University and College business Monty had to help his sister, recently widowed, to settle up at Livermere before she came to live with him temporarily at the Lodge. 'It certainly is and has been a grim time,' he told Gwendolen early in October. 'So far I have no news of anyone that I know well having fallen, but that is bound to come. As for Reims there is no doubt that it is pretty hopelessly spoilt: restoration can only complete the destruction. Nothing can really wash the Germans clean of that.'[2] He tried as far as possible to preserve the pattern of the old days: he had his 'usual people' at King's for Christmas, after which he took Grace to Bembridge, Sydney's house on the Isle of Wight, and stayed there until 12 January, 'as much of a family party as we can muster and no obligations to do more than take walks'.

The Lent Term began with only some 1,200 undergraduates—forty in King's—but 20,000 or so troops scattered in and about Cambridge. A black-out was enforced—'no lights to be seen in courts or streets, and they tell me it is difficult to get into or out of the town—gates across the road, for motors I suppose'. As the number of undergraduates continued to decline, Monty's official duties actually began to decrease. He told Gwendolen in February: 'There are very few young men about in this University, but the machine runs on in some fashion'. The following month he wrote to say that 'We are empty enough but for soldiers: I must say I have been very thankful to have had occupations forced upon me all the time.'[3]

The comings and goings of the military provided some atmosphere of youth, and the cadets gave a certain liveliness to the place. But the gradual depletion of the undergraduate population could not be compensated for by these temporary infusions. 'Emptier and emptier grew the courts,' Monty recalled, 'slower and duller the pulse of life.' It is hard not to feel that throughout the war years there was a loosening of the bonds that had held Monty James to King's for so long, a gradual process of psychological preparation for departure, should the occasion arise. For what was King's, what was Cambridge, without its youth? 'It is hard to judge,' he wrote, 'but I think that, among those who saw no active service, they whose life was bound up with a University or a great school had some of the most poignant experiences of the War, in the constant partings with the young.'[4] And even when the war ended and youth returned, it would be difficult, if not impossible to recreate the conditions and atmosphere of pre-war Cambridge. Monty also probably realized that, in terms of the College's development, the tide was running in favour of such as Keynes, and that those who returned from the war and their successors would have little time for his Victorian world-view.

For the time being, though, Monty went on doing what was required of him officially and what little he could in the way of personal war work—putting up two wounded officers at the Lodge, visiting the hospital, writing letters to the front. But that he was able to consider leaving King's quite early on in the war is suggested by an entry in Arthur Benson's diary in 1915: 'I went for a walk with Monty . . . He was as nice as ever, but idle and indifferent. He would like to leave Cambridge and live in the country.'[5] This kind of attitude encouraged Arthur in refusing to believe that Monty felt deeply about the war or that he suffered in any way as a result of it. He even called Monty 'a lucky man, thrust into the Vice-Chancellorship—then the war—which has really lessened his work—and comes out of it with high credit. All this because he is calm, moderate, hates a fuss or a row, and always courteous. I don't think he has any opinions or feelings about the war—he wants to get back to cataloguing manuscripts and reading Dickens.'[6]

In October 1915 Monty gave his second resignation speech, which ended his period as Vice-Chancellor. The speech was still the talk of Cambridge a month later, as Gordon Carey told his brother Clive: 'Lapsley [G. T. Lapsley, a Fellow of Trinity and a close friend of Arthur Benson] last night was saying that he regarded it as "the finest literary product of the war".'[7] Monty had indeed found a voice for the occasion, as he had done all those years ago after the death of Seton Donaldson. He spoke in plain but passionate terms for the combatants, for the young victims and their families, for all those whose response to war had been swift and simple:

More than four hundred and seventy Cambridge men have fallen: a hundred and fifty of them, at least, should have been undergraduates still. For these no privilege that we can devise awaits. Yet the University bears them upon her heart, and will not, I know, neglect to perpetuate the memory of them in such sort that it may speak to the youth of England in time to come . . . To put into words the reverence that we owe to the young who have worked and suffered and died for us is beyond my powers: but my heart follows our departed sons with confidence into that state of life into which it has pleased God to call them.[8]

Amongst the Kingsmen lost that year, 1915, was Rupert Brooke, a Fellow since March 1913. Early in September 1914 Monty had received a note from him asking for a 'certificate of "good moral character" ', as he was 'applying for a commission in the Royal Navy Division with a very good chance of getting it'.[9] Monty wrote both an official and a personal letter of sympathy to Brooke's mother after his death. 'I am indeed almost heartbroken about Rupert,' she replied, 'who was unceasing in his thoughtfulness to me and was I believed going to do great things. In some ways he did violence to his feelings by going to fight—but he was firmly convinced of the righteousness of our cause; so he went, undeterred by me I am glad to say.' Monty also made special mention of Brooke in his Vice-Chancellor's oration: 'His is a name which will always bring back, beside the thanks due to the true poet, images of beauty, nobleness, and affection. No one, I think, must call that short life a tragedy which was so fully lived, and spent itself so generously upon all who came in contact with it.'

The following year (July 1916) Monty gave an address at the unveiling of the Roll of Honour of the Cambridge Tipperary Club; it was privately printed and widely circulated outside Cambridge. Ronald Norman wrote to say that it was 'written for the simple but should touch the wise'. The quiet liturgical dignity of Monty's prose, with its stately procession of monosyllables, perhaps draws our attention away from the fact that this commemorative public address is also a frank expression of personal belief:

Among much else that this war has taught us is its lesson about the dead . . . We have learnt in these days that the laws under which the world and our lives are ruled work gradually; and though the change of death is a sudden one, and the greatest that is possible to us, we do not and cannot think of it as making those whom we have known into wholly different beings. They are not at once made all-knowing and all-powerful. They have much to learn and—it cannot be otherwise—much to unlearn and be sorry for . . . To go to school once more in a new life, to have the crooked things of the old life made straight, and the blind eyes opened that they may see and desire the things that are more excellent than the best we dream of here; this is what we pray may be granted to every human soul; it is what we desire for our own souls, and it is what these have gained whom we commemorate here to-day.

But Arthur Benson had convinced himself, after hearing Monty's second Vice-Chancellor's oration widely praised, that Monty 'only thinks these things, he does not *feel* them'; for Benson, Lowes Dickinson, 'grey and leathery, ridiculed by all the loyal papers, and suffering acutely, holding on to peace, is a much more heroic figure. He is a martyr—Monty is only a sort of Caiaphas, trimming his sails to the wind.' Elsewhere he wrote of Percy Lubbock's admiration of Monty's 'silent agony and bleeding heart over the war—when Monty simply thinks as little about it as he can and is far more successful than most of us in forgetting it'.[10] Benson had little justification for pronouncing in this manner. He himself reacted strongly to the carnage and the moral coarsening that war brought, but still he was able to write: 'It's no use being too tragic or serious about it. The good evoked doesn't seem to me to justify the war—and, once over, I shall never think of it again.'[11] As for Monty, while he was incapable of agonizing over abstract principles and cared little for the purely political issues of the war, he was far from being indifferent to its effects. There were limits to what he would confess in Benson's company; but in letters to those, like Gordon Carey, who were exceptionally dear to him, it is clear that Monty was genuinely oppressed by the thought of what others were suffering while he remained in comfort and safety.

What Arthur Benson saw as indifference was a defensive assumption of equanimity in the face of extraordinary circumstances. Two months before Benson wrote sceptically of Monty's 'silent agony and

bleeding heart', Monty wrote to Gordon Carey: 'I wonder what they
will find for me as national service. I can't think, but shall be delighted
if *they* can.' In September 1915 he had told Clive Carey, then serving
in a casualty clearing station in France, that he had been 'doing some
of what I am pleased to call work, but in which I feel no pride when I
think of what other people are doing'. And to Eric Millar the following
October he wrote: 'I wish you the best of luck abroad and look forward
to meeting you again. Meanwhile you will be one of the many whom I
think of daily.' He also told Millar, in August 1917, that sleeping had
become difficult for him and that he now expected to lie awake for
some time.[12]

Amongst those he thought most about was Gordon Carey. Largely
on Monty's initiative, Carey had returned to Cambridge in 1913 after a
period of schoolmastering to work at the University Press. In May
1915 he embarked for France with a commission in the 8th Battalion
Rifle Brigade and on 30 July he was present at the horrendous and
unlooked-for liquid fire attack at Hooge. 'I had moved forward some
yards,' Carey later recalled, 'when out of the prolonged silence came a
hissing sound and suddenly the scene turned crimson. The effect was
not merely breath-taking but sense-taking: for a moment the only
thought in my head was "The end of the world—".'[13] The 8th
Battalion ended the day with four officers left out of twenty-three and
280 men out of 760. Carey was the only officer in his company to
survive. Afterwards his conscience unwarrantably charged him with
cowardice for chancing to turn briefly away from the front line just
before the attack, and he came to the brink of a nervous breakdown.
This was the background to a deeply sympathetic letter Monty wrote to
him on 6 August:

I can't say how much I would like to be by you when you are feeling depressed.
Of course you feel that you were nonplussed at the liquid fire and I love you all
the better for saying so: and I should like to know who would not have felt as
you do, or done any better. But I have a confidence in you that makes me quite
sure you are the right kind from one end of you to the other. Enough said, my
dear: if I were to go on as I could, you would be crying 'Come off the perch'.[14]

Monty sent Carey a copy of George Macdonald's *Phantastes*, 'which
for me has the property of taking me out of this world of
unpleasantness into another and more desirable, and I hope it may do
so for you'. Carey was shipped back to England, having been wounded
at Hooge, and eventually arrived in Cambridge to instruct trainee

officers at a unit based in Pembroke. He remained on light duty in Cambridge until the autumn of 1916, when he re-embarked for France. Just before he left, a note from Monty was delivered to his rooms in Corpus:

My dear Gordon,
I am no hand at expressing what I have at heart—but I do not think that matters as between you and me.
    No day and no night will pass without my thinking of you. You will let me know, as you can, what you are about: and so
    Dominus custodiat introitus tuos et exitus tuos
    ex hoc nunc et usque in saeculum.[15]

*   *   *

'Dreadful weather here,' Monty told Clive Carey in March 1916, 'snow, rain, wind, east wind . . . Benham and me cut off from our walks, elms blown down here and there: all these beastly Germans' fault.'
    There was no question in Monty James's mind as to where the blame for the war lay. He was not tormented by moral doubt: the justice of the nation's cause was only too apparent to him. It followed that he had little sympathy with the pacifists or conscientious objectors. He told Clive Carey in June 1916 that he was treasuring in a secret place a picture from the *Daily Graphic* of Bertrand Russell leaving the court after being fined £100 for the authorship of a leaflet attacking the imprisonment of a conscientious objector, 'and followed; mark this—followed by the Elder Strachey [Lytton] . . . Well, well, I think his little lot are taking the back seats which they have so richly earned (if the phrase be correct) and I do not care to think of them.'[16] As for the Germans, it touched a nerve when a place like Reims was deliberately destroyed. For Monty, such acts were more culpable and despicable by far than the uncomprehending barbarism of the Dark Ages. Germany, he said, had 'turned apostate, and to its lasting shame destroyed and dispersed what more ignorant men had spared. The mischief Germany has done—and it will be long before we learn the full extent of it—she has done with open eyes.'[17] After the war, the deep anger he had been hiding broke out in a letter to Clive Carey: '*Qui a voulu cette guerre?* I want to go on saying that to a German till he is sick in my presence. We who have not been out to fight or do anything have no right to be noble or forgiving: it is a miserable state, troublesome and corrosive. Let us not think about it.'[18]

Of his own part in the war he said simply: 'We sat in our empty house and watched the hosts go by, and we kept our lamp burning with however dim a flame, in faith that it should yet shine in full strength for generations to come.' This statement, in a sermon delivered in King's Chapel in 1919, perhaps explains why Arthur Benson thought Monty 'unheroic' and unfeeling throughout the war. It suggests that what Benson took for shallowness and complacency was actually a determined attempt to maintain pre-war life and values; to preserve a semblance of sanity in a world gone mad by being what he had always been and by refusing to give in to the anarchy of despair. It seems very likely indeed that Monty James saw his duty exactly as expressed in his 1919 sermon: to keep the lamp of civilized values burning.

*   *   *

Stuart Donaldson had died in October 1915 and was succeeded as Master of Magdalene by his old friend Arthur Benson, who was installed, with Monty present, on 9 December. Eight years earlier Benson had suffered a severe attack of crippling nihilistic depression—his 'black dog'—that had completely incapacitated him. In the summer of 1917 the symptoms began to recur. He and Monty were dining together in July and talking of Eton. Arthur afterwards wrote that he was 'utterly done, and I fear he saw how ill I was. I sent him away at 10 to 10—shall I ever see him again?' On 18 August Arthur was taken to a nursing home for the mentally sick at Ascot. He wrote an entry in his diary that day, and then no more until January 1918. In February of that year he sent a letter to Monty:

I met yesterday . . . a certain Miss Ellis . . . It seems she was, or is, a cousin of H. B. Smith's, and talked about him and you and Jem [J.K.] Stephen and Harry Cust, and the Ajax, which she saw at Cambridge. 'I suppose that Monty James', she said naively 'is the kind of person who is pointed out to strangers as a celebrity at Cambridge now?' I assured her it was so . . . This all made me think I would write you a line to say that I am still alive![19]

But Arthur was still suffering from sleepless nights and depression and did not leave Ascot until the end of 1919, and only then for lodgings in Hastings. It took him until the early months of 1923, by which time Monty had left Cambridge, to return to full health and his duties at Magdalene.

As Cambridge became ever more unfamiliar and cut off from its life-blood of youth, events began to draw Monty closer to Eton. The

Provost, Edmond Warre, was now in his eighties and growing ever more feeble and pathetic. The result of this incapacity was that it often fell to Monty, as *ex officio* Senior Fellow of Eton, to take the chair at meetings of the Governing Body. Early in 1916 he had to deal with the resignations of Francis Warre Cornish, the Vice-Provost, who was near death, and of the Head Master, Edward Lyttelton. Lyttelton's resignation had been the culmination of a far from tranquil head-mastership. In 1915 he had argued in favour of the internationalization of Gibraltar and his views on the war generally had been widely condemned as unpatriotic. Monty had found the whole business rather unpleasant and was doubtless relieved when Lyttelton was replaced in July by Cyril Alington, a former Master in College (though not an Old Etonian) who had come from the headmastership of Shrewsbury. Frank Rawlins became Vice-Provost and A. B. Ramsay was appointed Lower Master, which was particularly satisfying for Monty.

Apart from Eton business, Monty's life had little to enliven it. As he wrote to Clive Carey: 'In an ordinary year this would be about the last evening of the May Week. A distant band would be audible—the court might perhaps be burning with Chinese lanterns and the gravel crackling under the tread of tiny feet . . . Gordon is not likely to come in tonight, for he was here last night and is expected tomorrow, and short of him there is no one whom I care or expect to see.'[20]

In 1914 Sydney had retired from the headmastership of Malvern and in December the following year had accepted a residentiary canonry in Worcester Cathedral. He went into residence at Worcester in June 1916, and Monty visited him in his new house in the Close for the first time in July. Monty went regularly to services in the cathedral, feeling 'like the parish clerk who spent his holidays going to other churches to see how they did things'. He also made acquaintance with a parrot the family had been given: 'I can't say I think it takes to me: however, I love parrots.'

In the autumn there was a visit to Woodlands and then he had to accompany Grace in her move to Presteigne. From there he told Gwendolen that he had purchased some paper 'with a view of writing a story upon it to explain to Jane what I have heard from the owls and other neighbours, and how it came about that I was able to do so . . . ' This was the start of what was to become *The Five Jars*. After Christmas there was a hard frost and an opportunity for skating, which he had always enjoyed; but 'the agony of beginning' deterred him and he remained indoors, sitting by the fire until it went out. 'The house is straining every nerve to show how cold it can be and the drawing-room is quite uninhabitable.'

Generally, he had little company. In the summer of 1917, after an attack of shingles, he visited Woodlands again and spent more time at Eton, during which he took A. E. Housman, a Fellow of Trinity since 1911, exploring. The sense of stasis was still strong. 'Were it not for work having to be done and work that can be done in the way of Research—save the mark!—I should be puzzled,' he told Gordon Carey. That month there was a curious incident as he lay awake one night. At about two o'clock he heard taps at his window, 'which may well have been the magnolia outside—and then for several seconds an appearance of a curtain being pulled aside from the window again and again. I lighted up at once and watched, but there was no one: I could make nothing of it.'[21] Perhaps this was another indication of what Wedd (speaking of Monty) called 'the Celtic sense of the unseen' and of Monty's inability to entirely disbelieve in supernatural phenomena. Wedd had occupied rooms below Monty's in Fellows' Building for some years and recalled in his memoirs: 'At about two a.m. I used to knock the ashes of my pipe out by tapping on the mantel-piece. Monty told me how often and often when in bed he heard the tap, tap, tap, he used to lie shivering with horror. He couldn't believe it wasn't a ghost in his outer room, though he knew all the time exactly how the sounds were produced.'

With the new year of 1918 came six to eight inches of snow, and on 14 January news that the Master of Trinity, Dr Butler, had died. The Master had been an eccentric but stately survival from a lost age and his death came as a surprise to Monty. Nixon, who had provided so much hilarity for Monty and his contemporaries, had already gone. His death in February 1916 had been a sad loss, though 'it was not to be wished that he should have a helpless old age'.

In the spring Monty heard that Harold Lubbock had been killed—one of the hardest losses of the war for him. Another good friend, Geoffrey Tatham, was missing; and there was the insistent worry of Gordon Carey. 'The fact is', Monty told Carey, 'that when I don't plunge myself into some subject quite unconnected with the present I am for ever thinking of what is going on with you, and that dries my pen and incapacitates.'[22]

It was clear by this time that Edmond Warre could no longer defer his resignation from the provostship of Eton and soon it began to be rumoured that the post would be offered to Monty (it was a Crown appointment). The only foundation for the rumour, as far as Monty claimed to see, was that

whereas for a century or more the post has always been held by an ex-headmaster, it appears unlikely that it would in this case be offered to E. Lyttelton: and that the 'incapacity' of Warre has put me in the chair at the College meetings for this long time past. But it is a far cry from that to suppose that the Crown would pick out a bachelor who has been leading the life of a University don for thirty-six years.[23]

In fact, the probability that he would take Warre's place had been spoken of for some years. As far back as 1911 there had been talk of it, as Arthur Benson had recorded in June of that year. In 1915 Benson had been discussing the provostship with others and had concluded that it would probably go to Monty, even though, in Benson's opinion, Monty would 'do nothing for Eton; he simply wants to be quiet and peaceful'.[24] Then in 1916, after Lyttelton's resignation, Benson had been incensed at the attempts by Percy and Cis Lubbock to run Allen Ramsay for the Head Mastership, feeling that when this was achieved 'the three will job Monty with the Provostship'.[25]

On 13 May 1918, exactly thirteen years after he had been elected Provost of King's, Monty told Gwendolen that 'Old Warre has made up his mind to retire from the Provostship of Eton and I suppose that will occupy us to some extent when he does so.' A few weeks later Warre took the definite step of asking leave to retire.

'As for Eton news,' Luxmoore wrote on 15 May, 'the most important is the resignation of the poor old Provost... Who will succeed? We hope for Monty James, Provost of King's, but I don't suppose Lloyd George knows much of scholars. Perhaps the King is more interested now in the School and will settle. I hope it will be no courtier politician nor an invalid bishop.'[26]

CHAPTER 16

OLD FRIENDS AND YOUNG CREATURES
Eton 1918–1920

Well, it has materialized, this matter of the Provostry, (*praepositura*) of Eton . . . [I] will only say to you that there is a great deal in the prospect which is nice to look forward to in the way of being at a place containing many old friends and many young creatures.

M. R. James to Gordon Carey, 8 August 1918

ON 29 July 1918, Lord Rosebery sent a telegram to M. R. James intimating that the provostship of Eton would be offered to him. The formal offer of nomination was received the next day, and Monty lost no time in signifying his acceptance.

Cambridge had become a lonely place for him, and a visitor, he had told Gwendolen McBryde in May, was a rare bird. But at Eton that summer it had been 'a joy to be where people are carrying on and the ranks are not depleted'. To those who knew him best, Monty's immediate acceptance of the provostship probably came as no surprise. As Sydney wrote: 'Your latter years at King's have not been altogether congenial and I like to think of you as being in an atmosphere which will suit you entirely.'

He had not been the only candidate. Lord Rosebery himself had been favoured by Herbert Asquith; Walter Durnford had some claim; and W. R. Inge, Dean of St Paul's, perhaps the strongest contender apart from Monty, had even been led to believe that his appointment was likely.[1] But as far as Eton itself was concerned, Monty James was the ideal choice. Cyril Alington, the Head Master, was delighted when the formal acceptance became known; and so of course was Luxmoore, who wrote with relief: 'Deo gratias. What a weight of anxiety is lifted by your letter . . . anxiety for Eton more, perhaps, than for you. Yes, much more . . . It is not all easy. There are hindrances as well as helps. But you know the route and have already gathered the reins in your hand.' A. C. Ainger, a former division master of Monty's and a stalwart Etonian, commented drily to him that 'It was pleasant to read of your coming here this morning . . . We have been disquieted by various rumours of other appointments—and so can find satisfaction not only in what we have got but in what we have escaped.' Amongst younger friends, Ronald Norman, who fully shared Monty's sentiments towards Eton, felt 'something of the same pleasure which the marriage of two old friends occasionally, but rarely, gives. The lady in this case is my first love, and my affection for her grows more eager and deep rooted the longer I live. And for the man, I can say anyhow that time and absence do not make the heart grow any less fond.'[2]

At Cambridge, the response to Monty's departure was mixed. The fashion, Henry Jackson told his brother, was to bewail it; but Jackson believed that the right man would now be in the right place.[3] 'We shall miss you terribly, and I not least,' wrote Jackson, whose company Monty had much enjoyed over the years. 'But I am heartily glad that the offer has been made to you, and that you have accepted it . . . I have learnt to care more for Eton than for the King's of the present day. I am an old man and the King's of the sixties is one of my most precious memories.' A. E. Housman took a similar view: 'Though I am sorry on account of Cambridge and myself, I hope and believe that your choice is for your own happiness and I wish you prosperity and contentment in all your doings.'[4]

But others felt that Cambridge was losing one of its greatest figures and were dismayed that Monty could think of leaving at such a time, with the war not yet over. One of these, J. H. Clapham, congratulated Monty with a heavy heart and confessed that he would find it hard to forgive Eton: 'Cambridge, all in confusion, can so ill spare its best scholar and one of the very few heads of Houses who add to its reputation. And, not being an Etonian, I feel that Eton, who is not in confusion, and does not, I take it, really need our best scholar as Provost—however much she needs you—has been a bit greedy.'[5]

Two significant expressions of regret came from Kingsmen who had not been identified with Monty's circle: Nathaniel Wedd and Goldsworthy Lowes Dickinson. 'There is some comfort in thinking that you are not going to an alien foundation,' wrote Wedd, 'and that you will have leisure for your own work, but at present I have nothing but a sense of loss.' Three days later Lowes Dickinson typed out a note in which he stated that his predominant feeling was 'regret for the loss entailed to King's. It will not be easy for us—I think indeed it will be impossible—to find anyone so admirably equipped in the qualities needed for a Provost.'[6]

A eulogistic assessment of Monty's career at King's later appeared in the *Cambridge Review* on 18 October, in which he was described as 'a scholar of the type of Henry Bradshaw'. 'He had a genius for friendship,' said the *Review* of Monty, 'and there are many who see in "Monty" their guide, philosopher, and friend. With such a record, Dr James leaves a gap which none can fill, and we cannot but deplore his departure.' But it was E. G. Swain, perhaps, who best summed up the feelings of many who had known Monty James as Dean, Tutor, and Provost of King's:

Cambridge will long be unsettled, and when settlement begins, a great deal of it will lie outside your main interests and sympathies. I judged that you might not be unwilling to make this particular exchange. What many hundreds of us will feel is that it is the end, but for a few survivals, of King's as we knew it, you being a real link with the past. Your intellectual and other antecedents belonged to the King's of history, to enter into which has been the main pleasure and privilege of my life . . . I imagine that no one ever grows old at Eton, except by the reckoning, and although you will have reproaches heaped upon you at Cambridge, I feel sure that having had to consider the alternative of now or never, you have been wise in choosing now.[7]

He had spent thirty-six years at King's and inevitably there was some sadness and regret in leaving it, but not enough to overshadow the happiness he felt at being able to return to Eton. He described his feelings to Henry Jackson:

It is truly a very great pleasure, the prospect of being knit up so closely with Eton, which of all places holds perhaps the first place in my affections. But I begin to realize, though very imperfectly as yet, that it will be a great wrench to go from here after thirty-six years. But Cambridge is a place where one can keep a foot, and I refuse to think of this as a farewell.[8]

Eton was somewhere he would never want to leave. At Cambridge there had always been the submerged desire—brought on and exacerbated by administrative duties—to escape. Back in July 1911, weary of the provostship of King's, Monty had told Arthur Benson that he had 'no kind of sentiment for Cambridge, but he liked the idea of living alone in the country'. And soon after the outbreak of war, when Arthur had told him he was thinking of leaving Cambridge, Monty replied that 'he would be glad to do so himself and never set foot in it again'.[9] He was tied to King's by affection and duty; but his relationship with Eton was in the deepest sense personal: 'Once, in the night, talking of his affection for King's under the walls of Clare, he had stopped, pointed south-west and said, "But all my *sentiment* is over there." '[10]

So the emotional pull of Eton was strong, as was the negative effect of war on Cambridge life and the consequent feeling of inertia Monty experienced when King's and Cambridge were drained of under-graduates. Eton, he said, was the place for which he would least unwillingly leave King's, and 'if one time for leaving it could be easier than another, it was the moment when its life was at its lowest ebb, and there was least to be done there.' At Eton there would be youth to provide the atmosphere he seemed to need and in which he thrived.

Presumably, he did not recognize any clear imperative to stay on and play a part in the post-war government of King's; for if anything could have prevented him from accepting the provostship of Eton, one imagines that it would have been the sense of an inescapable duty to King's. He probably felt that the College, guided by the 'ungodly', would now move even further towards secularism and that to remain at King's as a representative of an older order would inevitably bring tension. There was certainly a feeling abroad that Cambridge as a whole, and not just King's, would need bold reforming spirits when peace finally came. As the *Cambridge Review* had maintained, apropos of Arthur Benson becoming Master of Magdalene: 'After the war Cambridge will be truly in the throes of a new birth. Then those responsible for the government of our colleges will be literally in the position of second founders. They will need to be men capable of receiving new ideas and carrying them into practice.'[11] By accepting the offer of Eton, Monty was avoiding this formidable challenge; but it was also an honest admission of his 'deeply Victorian' character. He would go to where his heart was and had always been, to a post and to an environment that everyone—even his critics—knew suited him perfectly.

Lionel Ford and Allen Ramsay were with him for his last Sunday in King's—11 August. There had probably been little time to brood during the several days that had been spent sorting through books and papers and generally clearing up. Leaving the Chapel was perhaps the hardest part of all.

He was installed as Provost of Eton on Michaelmas Day, 29 September—a Sunday. As soon as he entered School Yard he felt that he had come home. And there to welcome him, amongst many other friends, was his tutor. The next day he sent a description of the day's events—with some characteristic asides—to Gordon Carey, who was still in France:

All went as well yesterday as heart could wish. I knocked on the door of School Yard as the clock struck 10.30, having put on all the red things I could collect. The Vice-Provost was lurking within, instantly grasped my hand and led me up an avenue of boys to the statue of Henry VI, where such of the Fellows as were able to come were stationed . . . We then proceeded at once to the North porch of the Chapel, where, in the vestry, I presented my Royal Warrant, and made the declarations required by the Statutes. This was the work of less than five minutes, but in that time I ceased to be a Member of the Foundation of King's College. We descended the steps again into School Yard (which were lined by the Choristers in red cassocks) and halted on the platform near the bottom. The Head Master read me a Latin address from the Masters, the Captain of the School, another from the boys, the Captain of the Oppidans called for cheers (fortunately meeting with a response), and I replied to both addresses in the Latin tongue (old pronunciation). We dispersed, the College people to robe, the boys to their places in Chapel.

The rain then began . . . The Dean of Windsor with what I cannot consider the best of taste thought that the Handel anthem was the one blemish—it always had the same effect on him as a pianola, he said.

In Hall we had a loving cup administered by me severally to each person present, the seventy Collegers and the High Table. This was a revival on which I insisted. (The drink-habit cannot be begun too early.)[12]

He spent some weeks with Ramsay before 'camping' in the Lodge, which was being painted and cleaned. 'I'm preparing to sleep tonight in my Lodge for the first time', he told Sydney Cockerell on 25 October, 'far away from human aid if Jane Shore* chooses to visit me'. He spent hours sorting out his books, which to begin with he set out in rows on tables due to lack of shelf space. The job of sorting and shelving his library went on for some time: 'A shabbier and more variegated collection I doubt if anyone in my position ever owned—or more devoid of the ordinary works which fill most people's bookcases. No Macaulay, Carlyle, Grote, Gibbon, Byron, etc., etc. It comes partly of living next door to a library where they all were: just as I never used to buy port because I could get it from College: and now it is sadly to seek [sic].'[13]

---

* i.e. the ghost of Edward IV's mistress. There is a portrait alleged to be of her at Eton.

At the beginning of November there was still nowhere to put Gwendolen and Jane (who had not yet visited him) away from 'smell of paint and workmen'. He had already sent Gwendolen a description of his rambling and beautiful new abode: 'Roughly it is in the shape of a cross with very unequal arms. The lay-out is 100 yards from end to end, but that consists chiefly of large rooms. There are many pictures—portraits of Eton boys dating between about 1770 and 1850. In the front hall are two large bas reliefs from Nineveh given I suppose by Layard when he did the place up in the forties.' Of one room (the 'Magna Parlura') he wrote to Clive Carey: 'There is a panelled parlour with portraits of past Provosts, painful preachers, prominent politicians, pallid princes, pleasing paramours (Jane Shore), and prosperous persons.' To go to bed he had to traverse 'dark halls and empty chambers, in one of which I always expect to feel a scratch from a sharp fingernail on the sleeve of my coat—I don't know why and it is rash to set it down in writing, especially as it might work into a story.'[14]

The armistice between the Allies and Germany was signed on 11 November. At first, Monty could not quite believe that the war was over, though by the 13th it was beginning to percolate into his system 'like a healing balm'. Five days after the armistice, Walter Durnford became Provost of King's and ten days later Monty was elected to an Honorary Fellowship there by general consent. 'Very good of them to do it so promptly' was his comment.

The armistice brought a general release of tension at Eton as elsewhere, though Luxmoore felt 'more inclined to cry than to shout, thinking of all it has cost us. The boys are different. They paraded the town wrapped in flags and beating tomtoms and making those odious noises which nowadays are taken to express joy.' The outburst of festivities continued into December. On the 7th Luxmoore recorded that he had seen the Provost at Ramsay's 'with a paper crown listening to Punch and Judy!' 'He is very happy at being here,' Luxmoore wrote of Monty, 'very accessible to boys and all, but I wish he were married.'[15]

Monty celebrated Christmas at King's and was with Sydney at Worcester for New Year. On 27 December he attended a state banquet at Buckingham Palace for Woodrow Wilson and his wife, the prospect of which had made him suffer 'incredible anxieties'. Walter Durnford lent him a white waistcoat, 'but I shan't be able to get my hair cut I *know*', he told Sydney Cockerell the day before the banquet, 'and finding a bed in town is a terrible job. I'm afraid the King and Queen/One in red and one in green/Will cry aloud "You are not fit/You James to come to court a bit".'[16]

A number of special occasions marked the first year of peace at Eton. In February 1919, under the auspices of the League of Empire, there was a visit by over 200 overseas schoolmasters who had served in the war. They were received in Upper School by Monty, who asked them to look upon Eton 'not only as a collection of venerable and beautiful buildings, but as a centre—a nerve-centre—of the spirit of Eton. Remember that for somebody, somewhere in the world, every corner, every room, almost every stick and stone has some association which is woven into history—some memory that will be with him to the last moment of conscious life. Eton centres its magic upon the eye and the heart as well as the brain.'[17]

In May there was a grand visitation of Etonian generals; and then came the Fourth of June, the first since the war, and the first Monty had seen for thirty-seven years. It was an occasion, as the *Chronicle* observed, plainly deserving of fine weather, but the rain set in with determination and parasols had to be used as *parapluies*. After luncheon in Hall, Monty proposed the toast 'Floreat Etona' and addressed a distinguished gathering of guests, including HRH Princess Alice and the Earl of Athlone. His speech emphasized once more the paramount importance of Eton in his life: 'We did not make Eton—our Founder and our forefathers, and the spirit of youth that has for centuries haunted every foot of ground, every brick and stone and beam about her—these have made Eton, and she has made us.'[18]

A letter arrived a few weeks later from Oscar Browning (now domiciled in the Palazzo Simonetti in Rome) praising the Fourth of June speech and Monty's intention 'to give substance to an office which has hitherto been a shadow ... This is a very noble ambition and I respect you for entertaining it.' Browning then went on to speak of King's: 'Our beloved College has lost its literary distinction and devotes itself to Science men and medicals. What a destiny! Clapham tells me that the attraction is Barcroft [Joseph Barcroft, Lecturer in Natural Sciences], who knows more than anyone else in the world about deleterious gases. How awful! Every day I live I thank God for having given me a purely Classical Education.'[19]

Peace was officially celebrated at Eton on 19 July. The day ended with a torchlight procession and singing in School Yard. The Last Post was sounded from the roof of Upper School and answered from a distance: 'The boys all stood with torches raised and were perfectly silent. The rain which was continuous did not matter.'

With the end of the war came the need to erect permanent memorials to the thousand-odd Etonians who had died in it ('Memorial schemes jostle like a cubist picture,' Luxmoore wrote in December 1918). A bronze frieze to the fallen was placed under Upper School and unveiled on Founder's day 1921 (the 500th anniversary of Henry VI's birth) by Monty, who had composed the English and Latin inscriptions. He also took charge of publishing the Eton War List. Lower Chapel was furnished with memorial panelling, plaques, and tapestries, and a 'Golden Book' was placed in College Chapel. The most controversial piece of work, also in College Chapel, was the window designed by Monty for the 'Chapel of Sacrifice'. A description of the composition appeared in *The Times* in July 1924:

Its central feature is a large red cross which covers the entire width of the three lights, and is filled with figures of Christ and soldier saints and figures representing those who fell in the war. The idea of this is taken from Dante's vision of the Heaven of Mars in the *Paradiso*, where the souls of the warriors of Christ form themselves into a Cross of Light with the Redeemer in the centre. The Cross is encircled by a rainbow. In the outer spandrels are four small scenes, representing Deborah and the Sons of Israel, Jonathan dead on Mount Gilboa, Judas Maccabeus, and the Valiant-for-Truth crossing the River. In the tracery King Henry VI kneels before the throned Christ, presenting two boys (scholar and oppidan).

The design did not find general favour: even Monty's obituary in *The Times* made reference to this 'curious, rather Blake-like symbolic window' and noted that it failed to charm many at first, 'but with understanding and use its effect grows'. 'It is of course a new departure in glass,' Luxmoore wrote diplomatically to Monty. 'There is nothing like it elsewhere. It makes one gasp at first and has to be studied slowly and long ... What I hear generally—but I hear very little—is approval coupled with rubbishy criticism of details ... I don't say that I want this *kind* of work to institute a new school of glass painting. I don't. But it's amazing fine in a quite new way.'[20]

As well as supervising the Eton war memorials Monty composed the wording on the memorial scroll sent with a bronze plaque to the next-of-kin of the nation's war dead. In 1916 the General Committee in charge of the scroll had experienced some difficulty in deciding on the wording. After suggestions had been invited and received from Rudyard Kipling, Robert Bridges, Sir Henry Newbolt, Laurence

Binyon and others, Vincent Baddeley, an Admiralty member of the
General Committee, obtained leave to ask Monty's help. By return of
post they received the following draft, which was accepted with three
minor changes:

He whom this scroll commemorates was numbered among the sons of the
British Empire who at the bidding of their country left all that was dear to
them, endured hardness, faced danger, and finally passed out of the sight of
men by the path of duty and self-sacrifice, giving up their own lives that others
might live in freedom.

The remembrance of them shall long be honoured in the land which they
loved and died to save.[21]

*   *   *

It was curious, Monty noted in *Eton and King's*, that no translation of a
Provost from either of King Henry's Colleges to the other had ever
taken place: 'Four Head Masters at least had become Provosts of
King's; and, under the old dispensation, you would naturally find that
several Provosts of Eton had been Fellows of King's in their time. But
the precise thing that happened in my case was new.' The provostship
of Eton was a less demanding position than that of King's, for much of
the day-to-day administrative work fell on the Head Master. It was no
sinecure; but it was true nevertheless that after Cambridge, Monty
'swam into peaceful waters' at Eton.[22]

His duties included chairmanship of the Governing Body (a job he
was well used to), admitting Collegers, receiving royalty and other
distinguished visitors, oversight of the Chapel and its services, College
buildings and estates, and a certain number of civic responsibilities as
the leading citizen of the town of Eton, which ranged from judging the
merits of a large number of cottage gardens, of almost identical
appearance, to serving on the Eton Poor Estate Committee. 'I will not
say that it reminded me of any particular Syndicate or Board at the
University,' Monty wrote to Gordon Carey concerning a meeting of
the latter body, 'but at the same time I will not do such violence to my
love of truth as to say that it did not.'[23]

He seemed to find the proximity of royalty a little unnerving and did
not relish the frequent invitations to dine at Windsor Castle. His first
summons to the Castle was in the summer of 1919 and was described
to Gwendolen McBryde:

You left me *distrait* at the prospect of dining at Windsor but the clothes were
procured and the only real tantrum I had was when the taxi did not come and I

thought I should be late, which would have been a poor thing on a first appearance, and perhaps particularly as I was the only guest outside the castle. I sat between the Queen and Princess Mary. It was not difficult and I should be less put about on another occasion. The King talks without a break, the Queen not, but has plenty to say at short intervals.

His position as the titular head of Eton College inevitably brought with it many outside commitments and public engagements, some agreeable, others not. He complained to Eric Millar in December 1922 of having been obliged to go to Wolverhampton to distribute school prizes, 'a poor and expensive way of spending a day'. On such occasions he was usually expected to make a speech, one imagines with little enthusiasm. At Eastbourne College, where Gordon Carey was a governor,* in June 1926 he advised the boys never to drop their acquaintance with 'the best things' (this message runs through many of his speeches and sermons) if they wished to keep 'a mind that is worth having at all'. Another, and related, aspect of his view of education was conveyed in a speech made at Gresham's School in July 1928, when he spoke in defence of the humanities against 'modern invention or the most intimate knowledge of things that had no soul'.[24]

On another occasion, at the University of Liverpool in 1921, he turned his attention to teaching and urged the necessity of teachers being in love with their profession and of treating it as a pastoral office at the very outset—an emphasis that reflects his own career as a don at Cambridge. It was also important, he maintained, for the teacher to possess some special interest, which for Monty did not include 'municipal or parochial affairs, and personally I would divorce him [the teacher] from politics as I would the minister of religion'. He cited Henry Bradshaw to support his contention that expertise in one subject encouraged respect and sympathy for other, apparently unrelated, subjects, and he made mention of his own experience to illustrate the impropriety of applying standards of usefulness to the acquisition of knowledge:

In the branches of knowledge of which I have any experience, I have learnt to believe that no observed phenomenon is meaningless. I copy marks I do not understand, and names I have never heard, from the flyleaves of a manuscript; and ten years later I find that the mark is that of a famous ancient library, and the name that of a saint only honoured in a well-defined area; and so it is revealed where my book was written, and through whose hands it passed, and a

---

* Carey became Headmaster of Eastbourne in 1929.

little new chapter of history, perhaps of very appreciable value, becomes possible.[25]

A certain amount of national work also drew him away from Eton, such as the Royal Commission on the finances of Oxford and Cambridge, to which he was appointed in 1919. 'To Oxford for Commission,' runs a note in his diary. 'Stayed with Provost of Oriel. Dreary work hearing witnesses.' In 1926 he was involved in an even more uncongenial investigation—'a divorce case, if you please', as he wrote to Eric Millar. 'How various are the duties that Fate assigns.' The case was that of J. B. S. Haldane, the brilliant Cambridge biochemist, who had committed overt adultery with a journalist, Charlotte Hughes, in order to secure a divorce from her wayward husband. The University had felt obliged to deprive Haldane of his Readership on the ground that he had been guilty of gross immorality as defined by statute, and Monty was one of the five Judges Delegate (Walter Fletcher was another) appointed to hear Haldane's appeal. It is not surprising to find that, though the appeal was upheld, Monty was in the minority of two who voted against it.

As far as Eton was concerned, the Provost predictably had every intention of involving himself in the life of the school. Not that he wished to encroach upon the Head Master's domain: he cheerfully left educational and administrative affairs to Cyril Alington. Instead, he showed himself as eager as ever to mix with his juniors and he offered even the youngest inhabitants of Eton his hospitality, sympathy, and friendship. The Lodge became familiar to boys—Collegers and Oppidans alike—whose predecessors had probably never once stepped inside it. He could also be seen watching obscure races on the river or dull house matches on Agar's Plough with every appearance of interest, always genial, always approachable.

It is through the eyes of boys who knew Monty James as Provost and who enjoyed his hospitality at the Lodge that we gain the most vivid impression of his presence during his later years. Jo Grimond was one of many to be invited to supper at the Lodge, and he pictures Monty 'slumped at the head of a polished black table, his stiff shirt bulging, a lock of hair across his broad forehead which topped off a broad face, chatting in a desultory manner to boys, masters, guests, whoever took his fancy. It was his presence and his unspoken encouragement to get others to talk, rather than what he said, that enhanced him.' The thirteen-year-old Grimond was plied with claret and port and sent back to his house just before midnight, very slightly drunk. He describes Monty as 'the most impressive man I have ever met. It is impossible to compare him with Churchill or De Gaulle, wrapt about in the aura of their achievements. But in force of personality he struck me, perhaps because I was younger when I knew him, and knew him better, as more redoubtable than either.'[26]

The following impressions of Monty as he appeared to an Eton boy are from an unpublished account written for the present author by C. E. Wrangham, a former Colleger:

Supper might be followed by an hour or two in the drawing-room when, perhaps after some polite persuasion, he would read aloud. I remember once a ghost story, 'The Tractate Middoth', I think, and at other times thrillers (Edgar Wallace comes to mind) and —best of all—P. G. Wodehouse. This last was the most delightful but the most difficult, since the combined effect of his pipe, of his occasionally uncertain false teeth and of his uninhibited and infectious laugh, starting just before he reached the joke, which then became almost inaudible, led one into a state of mild hysteria . . . His public figure in long, shiny-black cassock, surmounted by preposital bands, was noble, but his countenance looked always human, never pretentious, and his wire-frame spectacles could often sit awry. Most human of all was the sight of him half-running across School Yard, somewhat frantically doing up his cassock-buttons, as the Chapel Bell approached its final peals. 'The Provost', said Luxmoore, 'may get up too late, but he will catch and pass the rest of us all.'

For John Lehmann, the Provost was a 'genial and amusing super-uncle' who treated the most lowly Eton boy as a friend and a gentleman. He seemed to live in a civilized and spacious atmosphere that reminded Lehmann of the eighteenth century and that appeared to have been untouched by the spirit of Dr Arnold. Indeed, says Lehmann, Provost James 'gave the impression of thinking all the dreaded paraphernalia of rules and taboos and marks and examinations rather ridiculous'.[27]

Cyril Connolly also used the epithet 'eighteenth-century' in connection with Monty James and the tradition of classical humanism he represented; but in Connolly's opinion, the Provost and those he favoured formed 'an inner culture' at Eton.[28] Invitations to the Lodge, however, were not secured on the basis of intellectual attainment. Gurney Lubbock wrote that

There was a constant stream of boys going to breakfast or dinner at the Lodge, and no special ability or distinction was needed to earn that deeply prized invitation. Sons of old friends were sure to be asked; and if one casually let drop the name of some modest and obscure but interesting boy, one knew that the name had dropped into the net of that vast memory from which no name escaped; and the invitation was sure to follow sooner or later.

The idea of an inner circle, partaking, as Connolly said, in 'the Eleusinian mysteries of learning', does not quite ring true. The 'ordinary' boy predominated, and if the Provost was selective, it was largely because of the practical impossibility of systematically inviting something over a thousand boys to the Lodge. As he told Gwendolen McBryde in February 1920: 'As the only day one can have boys to breakfast is Sunday, it takes a long time to get round.' But he took every opportunity he could: during Holy Week 1920, for instance, because Chapel was at a later hour, he was able to have boys in during the week. He delighted in schoolboy talk, but even so he realized 'what a Providence it is that I was never a housemaster'.[29]

As well as offering hospitality, the Provost took an interest in various school societies, particularly the Essay Society, to which he read ghost stories, and the Shakespeare Society, and in the Eton Scout Troop. The Shakespeare Society occupied a special place in his affections, being associated with his own school-days and with Luxmoore, who presided over it for many years. Just before his death in 1926, Luxmoore told Monty that he was getting too deaf to take charge of the readings and that he must find someone to take his place. 'It was clear that he wished for me. So there you are,' he told Gwendolen McBryde. 'That means Tuesdays 9–10 p.m.' He might write facetiously to Alwyn Scholfield that, 'Tomorrow evening the boys should begin reading *King Lear* to me, at which I shall cry quietly all the time, for though you may not realize it, the play is one which contains exceedingly *powerful* and *affecting* situations . . . ' But he rarely gave up his Tuesday evenings for other engagements, and his participation was total: 'The reading of a comedy would reduce him to helpless laughter: at the culmination of a tragedy, it was almost painful to witness his emotion.'[30] According to A. J. Ayer, 'Assigning the parts beforehand, he sometimes told us to omit certain lines, thereby drawing our attention to obscenities which we might otherwise have missed.'[31]

For the Eton Scouts (the troop had been started by A. B. Ramsay) the Provost wrote a ghost story, 'Wailing Well', which he read to them at camp in Dorset in the summer of 1927, 'with the result that several boys had a somewhat disturbed night as the scene of the story was quite close to Camp'.[32] That December the Scouts gave him a gold badge to wear on his watch-chain, giving him 'the privilege of fagging any Scout I meet in all the world. I think of beginning on them here and sending them to Layton's for a ½d bun five minutes before lock-up. It is grand to have a giant's strength and use it *like* a giant.'[33]

The effect on some of the boys who came to know the Provost well could be transforming: one reads of enchantment, admiration, gratitude, stimulation, laughter, and even love. 'He would guide you slowly into dinner', remembered one boy, 'with a heavy hand upon your shoulder: an appreciative listener and a brilliant talker, he would discourse on almost any subject you could raise, with superior knowledge, and raising others of his own, awaken new interests in you by his treatment of them. He was stimulating and not overwhelming. It was impossible to leave him without feelings of admiration which he had not for a moment intended to promote.'

For another—Bernard Fergusson, the late Lord Ballantrae—the evenings at the lodge at Eton remained 'one of the happiest memories of that happy place'. 'We shall husband', he wrote, 'not only his letters and the books he gave us . . . but every memory of his friendship, however trivial. We are young men [he was writing in 1936], and we have many friends yet to make before we are old; but none can dim our memory of our love for MRJ.'[34]

CHAPTER 17

UNDISCOVERED ENDS
Eton 1920–1936

The truth is I am a very immature creature, with not much clearer vision of life than I had when I left school . . . Friendships have been the saving clause—James's and yours, Harold Lubbock's, Ramsay's, Luxmoore's, Walter Fletcher's and not a few more, and so it is like to be to the end of the chapter.

M. R. James to Gwendolen McBryde, 13 January 1922

From quiet homes and first beginning,
Out to the undiscovered ends,
There's nothing worth the wear of winning,
But laughter and the love of friends.

Hilaire Belloc, 'Dedicatory Ode'

THE focus of the Provost's feelings towards Eton was undoubtedly the Chapel. Everything there, it was said after his death, 'must have touched the deep recesses of his soul—the dignified and orderly worship of God in accordance with a great tradition, the music which he loved, his reading of the Lesson, the presence of the School, all in this the great Church built by our Founder to whom he felt he owed a debt which could never be repaid'.[1]

Monty had not been at Eton long before he invited the choristers (boys from the town) to tea in College Hall: 'We went out on the roof of my clock tower in the dark, and I was glad none of them fell over. I had warned them that any boy who did would be expelled from the choir that moment.' He lavished great care on the services, music, and fabric of both College Chapel and Lower Chapel, which had been completed in 1891 and accommodated the Lower Boys. His most notable contributions to Chapel services were a new Bidding Prayer and a new Exhortation for the start of the Ash Wednesday Commination Service. He rarely missed either morning or evening services, while in the afternoons he would sometimes find himself practically alone with the choir. 'I don't object,' he said, 'though I doubt if I use the chance as well as I might.' His reading of the Lessons was both impressive and inspiring. It was generally thought that he preferred to read from the Old Testament: 'The stories in the Old Testament were indeed very real to him, so real that he found it increasingly difficult, in his declining years, to read certain passages without breaking down, and in the last year of his life some had to be omitted.'[2]

He contributed directly to the spiritual life of Eton by preaching in both chapels. He found it 'interesting but embarrassing' to preach, and he said he could only do it if the whole sermon was written out first. Some ninety of his sermons survive (at Cambridge), scribbled usually on lined foolscap sheets. Gordon Carey once suggested that he should consider publishing some of them, but when he looked through them Monty felt that they were all exactly the same. The range of topics covered was indeed limited—understandably, considering his audience; but their simplicity, the clarity of Monty's presentation and his majestic presence made them effective and powerful vehicles for expressing the beliefs he had held firm throughout his life.

'Preaching', Herbert James had written in *The Country Clergyman and His Work*, 'is God's great ordinance for saving souls.' Monty's aims were necessarily more modest than this in preaching to Eton boys; but he must have thought often of his father—and perhaps also of his own former indecision over ordination—as he wrote out his sermons and as he climbed into the pulpit. His father had also said that sermons should be 'the Bible in solution'. A deep personal relationship with the Bible shines through all Monty's sermons, but Eton also supplied him with an ever-present text, and the most moving—and most personal—passages in his sermons are those in which he evoked the vision of Eton that had formed the bedrock of his own convictions. One such passage occurred in a sermon given towards the end of his life, in 1933. The text was Psalm 77, verse 5 ('I have considered the days of old, the years of ancient times'):

There is a voice in this place which often recalls to me the gist of those words. After the work and play of your day you I think sleep sound: in later life one is apt in the small hours to wake and to lie waking for some few moments; and then it is that the voice speaks to me. Sometimes I do but note it and turn to rest again: at other times it will bring back memories and then I consider the days of old and the years that are past.

It is, you see, the voice of the College clock that I mean . . . If the clock is the voice of Eton, memories are the soul of it. What else avails to bind so strongly together those who have lived the school-life in the same years, or those of widely different ages who find when they meet far from here that they are fellow-Etonians? The clock is a fair symbol of considering the days of old . . . That considering is a thing which no man and no nation can afford to neglect. If you cast away all thought of your home and your upbringing, if you shut your eyes to all that the best of men have said and written and done, wherein are you better than the beasts? You have renounced knowledge, and with knowledge, reverence, and with reverence the power to believe what you cannot see, the reason to hope for anything better than you know, and the wish to love God and man for what they have done for you.[3]

He laid special emphasis on the sense of belonging to history—being part of 'the great procession, the pageant or, if you will, the stream of life that flows continually out of this place passing on to God'. Eton was the abiding mother—'the joyful mother of children' who had tried to show her sons the worth of 'work and Friendship and Love':

You who have been living within the range of the sound of the Eton bells and who are to come back within that range once more, come back with the intent to be good sons to this your mother. You whom life calls to listen to other voices, do not forget these. They have spoken to your ears at sundry times and in divers manners, the living song of Eton. I hear them myself at times when I am well nigh the sole inhabitant of the Cloisters and when the fields and the river, the courts and the houses are empty of you and of your voices. It is perhaps at such times that these places are fullest of memories: that I recall most clearly the figures that moved about them when first I came.[4]

Monty's devotion to the collegiate church and his scholarly interest came together in the uncovering of the fifteenth-century wall paintings, which he had first read about as a boy in Maxwell Lyte's *History of Eton College*. The paintings (executed between 1479 and 1488) filled up a blank expanse of stonework between the tops of the original stalls and the string-course under the windows. In the middle of the sixteenth century they were covered over by whitewash and subsequently, in 1700, by panelling. The mutilated remains came to light briefly in 1847 when the interior of the Chapel was undergoing restoration, and pencil drawings were made by R. H. Essex; but the paintings (which aroused Provost Hodgson's 'intense dread of Romanism')[5] were soon hidden from view again by new 'Gothic' stall canopies.

Soon after returning to Eton as Provost, Monty suggested to the

Governing Body that the existing stalls should be altered or removed, his intention clearly being to expose the paintings. But he did not get his way until 1923, when the stall canopies were removed, to the consternation of many Old Etonians, Arthur Benson among them. 'The ashlar walls, where the frescoes are, with the stalls removed are hideous,' wrote Benson, 'bare, bleak, comfortless, like a palaeolithic cave. The frescoes wretched and conventional stuff.'[6]

Monty, of course, did not agree. 'In these paintings', he said in *Eton and King's*, 'Eton possesses a treasure which is, honestly, unrivalled in this country and in France.' As the paintings could not be allowed to remain in their mutilated condition, E. W. Tristram was commissioned to paint restorations on panels that covered the damaged surfaces. The panels for the north wall were finished and put up in 1927; those for the south wall in 1928.

*   *   *

On Founder's Day 1919—the first to be celebrated at Eton since the war—Monty (with Ramsay's help) revived the Founder's Pageant and the Boy Bishop's Play, an ancient custom that had been in abeyance at Eton since the sixteenth century (6 December was St Nicholas's Day as well as Henry VI's birthday). The play (which was somewhat in the Grand Guignol spirit of Monty's earlier productions for the King's choristers) was acted by Lower Boys in fifteenth-century costume in College Hall. Monty wrote the prose sections of the Latin text, Ramsay the verse. When it was over, Luxmoore felt that there had been 'something a little unsatisfactory in all the old 'uns sitting over wine and cigars (in Hall!) and having in the little boys to amuse them. So the old Cardinals might ring for dancing girls!'[7]

There were four 'Plays of St Nicholas' in Latin, 1919–22, and one (in 1925) in English. In 1923, 1924, and 1926 (when the practice ceased) the play was replaced by the Boy Bishop's Sermon, written by Monty in period English (both plays and sermons were privately printed at Eton). The first sermon, spoken by the leader of the Lower Chapel choir, contained the line: 'I hear of you, Master Provost, that ye write fond idle tales.' The Provost's third collection of ghost stories, *A Thin Ghost*, had been published at the end of 1919, containing stories mostly written at Cambridge. Oscar Browning wrote to him to say: 'I don't care for your thin ghost, nor do I think it good. Perhaps I am not clever enough to understand it—but you have a charming style.'[8] The inimitable O.B. did not live to see another volume of stories by his former Provost. He died in Rome on 6 October 1923. Monty marked the date without comment in his diarty.

Oscar Browning's old adversary Edmond Warre died in January 1920, at Eton. 'That terrible penance of death in life is ended at last,' wrote Luxmoore. Three months later Frank Rawlins died and was succeeded as Vice-Provost by Hugh Macnaghten (Luxmoore had been approached, but being in his eightieth year had turned the offer down). Macnaghten and Monty James, said Cyril Alington, were as unlike as two Etonians of precisely similar training could well be:

Both wrote books about Eton,* and neither could endure to read the other's work, for Hugh thought Monty frivolous and Monty knew Hugh to be sentimental. The one went to bed very late and rose as late as decency permitted: the other retired soon after dusk, and was up with the lark, and I need hardly say that it was the early riser who was the most uncharitable in his judgement of his colleague's idiosyncrasies.[9]

The following spring Monty paid a vist to Aldeburgh, his first since the summer of 1902 with James McBryde, and went about on his bicycle in bright sunshine and a cold wind: 'It changes little: I tell the inhabitants with only too much truth that I knew the place fifty years ago.' Wyndham House, his grandmother Caroline's former home, was up for sale: 'I think I must summon courage to go over.'[10] He went back to Aldeburgh regularly thereafter, almost to the end of his life. He did not seem to mind being often alone in a place so full of memories. 'My remarks', he writes in April 1927, 'have been confined to saying Good-morning and thank you. The only more extended converse has been with the man who sells and lends detective stories.' There was a gratifying experience in April 1933 'of going into a shop to buy paper . . . and of the man taking a volume from the shelf and saying "Do you know this book at all, sir?" and of being able to reply, "Yes, I wrote it".'

By February 1920 he had finished *The Five Jars*, the tale written for Jane McBryde (the 'young person' of the half-title) and begun in 1916. He sent the story, with some illustrations by Gwendolen, to Edward Arnold, who was 'entirely charmed', though he did not think that Gwendolen's pictures would reproduce. Monty was disappointed, 'for

---

* Macnaghten's *Fifty Years of Eton* was published by George Allen and Unwin in 1924, two years before Monty's *Eton and King's*.

nothing could be better of their kind'. An illustrator called Gilbert James (no relation) eventually produced seven pictures for the book (which was published in 1922), none of which Monty thought much of.

The Five Jars develops at length the kind of fantasy Monty had been fond of devising *ad libitum* in his letters to Jane, and to Sibyl Cropper. Typically, the metal plates that close each jar have each a Latin inscription. Just as typical is the comment that follows: 'Now, years ago, I took great pains to learn the Latin language, and on many occasions I have found it *most* useful, whatever you may see to the contrary in the newspaper.' As well as the correspondence with Jane and Sibyl, there exists what is perhaps another antecedent of *The Five Jars*—an unfinished story (written in or about 1885) of a little girl called Anna Maria Wiggins, a compound of Lewis Carroll's Alice and Little Red Riding Hood, who seems to have taken her name from Monty's aunt, Anna Maria Horton. The tone of this story is very similar to that of *The Five Jars*, and Monty uses the same opening device of a stream running through a wood. Anna Maria traces the stream to its source, a spring issuing from the base of an oak tree, just as in *The Five Jars* the narrator finds 'a kind of terrace, pretty level and with large old trees growing upon it, mainly oaks ... There was no more stream, and I found what of all natural things I think pleases me best, a real spring of water quite untouched.'[11]

The Five Jars has not become a classic of children's literature in the way that the ghost stories have established themselves in the tradition of English supernatural fiction. It sold slowly and remains a charming curiosity. But it clearly shows the richness and fluency of Monty's imagination and also the degree of empathy he enjoyed with the world of the young. The book was reviewed in the *Chronicle* on 2 November. The reviewer described how he had heard from the Provost that his new book was 'for juveniles': 'I asked him if he meant people even younger than me, and he said that he did. He was wrong.' A rather eccentric estimate of the book was expressed by Nathaniel Wedd in his unpublished memoirs. Wedd felt that in *The Five Jars* the lid of Monty's mind was partly lifted, revealing its 'repressed workings'. Wedd called it 'a very notable work, too little known, with as much speculative suggestion as would if expanded and inflated and expressed in the technical German jargon make its author a great name in the ranks of the professional thinkers'.

Monty published nothing else in the same vein as *The Five Jars*. Soon after it was published he wrote to Gwendolen: 'I am uncertain whether to go on with the topic of the Five Jars: something no doubt could be done, but there is always a risk (apart from that which attends all sequels) of getting involved in further definitions of what relation the small people have to the world in general—which might bring in politics and religion before you could say knife.'

Besides *The Five Jars* and the ghost stories, two other books made Monty known to a more general readership. The first was *Abbeys* (1925), one of three books commissioned by the Great Western Railway on the architectural antiquities of its area (the other two were *Castles*, by Sir Charles Oman, and *Cathedrals*). The G.W.R. provided Monty with a car and driver and, with Ramsay as a companion, he set off early in August 1924 to examine the sites. He began to write up the book that October and had virtually finished it by the end of November. Monty clearly found the job a congenial one and he provided a text that was delightfully informal in tone but authoritative in content. The Introduction shows him at his most relaxed:

Your mental picture of the monk should not be that of the fat man holding his stomach and bursting with laughter at a good story, or brandishing his goblet in the conventional attitude of the stage carouser. Nor need you fly to the other extreme and figure them all as pallid ascetics passing their lives on their knees. There were monks of both sorts, no doubt: but the bulk of them were steady prosaic men, perhaps more like the Fellows of Colleges in the eighteenth century than anything else. Whatever the venal commissioners of Henry VIII may have said, the monasteries were not hotbeds of crime and luxury. Many were somnolent, many were insolvent, few were evil. You need not trouble yourselves to say when you see the refectory or the cellar, 'ha, ha! those old monks knew what was what!' Nor need you be shocked when you are shown the opening of a subterranean passage and told that it leads to a nunnery five miles off. You may rest assured that it is really the main drain of the establishment.

Five years after *Abbeys*, in 1930, J. M. Dent published Monty's *Suffolk and Norfolk*, in almost identical format and, like *Abbeys*, lavishly illustrated. The subtitle describes the book accurately as a 'perambulation' round two English counties that the author knew and loved well. Part of the perambulation takes the reader to Livermere, and we are asked to 'forgive a little expansiveness here: from 1865 to 1909 the rectory was my home, if not my dwelling-place'. He then briefly noted the changes he found there with resignation: 'The Livermeres and Ampton are in one hand now, Livermere Hall is gone, and many oaks in its park are cut down . . . But village and park have some beauties left.'

Monty still saw Arthur Benson from time to time, and Arthur, in spite of his affection, continued to find fault (in his diary) with Monty's way of running things. In July 1924, when Monty had been Provost of Eton for six years, Arthur heard from his friend Geoffrey Madan that Mrs Alington believed there was 'something wrong at Eton, a complacent tendency to sit still and see the apples ripen. Monty is courteous and delightful but would do anything to avoid a row or a crusade or anything which raises the mental or moral temperature . . . Mrs A says "Even Cyril [Alington] is touched by the spirit of inertness".' Arthur thought all this might be true; it was after all, the substance of his former criticisms of Monty as Provost of King's. But he remained impressed by the typical Eton product, which he thought 'only unfortunate in thinking of the intellectual element as stuffy'.[12]

Arthur saw Monty that November at a Family dinner in Cambridge and thought his old friend looked 'rather pursy and elderly'. The following month he was at Eton to read a paper on 'Vulgarity' and went to the Lodge with Ramsay:

Here in a panelled room we found Mrs Woodhouse [Grace], who fled with cries of alarm. The panels of this room have been cleaned, which makes them slovenly and hideous, and quite destroys the effect. This is like Monty—he has no sense of beauty or decorum, only of interest. The room is simply mean . . . Monty very kind and cheerful . . . What remains in my mind is a wonderfully affectionate and brotherly welcome, and I feel that a bit of my heart is rooted at Eton, though I am not an Eton product . . . I think Eton offered me its best, and I couldn't or wouldn't take it.[13]

In June the following year (1925) Arthur suffered a severe heart attack. He recovered consciousness, but a few days later his mind began to wander and he died just after midnight, on 17 June. A letter from Fred Benson on the 19th told Monty that Arthur 'was always so fond of you'.

An old pupil of Arthur's, E. H. Ryle, of Bell's the publishers, immediately laid plans for a memorial volume, to consist of reminiscences by various friends. But Fred was strongly against the book coming out so soon (he was himself 'absolutely pledged to a book on family affairs coming out before long') and wrote to Monty to say that 'Gosse feels this very strongly and quite independently of me, and I hope you *will* agree with us'.

Monty did not appear to agree. At any rate, he soon wrote what he called 'the screed about Arthur Benson' and sent it to Ryle to be typed. A copy of the typescript arrived on 12 August with a note from Ryle:

I am afraid the superior 'lady typist' sent it [the manuscript] back to my clerk with a note to the effect that she wished these 'University Gentlemen' could write better—and that she, at any rate, wouldn't send any son of hers to the University—prize waste of money in her opinion! But if you can bear up under this criticism, I should be grateful if you would correct the typescript, and fill in the lacunae.

Monty's short essay, 'Trivial Reminiscences, Early and Late', began the volume that Bell's published that year, *Arthur Christopher Benson, As Seen By Some Friends*. It recalls, with patent affection, the times they had shared at Temple Grove, Eton, and King's, ending with a few brief memories of Benson's later career as a Fellow and then Master of Magdalene. 'It is not easy', Monty confessed, 'to write with balance and proportion of an old and beloved friend who has, for over fifty years, been a part of one's life: and the fact that that friend is one who has written most copiously about his own experiences, surroundings, views, and emotions does not make the business easier.' He regretted that Arthur had never written a book of frankly comic content, for he suspected that future generations, deriving their idea of A. C. Benson from such books as *The Golden Thread, Beside Still Waters*, or *From a College Window*, would see him as 'a pale and ghost-like figure, bowed with *Weltschmerz*, and seldom speaking but in a level musical tone', whereas in fact he was 'capable of boisterous mirth and amused by jokes of a simplicity as elemental as the butter slide at the pantomine'.

Although Arthur had criticized Monty frankly in the privacy of his diary, he had found in his company a source of deep contentment and not infrequent amusement. In December 1905, for instance, he had written:

In the afternoon Monty came for me just as I was going to bike—so we walked together by Coe Fen, the avenue, and out to Cherry Hinton . . . Monty, this great academical dignitary, in loose grey suit, white Homburg hat, small, ill-tied shoes, shuffling along merrily, pleased me. We rambled along inconsequently in talk as we are wont to do—always quite delightful. He is one of the few people to whom I can and do say exactly what I think and as I think it. He never misunderstands, is always amused, always appreciative.

And many years later, near the end of his life, Arthur still found Monty a pleasure to be with, writing: 'What a *comfortable* person Monty is . . . I am completely at ease with him as I am with few people.' In Monty's tranquil and affectionate ways there was, as Arthur wrote, 'an atmosphere of home'.[14]

In May 1925 plans had been laid for 'a little Hans Andersen book', for which Arthur was to supply an essay on Andersen and Monty translations of some of the stories. Arthur's death put an end to the project, but in April 1927 Monty took a volume of Andersen with him to Aldeburgh intending to do some translations. His interest in Danish went back to the Scandinavian holidays with McBryde at the turn of the century and was perhaps revitalized by a trip to Denmark in 1923 with Walter Fletcher. The following year we find him translating two stories for a Colleger (John Maud, later Lord Redcliffe-Maud) to recite at Speeches on the Fourth of June. By July 1929 he had contracted with Faber and Faber for a selection of his translations to be published. The book appeared the following year. The Preface stated that Monty's reasons for adding to the already considerable pile of Andersen translations was simply 'that I am very fond of the originals, and do not think that justice has been done to them by any of the versions I have come across'. His book was, he said, 'in the nature of a tribute to a beloved author, an admirable people and a most delightful country'.

A Warning to the Curious, containing six stories written during the provostship of Eton, came out in October 1925. By the end of that month Monty had also written a large portion of his reminiscences, published a year later as *Eton and King's* (Sydney's *Seventy Years* was issued as a, much inferior, companion volume). He had begun the book at Moor Place, Ronald Norman's house; by the end of October he told Alwyn Scholfield: 'Do you know, I have written an immense deal of stuff, and find myself almost incurably frivolous? I find it also quite impossible to dilate upon the excellencies of my living friends. Shyness restrains the pen.' By the end of November he had filled some 380 pages of manuscript, and it was sent to be typed just before Christmas. The public, he thought, would find the book 'esoteric'; as for himself, the process of writing it had been an interesting experience:

I had never thought myself likely to write such things. I postponed the attempt to do so for a long time, and found it difficult to make a beginning. Then—I suppose it is the oldest of stories—when the pencil had begun to run along the lines, the doubt was whether I should ever be able to stop it. Doors opened in obscure parts of the brain, and people and scenes and dialogues, many more than I supposed I kept there, peeped out and insisted on being marked down.

Eton and King's was not intended to lay bare the heart of its author to a curious world; it stops far short of what the modern mind conceives of as autobiography. To this extent, *Eton and King's* is a deeply frustrating book, though in an indirect way it tells us a great deal about its author. Luxmoore, who knew Monty as well as anyone, saw clearly that the book's superficial blandness might mislead people:

I tell J. Lehmann that it's a misleading book for a freshman lest he think he can lie abed and know everybody worth knowing and never seem to work. MRJ's amazing power of acquisition is very rare and even with him I sometimes wish there were more sense of strain for ideals shewn in the book, which of course has guided him from the first, but his reticence of all about his home and his 'inner life' (so called) may make some think it is not there.[15]

One of the least sympathetic readers of *Eton and King's* was Lytton Strachey, to whom the book seemed 'a dim affair'. He found in it 'vapid little anecdotes and nothing more. Only remarkable as showing the extraordinary impress an institution can make on an adolescent mind. It's odd that the Provost of Eton should still be aged sixteen. A life without a jolt.'[16] It might be expected that *Eton and King's* (subtitled 'Recollections, mostly trivial'), with its reverence and innocence, would have little appeal for the author of *Eminent Victorians*, but Strachey had gone to the heart of the matter. In one fundamental respect, *Eton and King's* is a remarkable book: it is perhaps unique in English literature for showing with what completeness an educational institution can infuse ideals and mould—indeed almost create—a personality. The avowed motive for writing the book was 'to show cause for the gratitude which I feel for the two great foundations of King Henry the Sixth', and in the stately Epilogue the 'trivial' is finally abandoned when this motive is contemplated directly:

I allow myself to dwell on the thought of the real greatness, and augustness, of the ancient institutions in which I have lived: to which I have owed the means of gaining knowledge, the noble environment that can exalt the spirit, the supplying of temporal needs, and almost every single one of the friendships that give light to life . . . Centres of light let both of them be, and let both be dear through life to their sons, as mothers of the happiness of youth.

Yet it is the shaping spirit of Eton, more than the influence of King's, that emerges most clearly and emphatically from these recollections. Because maturity had not embittered him in any way, he did not yearn for a lost golden age of youth and therefore did not exaggerate the contentment he had experienced as a Colleger. His vision of Eton is unencumbered by sentimentality, just as his reverence for the past avoids romantic posturing by being the expression of a personal, and hence moral, relationship with history. His attachment to Eton did not simply feed off a reservoir of passive memories but was invigorated by a continual renewal of what had formerly moved and inspired him:

To-day I admitted five new Collegers, thereby marking for them probably the most important stage that they will arrive at till they are married or die . . . I only hope that when they come to the day of leaving, and march off, as most of them will, past Upper School and Chapel towards the station on their way to Camp, they will be carrying with them a treasure of memories as precious and enduring as I did when I went by that road.[17]

The book's dedication, fittingly, was 'To the friends whose names appear and do not appear in these pages'—for he had confined himself in the main to writing only of the dead: consequently there is no mention of Walter Fletcher, Gordon Carey, or a host of others. 'You certainly are included in the dedication,' he told Gwendolen McBryde, adding apologetically: 'But you know I am no hand at expressing myself.'

Eton and King's was naturally of most interest to those who knew the Provost and were familiar with his world. It made Luxmoore laugh more than 'in many years put together'; but he could not understand 'how being so much with me at your impressionable age you escaped so completely the least taint of prig, crank or idealist. Oh I don't say that I wouldn't have liked a touch of the visionary complaint . . . but generally the air of kindly bonhomie, enjoyment of quaint character and the strange tide of work and achievement flowing on all the time underneath is quite extraordinary. But for the fruits it would be incredible.'

*   *   *

In 1916 Monty had been elected to The Club and in 1917 to Nobody's Friends, two select London dining clubs. To some degree, these replaced the convivial donnish gatherings that he had enjoyed so much at Cambridge. Nobody's Friends was perhaps the more interesting. It had been founded in 1800 by a William Stevens (who modestly called himself 'Nobody') for 'persons of the first station for talent and worth in the three learned professions and others of a literary bent'.[18] The club met three times a year and Monty's fellow members included Stuart and St Clair Donaldson, Cyril Alington, Sydney James (elected in 1928), W. R. Inge, and A. B. Ramsay (elected in 1934). Monty's inaugural speech contained this tongue-in-cheek assessment of his qualifications:

I justify my presence here on the simple grounds that I am extremely good, that I write an excellent hand, am most regular in dealing with my correspondence and accounts, rise early by preference, play and sing delightfully, keep my books and papers in perfect order, am punctual in paying and returning calls, and (upon the authority of a professional judge of handwriting) am keenly interested in mathematics, economics, and problems of social order.[19]

Meetings of learned societies also took him to London. Since 1909 he had been a member of the Roxburghe Club, the oldest existing society of bibliophiles in Great Britain, and probably in the world. He was sole editor of eleven books published under the Club's auspices and collaborated in three more. One of the Club's historians, Nicolas Barker, has written: 'The contribution of Dr James and its influence is the most important feature in the history of the Club not only in this century, but in the whole of its history.'[20]

Besides his Roxburghe Club editions, Monty's last years saw the usual steady flow of scholarly publications, ranging from the last of his Cambridge manuscript catalogues to numerous articles and reviews. In 1923 he published the first English translation of Walter Map's *De Nugis Curialium*, a book that had fascinated him since his school-days, for the Honourable Society of Cymmrodorion. Some of the passages he had found 'too odious to translate': for instance, he omitted several clauses in the long episode of Sadius and Galo (Dist. III, ii), and elsewhere he 'disguised' certain phrases of a salacious nature. 'Map was not a great offender, for his age,' he wrote, 'but his public were amused at things which really do not amuse us.' No doubt this now seems like 'Victorian' prudery; but Monty was no prude, in any accepted sense of the word. He may have been ignorant of certain matters and indomitably reticent, but his inability to face translating some of the passages in Map reflects the high standard of his moral education—a standard which he always adhered to—and the *purity* (another of his old-fashioned virtues) of his mind.

On another occasion, however, he managed to overcome his scruples to a certain extent in the interests of scholarship. This was in connection with the Egerton Genesis, a manuscript containing many illustrations to the book of Genesis. 'There are two or three—perhaps half a dozen—of the scenes which I should think twice about reproducing,' he told Sydney Cockerell. 'Certainly they ought to bring a blush to the cheek of the young person. Yet as a whole the book *ought* to be done.' He continued to work on the Egerton Genesis illustrations and produced a facsimile edition (with monochrome plates) for the Roxburghe Club in 1921. He described the manuscript to Eric Millar as 'that very improper Genesis which I think is just the right book to preserve in a limited edition . . . I should say it was done by a Japanese convert to Christianity who was a previous incarnation of Aubrey Beardsley and wrote in an English hand.' In the Introduction to the Roxburghe edition he publicly excused himself from 'describing in any detail the not infrequent coarseness which the artist has permitted himself'.

Monty's most widely read work of scholarship was undoubtedly *The Apocryphal New Testament*, published in 1924. His aim had been to provide the English reader with 'a comprehensive view of all that is meant by the phrase, "the apocryphal literature of the New Testament" '. For biblical and patristic specialists the book has been largely superseded by W. Schneemelcher's 1959 edition of Edgar Hennecke's *Neutestamentliche Apokryphen*. But Monty's work remains in print, the lucidity of its editorial matter in combination with the quality of the translation (executed in the general style of the Authorized Version) making it a readable and accessible volume for the English reader.

In July 1925 Monty became a Trustee of the British Museum. 'It is indeed a satisfaction to me to be enrolled among the Trustees,' he wrote in reply to a letter of congratulation from Eric Millar. 'Whether, when I go through the Department of Manuscripts with a toothcomb in one hand and an axe in the other you will continue to feel that all is for the best, who knows?' The major event of his trusteeship came in 1933–4: the acquisition by the Museum of the Codex Sinaiticus, the manuscript of the Greek Bible discovered in the monastery of St Catherine on Mount Sinai. It had been owned by the Tsar of Russia but the Soviet government was willing to sell it for £100,000. The first half of this gigantic sum was guaranteed by the British government, the balance had to be found. Gwendolen was told by Monty in January

1934 that 'The Museum welcomes donations. The Beaverbrook Press—gutter—is making itself awkward and trying to put people off.'[21] He was also roused by 'a mean philippic about the Codex by Aldous Huxley' in the *London Mercury*—in the same number as Mary Butts's article on his ghost stories and as 'a panegyric on James Joyce, that prostitutor of our language'.[22]

He disliked the fact that for some people the acquisition of the Codex had become a political matter: he told Eton boys in a sermon that 'to a lamentably large extent, politics are sordid things, or at least are mixed up with very sordid things'. On the other hand, acquiring the Codex was 'a unique—really unique—opportunity, and it is one which the nation at large honours itself by taking'. Among changes and chances, he said, 'we cling to our traditions; and of those traditions one of the most precious and most honourable is our reverence for the Bible'. He contemplated no formal collection, but he arranged for a box to be placed at the entrance to School Yard.[23]

As a result of his scholarship, his position at Eton and certainly of his ghost stories, the Provost was a nationally known figure and several distinguished men of letters were numbered among his acquaintances. He had known Sir Edmund Gosse and A. E. Housman from his Cambridge days; he also knew Walter de la Mare, George Bernard Shaw, and J. M. Barrie. Four of Barrie's adopted sons had been at Eton—the last, Nico Llewelyn Davies, had entered Hugh Macnaghten's house in 1916—and the school always had a romantic fascination for Barrie himself. In May 1925, Barrie asked Monty: 'Did you know that "Captain Hook" was an Etonian? I ought to tell the boys of his career there, strange, agonizing.' Barrie wrote a short piece, 'Captain Hook at Eton', but did nothing with it until 1927. He was Monty's guest for the Fourth of June that year and a month later, on the eve of the Eton and Harrow match, he read the piece on Captain Hook to the First Hundred.[24]

The General Strike of 1926 appeared to have little effect on the Provost of Eton. Walter Fletcher brought him 'optimistic reports from those in authority as to the duration of the strike: but I don't know'. Was it unconcern or just a sense of realism that was expressed in a letter to Eric Millar: 'In the midst of all these General Strikes and what not, the pale student is still bending over his book and now wishes to know what became of two books in the Henry Perkins sale of 1873 . . .'? The main effect of the strike on the Provost's placid life was that, with Alington and the rest of the masters, he was enrolled as a special constable: 'The police sergeant at a table said "Mr James, forward, please." There was no movement. Dr James had been Provost, first of King's and then of Eton, since 1905. Then there came an agitated whisper: "Mr Provost, Mr Provost, I think he must mean you." The Provost was then enrolled.'[25]

An event of much more significance for Monty was the death of Luxmoore in November 1926. His tutor had been a link with the Eton of his boyhood and youth and with the old home circle at Livermere; in many ways, too, Luxmoore had acted as a kind of father-figure since Herbert James's death in 1909, always within reach and supplying a sense of security by the way he continued to watch over—and occasionally gently criticize—his pupil's career. For Monty it was 'a dreadful loss . . . but if it was to come it couldn't have come more kindly'. On the 12th an appreciation by him was appended to Luxmoore's obituary in *The Times*:

I do not think that any more desolating loss could have befallen Eton than the removal of Henry Elford Luxmoore. For more years than I can readily reckon he has been the beloved patriarch of the place and has stood for every cause that was beautiful and kindly, noble and Christian . . . Austerity there was in him, towards himself no less than towards others; but how much humour— oftenest and most delightfully directed against himself; how unfailing a sympathy with the young! . . . The garden which he culled out of nothing into beauty, and on the gate of which he wrote 'Et amicorum', is the best of visible memorials of him: the memorials that are not seen are set up in the hearts of many.

Luxmoore's Garden, referred to here, was eventually taken over by the College formally in 1933. Monty told Gwendolen McBryde in May of that year: 'An oak "shelter" is also being put up in my tutor's garden, and of course I have to write inscriptions and also open it . . . I am tired of writing inscriptions, however needful.' A more personal memento was the publication in 1929 (privately by the Cambridge University Press) of a selection of Luxmoore's letters made by Monty and A. B. Ramsay—'a precious record', wrote Monty in his brief Preface, 'of a wonderful man'.

*   *   *

The last decade of M. R. James's life passed peacefully and without any tragic intrusions. Only the inevitable loss of old friends brought him sadness from time to time. Henry Babington Smith had died back in 1923; in 1932 he lost Lionel Ford, and the following year Walter

Fletcher died after an operation. 'So little do I visualize the loss of Walter', Monty told Gwendolen McBryde, 'that I found myself thinking at Cambridge, Really I must write and tell Walter that at the funeral the Master of Trinity had his neck tie well up over his collar.' In an appreciation for *The Times* Monty, who had known Walter for over forty years, described him as 'the truest and kindest of counsellors and sympathizers . . . magnificently keen in appreciation of all that is best in the works of God and man'. He contemplated writing a memoir of Walter, but the undertaking seemed 'appallingly difficult'. What he did write, three and a quarter pages of printed text, appeared as the Foreword to a 'personal biography' of her husband published by Maisie Fletcher in 1957.

Both Ber and Grace outlived Monty. Ber never married and he remained on affectionate good terms with Monty all his life. His obituary in *The Times* (15 August 1939) gives us the man: 'He was a versatile soul excelling in pleasurable occupations. A keen collector of Chinese *vertu*, a fisherman of many waters, a capable carpenter, a good shot and an excellent raconteur.' Sydney, who had become Archdeacon of Dudley in 1921, collapsed and died, at the age of seventy-eight, in February 1934. He passed, Monty said, 'most calmly. There was neither sound nor movement.' Just over two months later, on behalf of 'the narrowing circle of pupils of the ever beloved Luxmoore', Monty had to write a short memorial notice of (Sir) George Duckworth for *The Times*; and then, at the end of 1935, towards the close of his own life, came 'a crusher': the death of St Clair Donaldson, Bishop of Salisbury since 1921.

But many younger friends remained, to visit Monty at Eton and offer him hospitality and companionship in their own homes; and the pace of Monty's life was such that he could now devote time to such pleasurable pursuits as researching into Sherlock Holmes: 'the collected volume has many points of interest, chronological and others, e.g. from 1891 to 1894 Sherlock was supposed dead. Yet we have a case in March '92 . . . '[26] There was also time to indulge his taste for the lighter forms of literature. He particularly loved P. G. Wodehouse; the words of 'the master' sprang instantly to his mind in January 1935, when he invited Gordon Carey to spend a night at the Lodge: 'You will find me, if extant, in a very hobbling condition: perhaps your words may be those of the Curate (in *A Damsel in Distress*—PGW) to Lord Belpher—"Sad piece of human wreckage as you are, you speak like an educated man".' He had little time for writers such as Aldous Huxley or James Joyce; but he allowed the Shakespeare Society to read J. M. Synge's *Playboy of the Western World* and wondered if *The Good Companions* was worth reading. He was glad to hear that there were no 'matrimonial complications' in it. Dorothy Sayers was also a great favourite. In October 1935 he reported reading 'the *Nine Tailors*, the *Unpleasantness at the Bellona Club*, the *Unnatural Death*, *Clouds of Witness* and others now procurable at 2/6. She is a remarkably successful writer, I must say; though ever and anon she does introduce intolerable people like Dian de Momerie in *Murder Must Advertise*. I could do no less than congratulate her on having that lady's throat cut.'[27]

As for supernatural fiction, he kept up his acquaintance with Le Fanu, receiving in November 1929 a new edition of *In a Glass Darkly*: ' "Green Tea" and other things—I write at night—and just now as I re-entered my room what should I see but a toad hopping across the floor. Fortunately a smallish toad. It has retired behind the curtain near the door. Will it clasp my leg as I go out? and what does it portend?' He grew more and more unsympathetic, however, towards the development of modern ghost stories. It surprised him 'how great is the supply, I won't say demand, for collections of ghost stories. They sent me one the other day—dreadfully bad I do think, about squalid people written in terms which really mean nothing to me.'[28] Proofs of his own *Collected Ghost Stories* began to arrive early in 1931, and the volume was published in April. At Cambridge that Christmas he tried to write a story ('The Experiment') for the *Morning Post*, but the result did not please him: 'the limits of space are tiresome and I don't know if they will take it—I'm not sure I would in their place.' He often now made his way to Cambridge for Christmas, which was spent not in King's, but at Magdalene, where A. B. Ramsay had been Master since Arthur Benson's death in 1925.

As well as keeping up an extensive personal and official correspondence, there were also 'various insane and sane inquiries' to be answered. An example of the former, perhaps, was a letter from 'a native of Wisconsin who asks me to send him a list of books on antiquarian subjects, and feels it could be as comprehensive as it is possible to make it: assigning as a reason that he has "been fortunate enough to have access" to my ghost stories. He is evidently one of those who feels that there is no harm in asking.'

The annual excursion to Aldeburgh in the spring increasingly became an occasion for pure self-indulgence as even Monty's enormous fund of energy began to diminish with age. In April 1930 Aldeburgh was preceded by a trip to Lyme Regis with Ramsay, but Monty was unable to pretend that he liked 'walking down the side of a house to the Cobb and then walking up again. Amazing, these disabilities of age, but what is the use of saying so? I shall sit out on a bench in the garden and read Homer if I don't read something else—or play patience.'

Part of that summer was spent at Kilkerran, Bernard Fergusson's home in Ayrshire. 'Dinner on the first evening', recalled Lord Ballantrae, 'went only moderately well.'

My mother did her best, chattering away as was her wont; my father was polite but reserved. We forgot to warn the Provost that breakfast at nine was preceded by family prayers ten minutes earlier; and the atmosphere was not improved when the door opened, and the Provost came in when we were all on our knees, our hands on our chins, our elbows on our chairs, and our rumps facing the door.

The dining-room at Kilkerran was hung with portraits of Fergusson ancestors, interspersed with eighteenth-century Italian scenes:

As my father, still in rather grim mood, was dolling out the porridge, the Provost was standing in front of one of these pictures, which portrayed a number of men and women with no clothes on eating grapes in a woodland grove, mumbling to himself.

'I didn't quite catch what you said, Mr Provost?' said my father, his porridge ladle in mid-air.

'I was saying,' said the Provost, 'that I like the picture, but I wouldn't have liked the party.'

There was a pause; then my father guffawed; and from then on my father took him to his heart. I heard him say to my mother after breakfast: 'I don't mind how long that man stays.'[29]

From Kilkerran Monty travelled down to Goodnestone, where Grace now had a cottage; and then on to Vincent Yorke at Forthampton Court, ending up at Orchard Wyndham in Somerset, 'where dwells William Wyndham who gave us the little organ':

A strange household—stout and bearded William, who repeats the beginnings of his sentences twice or thrice. Old Mother Wyndham, thin and deaf and silent. Three Misses Wyndham of mature age. An ancient house full of various bad pictures in massive frames. Smoking room kept locked (but unlocked for me, and smoking permitted in the Library). I don't know whether more than two days would have been better or worse.[30]

If only Monty had allowed himself to write more often with such freedom. A diary in this style would have been a joy to read, for it is clear that he had an eye for detail and an almost Bensonian flair for succinct and telling characterization. Another economical sketch was sent to Gwendolen McBryde in September 1932, describing 'two old Miss Neaves from Edinburgh, both very amusing and well read, one pretty deaf, the other not so, with a great display of whisker'.

*   *   *

'I have some reason to think that the Birthday Honours may be interesting,' Monty had told Gwendolen on 30 May 1930.

On 3 June the newspapers revealed that Dr M. R. James had been awarded the Order of Merit—'about the only Honour left', in Charles Tennyson's opinion, 'which is really worth having, and it will be an infinite pleasure to all your friends that your claim to it should have been recognised'. 'Ah well,' wrote Cis Lubbock, 'that's what comes of all the learning and wisdom that's in that little head of yours.' Eric Millar was told by Monty:

'Everybody is so kind and I am so happy' was what Arthur Benson used to quote of some Eminent Person on a parallel occasion. But can I truly say this when my friends take occasion to mingle the bitter with the sweet in their letters. Exactly what you meant by the phrase 'We are all so surprised' I do not care to ask . . . And let me tell you that not a sixpence has changed hands over the transaction: the cheque I sent the Prime Minister was for something *quite* different.

One of the first messages of congratulation to be received was from Sydney Cockerell, who was told: 'You may figure to yourself that the Lower Boys can't be disabused of the impression that OM merely stands for Old Man, and say that it tells them nothing new.' The OM was the supreme accolade of the Provost's distinguished career; but he also had honorary degrees bestowed on him: the DCL from Oxford in 1927, and the DD from Cambridge in 1934.*

In the spring of 1933 Cyril Alington was offered and accepted the deanery of Durham. Alington had had a high regard for Monty and made him the subject of several pieces of sprightly versification. His book of verses, *Eton Faces Old and Young* (1933), was dedicated to

---

* He already had honorary doctorates from Dublin (1907) and St Andrews (1911). In 1918 he had received the Belgian Order of St Leopold.

'M.R.J.' and prefaced by the following, perhaps the best of all the informal tributes to Monty James's accomplishments and charm:

O highest of Eton officials!
O student and scholar and sage!
I steal your auspicious initials
To grace an Etonian page,
For *quicquid agunt Etonenses*,
Whatever Etonians do,
Though others it often incenses
Finds charity, Provost, from you.

Obscure and illegible charters,
Miss Milligan, abbeys and art,
State criminals, murderers, martyrs
Are dear to your catholic heart;
Courts know your knee breeches and buckles,
The public your *flair* for a ghost,
But ah! your inaudible chuckles
Appeal to your intimates most!

In speech you can skilfully season
With salt any butter you spread:
Your reading surpasses all reason:
Your writing can rarely be read:
From cheap and ephemeral fiction
You learn (it appears) to compose
In fine and appropriate diction
A stately liturgical prose.

From Handel or Daniel or Dickens
You turn to piquet and a pipe,
Or hatch intellectual chickens
Of ev'ry conceivable type,
Or patiently seek to unravel
The deeds of the Provosts of yore,
Rous, Westbury, Lupton and Savile,
Godolphin and Wotton and Warre.

From these and from similar labours
If ever a moment be free,
You turn to be kind to your neighbours,
And one in particular—me:
Your attitude makes me so bold as
To offer—for better or worse—

A book which can only be sold as
Some Head-Magisterial verse.

Alington's departure left Monty with the problem of finding a new
Head Master: 'Dimensions say 6 by 2½ by 2. I appear to do little but
write letters on the subject—sober? industrious? willing? of tidy
appearance?' After a great deal of deliberation, the post was offered to
Claude Elliott, Tutor of Jesus, Cambridge, with whom Monty worked
well for the three years of the provostship that remained to him.

Throughout 1934 he had difficulty in walking very far. At
Aldeburgh that year he did little but pace short distances along the sea
front and read thrillers. He had had trouble with his legs for some time
after tearing a muscle in 1926 and had undergone a variety of
treatments. By the spring of 1934 his mobility had become considerably impaired and he complained of being 'horribly supine . . . I have
gradually but distinctly lost my capacity for walking, and half a mile or
so is as much as I can contemplate'. With this went a disinclination to
work. From Aldeburgh he wrote to Sydney Cockerell: 'I eats well and
sleeps well, but once I get a sight of a job of work I go all of a twitter.
There is however comfort in the works of such writers as T[homas]
Hearne, Fanny Burney, and P. G. Wodehouse.' The situation was
much the same in the autumn: 'I don't walk or work any better but it is
no good making a song about it.'

Christmas that year, spent at Eton, was one of the most uneventful
he had ever spent. He listened to the Christmas Eve service of lessons
and carols from King's (which he always thought was rather contrived)
on the wireless and hardly stirred from the Lodge, except to attend
Chapel. He felt well enough to spend a few days in Torquay with a
party of friends in January, but he could not deny that he felt 'feeble
and horribly indolent'. A letter to Gwendolen McBryde in March 1935
captures the sense of slightly bemused melancholy that now occasionally came over him:

I look over the intervening sea of jobs to the distant shore of country—first, I
think the sea breeze of Aldeburgh and then I hope westward. Gow speaks of
joining me and of bringing an undergraduate: all I have specified is that he
must not fill my bed with bunches of sea urchins in the lightness of his heart.
Starfish are also barred. R. Norman and Ted Butler offer themselves for brief
visits next week. And so one might go on shedding shreds of information . . .
But so barren is the mind just at present that I think I'd better desist: the
crossword this morning had absolutely no message for me.

In January 1936 he made his way with some difficulty to an annual gathering of friends at Kew, but after being taken ill there he was ordered to stay in bed for a month. A heart specialist was called in and there were further complications arising from a prostate condition that he had refused to have treated by surgery.* But by the 22nd Grace, who was now living at the Lodge, believed that all was well: 'The doctor is pleased with him . . . Monty smokes a bit, reads a bit, and sleeps a good deal.'[31] Towards the end of February a letter arrived from Eric Millar:

A few of your many friends have been conspiring together during your illness to see whether we could do anything towards relieving some of the boredom of it all. We had an idea that a radio-gramophone of the latest type might help a bit in that direction, at least during your convalescence, and have taken the liberty of ordering one and having it installed in the hope that you would perhaps not take unkindly to it after the first shock.

As spring began to break beyond the windows of the Lodge, Monty remained indoors, hoping that he might be allowed to go to Aldeburgh and on to Canterbury with Ramsay. But both trips were forbidden by 'the medical faculty'—'I don't doubt rightly', he admitted, 'and I have to do the best I can on my feet, which respond but ill to my calls on them'. He wrote to Sydney Cockerell towards the end of April: 'I go on grovelling in bed, and there seems no definite end. I naturally ask myself whether this doesn't point at giving up my present job. So far I am not encouraged by my colleagues. But I don't feel useful, and I am much bored.'

Cockerell paid a visit to Eton early in May and was quite heartened by Monty's cheerfulness. 'He was in far better form than when I saw him in February,' he told Eric Millar. 'Indeed I should not have known that he was a sick man . . . Your musical enterprise was greatly justified and I hope he will get more and more pleasure as a result of it.'

A portrait of Monty by (Sir) Gerald Kelly was finished in time for the Fourth of June 1936. 'Time alone will show', wrote Kelly on 6 June, 'whether, in the general opinion, it is a good or indifferent portrait of you.' But for M. R. James there was no more time. He made a brief appearance at Speeches on the Fourth of June and returned to the Lodge. The end came peacefully eight days later, at

* Three friends (James McBryde, Eustace Talbot and Walter Fletcher) had died after operations. Professor Charles Fletcher, in a personal communication, believes that if his father had been alive he would have persuaded Monty to have surgery.

three o'clock in the afternoon on Friday 12 June, just as the Nunc Dimittis was being sung in Chapel.

Monty left the beloved confines of the Cloisters and School Yard for the last time on the following Monday, 15 June. After a service in Chapel, during which the Dead March from Handel's *Saul* was played and the choir sang the prayer of Henry VI, 'Domine Jhesu Christe, qui me creasti', the coffin was taken to the town cemetery, where Luxmoore already lay. There, in bright sunshine, Cyril Alington said prayers over the grave and a hymn, 'Jesus lives! No longer now can thy terrors, death, appal us', was sung.

Thirty-two years earlier, Monty had concluded his Preface to *The Story of a Troll-hunt* by dedicating the book to the memory of Will Stone and James McBryde, 'Now no longer sojourners, but citizens'. The text on his own gravestone (Ephesians 2:19) echoed that dedication: 'No longer a sojourner, but a fellow citizen with the saints and of the household of God.' Three days after the funeral Grace wrote to Eric Millar:

The radiogram proved such a pleasure to him, and I can see him now, after dinner, in Election Hall, listening so intently, with his pipe in his mouth, and matches strewn around . . . If you could have seen him afterwards, you would have rejoiced—every line gone, looking a young man again, and a most beautiful profile——and strangely enough—and yet not so strange—a great likeness to my mother appeared. I feel sure that he looks like that in Paradise.[32]

POSTSCRIPT

ON 9 November 1936 there was an auction at Sotheby's of some of Monty's books and fourteen holograph manuscripts of the ghost stories — 137 lots in all. The holographs comprised:

'The Mezzotint'
'The Ash-tree'
'Count Magnus'
'The Treasure of Abbot Thomas'
'"Oh, Whistle, and I'll Come to You, My Lad"'
'Mr Humphreys and his Inheritance'
'Martin's Close'
'The Stalls of Barchester Cathedral' (called 'The Cat of Death')
'A Warning to the Curious'
'The Uncommon Prayer-book'
'The Story of a Disappearance and an Appearance'
'An Episode of Cathedral History'
'Casting the Runes'
'The Rose Garden'

The fourteen manuscripts fetched just over £140. Monty's friend Owen Hugh Smith bought four ('Abbot Thomas', 'Mr Humphreys', 'Martin's Close', and 'The Uncommon Prayer-book'), all of which are now at Eton. The British Museum acquired 'Casting the Runes' (now Egerton 3141), a missing folio of which was later found amongst Monty's papers at King's and presented to the Museum by the Provost and Fellows through A. N. L. Munby in 1948. A note by Eric Millar in the *British Museum Quarterly* later stated that the purchase had been felt to be especially appropriate 'as the scene of the actual "casting" of the runes is laid in the Students' Room, in which the author was for so many years a familiar and honoured figure'. Interestingly, Maggs Brothers Limited were bidding at the Sotheby's auction|on behalf|of Maynard Keynes, who had written to them in October expressing particular interest in '"Oh, Whistle"', 'Martin's Close', 'The Uncommon Prayer-book' and 'Casting the Runes' and indicating that he was contemplating spending about £20 altogether. Keynes was unable to secure any of them, although he did manage to buy (for £4.10 *s*.) 'An Episode of Cathedral History' and 'The Story of a Disappearance and an Appearance', which were later bequeathed to King's College Library.

NOTES

ABBREVIATIONS

1. *People*

ACB	Arthur Christopher Benson
GVC	Gordon Vero Carey
SCC	Sydney Carlyle Cockerell
WMF	Walter Morley Fletcher
GRJ	Grace Rhodes James
HJ	Herbert James (MRJ's father)
MEJ	Mary Emily James
MRJ	Montague Rhodes James
SRJ	Sydney Rhodes James
HEL	Henry Elford Luxmoore
GMcB	Gwendolen McBryde
JMcB	James McBryde
HBS	Henry Babington Smith

2. *Published Sources*

Bright Countenance   Maisie Fletcher, *The Bright Countenance: A Personal Biography of Walter Morley Fletcher* (1957).

Cam R   *Cambridge Review.*

CGS   *The Collected Ghost Stories of M. R. James* (1931).

Clapham   Obituary notice of M. R. James by J. H. Clapham, *Cambridge Review*, 9 October 1936.

Country Clergyman   Herbert James, *The Country Clergyman and His Work*, six lectures on pastoral theology delivered in the Divinity School, Cambridge, May Term, 1889 (1890).

CU Reporter   *Cambridge University Reporter.*

ECC   *Eton College Chronicle.*

ECC obit   Obituary notices of M. R. James in the *Eton College Chronicle*, 18 June 1936.

E&K   M. R. James, *Eton and King's: Recollections, Mostly Trivial* (1926).

Gaselee   Sir Stephen Gaselee, 'Montague Rhodes James', *Proceedings of the British Academy*, 22 (1936), pp.418–33.

GSA   M. R. James, *Ghost Stories of an Antiquary* (1904).

Letters   *Letters of H. E. Luxmoore*, edited by M. R. James and A. B. Ramsay (1929).

LTF   *Montague Rhodes James: Letters to a Friend*, edited by Gwendolen McBryde (1956).

Memoir   S. G. Lubbock, *A Memoir of Montague Rhodes James, with a list of his writings by A. F. Scholfield* (1939).

Newsome   David Newsome, *On the Edge of Paradise. A. C. Benson: The Diarist* (1980).

Pfaff   R. W. Pfaff, *Montague Rhodes James* (1980).

Ramsay   Obituary notice of M. R. James by A. B. Ramsay, *Eton College Chronicle*, 25 June 1936.

Seventy Years   Sydney Rhodes James, *Seventy Years: Random Reminiscences and Reflections* (1926).

Times obit   Obituary notice (anon.) of M. R. James, *The Times*, 13 June 1936.

TLS   *Times Literary Supplement*.

'Trivial Reminiscences'   M. R. James, 'Trivial Reminiscences, Early and Late', in Ryle, E. H. (ed.), *Arthur Christopher Benson, As Seen By Some Friends* (1925).

3. Unpublished sources/location of material

This list also serves as a general indication of the nature and extent of the unpublished sources on which this book is based. It is by no means complete in this respect, but I shall be happy to supply specific references to any reader who desires them.

ACB: Diary   The manuscript diary of A. C. Benson, in 180 volumes, at Magdalene College, Cambridge (Pepys Library).

BL   British Library, Department of Manuscripts (MRJ's letters to Sydney Cockerell and Eric Millar).

Carey   Material in the possession of Hugh Carey.

CUL   Cambridge University Library, Manuscript Room (the CUL deposit includes James family papers; letters from MRJ to members of his family 1873–1909 and to A. F. Scholfield; letters to MRJ; notebook/diary; sermons; miscellaneous papers; lectures and addresses; letters from MRJ to various correspondents, e.g. Francis Jenkinson and John Neville Keynes).

Eton   Eton College, Windsor, College Library (miscellaneous papers and letters; cuttings, off-prints etc; many copies of MRJ's books; some ghost story holographs).

Fitzwilliam   Fitzwilliam Museum, Cambridge, Department of Manuscripts and Printed Books (104 notebooks in 23 groups, predominantly on scholarly subjects).

Hopkinson   Material in the possession of Mrs Anne Hopkinson.

KCC   King's College Library, Cambridge (KCC sources include miscellaneous correspondence to and from MRJ; printed papers, programmes and cuttings; holographs of seven of the ghost stories; typescript copies of MRJ's letters to Sibyl Cropper; O. L. Richmond's reminiscences of MRJ; typescript of Sir Shane Leslie's biography of MRJ; holographs of MRJ's letters to Gwendolen McBryde; MRJ's letters to Gordon and Clive Carey; unpublished memoirs of Nathaniel Wedd).

Nobody's Business   *Nobody's Business: An 80th-year Report.* The unpublished (handwritten) autobiography of G. V. Carey, in the possession of Hugh Carey.

Richmond   The unpublished reminiscences of Oliffe Richmond (typescript), King's College Library, Cambridge.

Trinity   Trinity College, Cambridge, Wren Library (includes letters from MRJ to Henry Babington Smith and others; diary of Henry Babington Smith).

Wedd   Unpublished memoirs of Nathaniel Wedd (typescript), King's College Library, Cambridge.

West Sussex   West Sussex Record Office, Chichester (MRJ's letters to Leo Maxse).

1. *FIRST BEGINNING.* 1862–1873

1 Hugh Paget, 'The Early History of the Family of James of Jamaica', *Jamaican Historical Review*, I (1945–8), p.273. See also V. L. Oliver, *Notes and Queries*, 11th series, 10 (1915), p.56.

2 E. C. Hawtrey to HJ, 14 November 1842, CUL.

3 KCC.

4 CUL.

5 MRJ to GRJ, 17 January 1888, CUL.

6 *GSA.*

7 *Country Clergyman*, p.12.

8 *Memoir*, pp.6–7.

9 Fitzgerald, *Memoir of Herbert Edward Ryle*, p.11.

10 *Country Clergyman*, pp.45–6.

11 F. G. Bettany, *Stewart Headlam* (1926), p.24. Headlam went on to found the Guild of St Matthew in 1877, a fusion of Maurice's ideas and the social aims of the successors to Tractarianism. He was the prototype for Morell in Shaw's *Candida* (1894).

12 Sermon preached in Lower Chapel, Eton, 3 December 1933, CUL.

13 Notebook dated 22 March 1872, CUL.

14 Sermon, 3 December 1933, CUL.

15 MRJ to GMcB, 7 April 1921, KCC.

2. *TEMPLE GROVE*. 1873–1876

1 Notebook, 1885, Fitzwilliam.

2 A. C. Benson, *Memories and Friends*, p.41.

3 Ibid., p.28.

4 Byrne and Churchill, *Changing Eton*, chapter 1 *passim*. For a general historical account of Temple Grove see Batchelor, *Cradle of Empire*.

5 Report for February 1875, CUL.

6 MRJ to HJ, March 1875, CUL.

7 MRJ to MEJ, July 1876, CUL.

8 *E&K*, p.14.

9 Ibid., pp.10–11.

10 Trevelyan, *Grey of Fallodon*, pp.7–8.

11 L. S. R. Byrne to MRJ, 31 July 1918, CUL.

3. *JAMES KS. Eton* 1876–1877

1 C. E. Chambers to MRJ, 17 November 1926, CUL.

2 Macnaghten, *Fifty Years of Eton*, p.79.

3 Balston, *Dr Balston at Eton*, pp.39–40.

4 Nevill, *Floreat Etona*, p.290.

5 Lyttelton, *Memories and Hopes*, p.40.

6 'O.E.' (Henry Salt), *Eton Under Hornby*, p.13.

7 Macnaghten, *Fifty Years of Eton*, p.98; *ECC*, 27 November 1924.

8 Browning, *Memories of Sixty Years*, p.16.

9 HEL, 'Address on Education', 1919 (*Letters*, p.254).

10 For Browning's own account of his dismissal see his *Memories of Sixty Years*, pp.221–4. For a more objective assessment see H. E. Wortham's *Oscar Browning*. Luxmoore sympathized with a great many of Browning's efforts at Eton, but he told MRJ some years later: 'There always was about O.B. just something a bit greasy, which made one feel insecure of the complete cleanness of his sincerity and motives.' (n.d., CUL).

11 Lubbock, *Shades of Eton*, p.171. Cf. Jones, *A Victorian Boyhood*, p.184, where Luxmoore is described as 'a lone standard-bearer for aesthetics'.

12 HEL, 'Eton: The Old and the New', *Quarterly Review*, 455 (April 1918), pp.311–12.

13 Hill, *Eton and Elsewhere*, pp.171–2.

14 HEL to MRJ, 'Sun 5' 1882, CUL (*Letters*, p.6).

15 MRJ to MEJ, October/November 1878, CUL.

16 *E&K*, p.32.

17 See Newsome, p.30.

4. *THE LEARNED BOY. Eton 1877–1880*

1 MRJ to HJ, 12 October 1877, CUL. For the ritual of keeping Chamber fire alight see Parker, *Eton in the Eighties*, pp.7–9.

2 *E&K*, p.82.

3 MRJ to HJ, 23 October 1878, CUL.

4 MRJ to HJ, March 1879, CUL.

5 HEL to HJ, 8 August 1879, CUL.

6 HEL to HJ, 20 December 1878, CUL.

7 MRJ to HJ, 30 March 1879, CUL.

8 HEL to HJ, n.d. Enclosed in a letter from HJ to SRJ, 31 March 1879, CUL.

9 HJ to SRJ, 31 March 1879, CUL.

10 MRJ to HJ, 2 April 1879, CUL.

11 HEL to HJ, 20 December 1879, CUL.

12 Notebook, Fitzwilliam.

13 MRJ to HJ, March 1879, CUL.

14 Birley, *History of Eton College Library*, p.33.

5. *SIXTH FORM. Eton 1880–1882*

1 *Seventy Years*, p.55.

2 'Trivial Reminiscences', p.6.

3 *E&K*, p.55.

4 *Eton Rambler* (No.4), 21 June 1880. The Eton set of this short-lived periodical has the contributors' names supplied by Arthur Benson.

5 MRJ to HJ, 10 October 1880, CUL.

6 MRJ to his parents, 3 February 1881, CUL.

7 College Debating Society Journals, vol.13, pp.55–6, Eton.

8 Ibid., vol.14, p.147.

9 The paragraph was sent to HJ, 25 May 1881, CUL.

10 Cust, *History of Eton College*, p.263.

11 Parker, *Playing Fields*, p.308.

12 Eton Society Journals, vol.70 (1881), 14 and 28 November, Eton.

13 MRJ to HJ, June 1882, CUL.

14 SRJ to Harry Cust, 25 May 1882, Cust Papers, Belton. I am grateful to Paul Chipchase for this reference.

15 *The Times*, 9 December 1935.

16 MRJ to HBS, 21 September 1882, Trinity. A letter of sympathy from Babington Smith to St Clair Donaldson shows that MRJ was not alone in responding to Seton's death in this way. 'I hardly knew your brother at all,' wrote Babington Smith. 'I wish that I had known him better — but now I feel as though he had been my friend; and indeed he is my friend — one who has done for me the best office of a friend, in opening my eyes, and in shewing me what the object of my life should and may be, by the way in which he followed the object of his.' (7 June 1882, Trinity)

17 MRJ to HBS, 12 January 1883, Trinity.

18 J.E.C. Welldon in Dimont, *St Clair Donaldson*, p.13.

19 *The Times*, 9 December 1935.

20 Papers concerning Seton Donaldson, James Papers, CUL.

21 ACB to MRJ, n.d. (1882), CUL.

22 ACB to MRJ, n.d. (1882), CUL.

23 *E&K*, pp.53–4. This passage was quoted by Walter de la Mare in his anthology *Behold This Dreamer* (1939).

6. *KINGSMAN. King's College, Cambridge* 1882–1883

1 MRJ to HBS, 7 September 1882, Trinity.

2 Ibid.

3 MRJ to HBS, 21 September 1882, Trinity.

4 Ibid.

5 GRJ to MRJ, October 1882, CUL. It had been a difficult decision for Herbert, especially after receiving a long letter from Bishop Ryle of Liverpool urging him to accept the Prescot living — 'in many ways an offensive production', wrote Grace of the Bishop's letter.

6 MRJ to HBS, 2 October 1882, Trinity.

7 Augustus Austen Leigh, *King's College*, pp.273–4; Winstanley, *Early Victorian Cambridge*, pp.236–7.

8 Wilkinson, *A Century of King's*, p.6.

9 In *Walter Durnford: Three Tributes*.

10 'Trivial Reminiscences', p.10.

11 Wedd, p.42.

12 Walter Frere to MRJ, January 1936, CUL.

13 H. F. Stewart in Dimont, *St Clair Donaldson*, p.16.

14 MRJ to HJ, 25 January 1883, CUL.

15 HBS, Diary, 23 January 1883, Trinity.

16 *E&K*, p.145.

17 MRJ to MEJ, 12 December 1882, CUL.

18 MRJ to HBS, 29 December 1882, Trinity.

19 Chitchat Minute Books, note dated 23 September 1918, CUL.

20 Notebook, 1885, Fitzwilliam.

21 MRJ to MEJ, 17 October 1886, CUL.

22 E. F. Benson, *Our Family Affairs*, p.233.

23 Alington, *Lionel Ford*, pp.14–16.

24 Ibid., p.11.

25 Ibid., p.19.

26 Esher, *Cloud-capp'd Towers*, pp.54–5.

27 Prothero, *Memoir of Henry Bradshaw*, p.389.

28 Esher, *Cloud-capp'd Towers*, p.55.

29 *E&K*, p.119.

30 Ibid., p.120.

31 *Seventy Years*, p.85.

32 *E&K*, p.150.

33 Walter Durnford to MRJ, May 1883, CUL.

34 MRJ to his parents, 11 June 1883, CUL.

35 Graves, *Hubert Parry*, vol.II, p.250.

36 Stanford, *Pages From an Unwritten Diary*, p.187.

37 Review in *The Standard*, MRJ's cutting, KCC.

38 Baillie, *My First Eighty Years*, p.48.

7. *A DON IN THE MAKING. King's* 1883–1887

1 *E&K*, p.141.

2 KCC. The story, which may have been written to be read aloud, and a related fragment are both undated. A perhaps not unrelated curiosity may be noted here. Amongst the things MRJ kept from his undergraduate days were copies of a May Week ephemeral, *The May Bee*, which ran from 4 to 11 June 1884. This contained a serial in the first four numbers called 'A

Lurking Danger: A Tale of King's Chapel', about an anarchist plot to blow up the Chapel during the May Week service. A former assistant librarian of King's, Donald Loukes, put forward the suggestion that this story might be by M. R. James. There are certainly many typical touches to the narrative and, as I have personally verified, the author shows the kind of detailed knowledge of the Chapel's structure, particularly of the upper areas of the roof, that MRJ would certainly have possessed. There is, unfortunately, no direct evidence to ascribe the authorship to him.

3 MRJ, obituary notice of Sir Charles Walston, *The Times*, 24 March 1927.

4 MRJ to MEJ, 14 March 1883, CUL.

5 MRJ to his parents, October 1886, CUL.

6 MRJ to his parents, 13 May 1888, CUL.

7 HJ to MRJ, 31 July 1883, CUL.

8 St Clair Donaldson to MRJ, 26 September 1884, CUL.

9 MRJ to GMcB, 13 January 1922, KCC (*LTF*, pp.108–9).

10 ACB to MRJ, n.d. (1882), CUL.

11 St Clair Donaldson to MRJ, 26 September 1884, CUL.

12 *E&K*, pp.151–2. The double tricycle MRJ later rode, in the early 1890s, was arranged differently — more like a tandem, with MRJ usually taking the front steering position.

13 MRJ to his parents, 1 September 1885, CUL.

14 MRJ to HJ, 17 August 1883, CUL.

15 *E&K*, p.112.

16 MRJ to MEJ, 31 October 1885, CUL.

17 *E&K*, p.198.

18 MRJ to his parents, 12 March 1887, CUL.

8. *FELLOWSHIP. King's* 1887–1889

1 MRJ to his parents, 1 May 1887, CUL.

2 MRJ to his parents, 21 May 1887, CUL.

3 *Memoir*, p.28.

4 *CU Reporter*, 22 November 1887.

5 Hogarth, *Accidents of an Antiquary's Life*, p.11.

6 MRJ to MEJ, 17 January 1888; 4 February 1888, CUL.

7 MRJ to his parents, 15 February 1888, CUL.

8 *E&K*, p.194.

9 MRJ to his parents, 15 February 1888, CUL.

10 ACB: Diary, 22 September 1906.

11 MEJ to MRJ, 19 June 1889, CUL.

12 William Austen Leigh, *Augustus Austen Leigh*, p.231.

13 *Pall Mall Gazette*, 8 March 1889.

14 Typewritten copies of letters between Oscar Browning, Arthur Tilley and G.W. Prothero 'on a College matter', J. W. Clark's Cambridge collection, CUL.

15 MRJ to his parents, 12 March 1889, CUL.

16 Ibid.

17 Wedd.

18 *Granta*, 15 March 1889.

19 MRJ to his parents, 12 March 1889, CUL. In fact, of the six people who had ducked Ross only one (Arthur Tilley's younger brother) had been an Etonian.

20 Bruce Dickins, 'Robert Ross at King's', *Cam R*, 23 January 1960, pp.268–9.

9. *THE DEAN. King's* 1889–1892

1 Notice dated 22 November 1889, KCC.

2 *CU Reporter*, 19 February 1889.

3 *Cam R*, November 1889.

4 MRJ to his parents, May 1890, CUL.

5 *E&K*, p.227.

6 Ibid., p.229.

7 Ibid., p.232.

8 *Nobody's Business*, pp.19–20.

9 Ibid., pp.36–7.

10 Furbank, *E. M. Forster*, vol. 1, p.53.

11 Tennyson, *Stars and Markets*, pp.93–4.

12 *Memoir*, p.21.

13 Wedd, pp.35–9.

14 *Bright Countenance*, pp.9–10.

15 Professor Charles Fletcher, personal communication.

16 *E&K*, p.218.

17 MRJ, Preface to James McBryde, *The Story of a Troll-hunt*.

18 MRJ, in *Eustace Talbot: Some Recollections*.

19 MRJ to HJ, Lent Term 1891, CUL.

20 MRJ to Leo Maxse, 14 September 1891, West Sussex.

21 ACB: Diary, 30 January 1904.

22 Printed notice, December 1904, CUL.

23 Clapham.

24 MRJ to HJ, January 1900, CUL.

25 Gaselee.

26 *E&K*, p.200.

27 Pfaff, p.172.

28 Barker, *Publications of the Roxburghe Club*, pp.53–4.

10. DR JAMES. *King's* 1892–1900

1 *GSA.*

2 MRJ to MEJ, 18 July 1892, CUL.

3 MRJ to his parents, 26 September 1892, CUL.

4 *E&K*, p.153.

5 MRJ to his parents, 8 September 1895, CUL.

6 *E&K*, p.219.

7 Ibid., p.220.

8 *GSA.*

9 MRJ to HJ and GRJ, 18 August 1901, CUL. The conclusion of 'Number 13' was perhaps added after this 1901 trip, since it mentions both the library at Uppsala and the Salthenius contract.

10 MRJ to Francis Jenkinson, 4 June 1889, CUL.

11 MRJ to Leo Maxse, 5 January 1892, West Sussex.

12 MRJ to JMcB, March 1899, KCC.

13 *Memoir*, p.6. Lubbock mistakenly states that MRJ's mother died in 1899.

14 *GSA.*

15 HEL to Lord Lytton, 26 December 1899 (*Letters*, p.77).

11. CHANGES. *King's* 1900–1904

1 ACB to MRJ, 12 November 1901, CUL.

2 MRJ to HJ, 25 October 1900, CUL.

3 MRJ to HJ, July/August 1901, CUL.

4 Augustus Austen Leigh to MRJ, 1 April 1901, KCC.

5 A. H. Cooke to Augustus Austen Leigh, n.d., KCC.

6 Augustus Austen Leigh to MRJ, 30 May 1901, KCC.

7 MRJ to HJ, 25 May 1902, CUL.

8 ACB: Diary, 18 October 1902. Arthur's brother, E. F. Benson, had achieved considerable success as a novelist with *Dodo* (1893).

9 Storrs, *Orientations*, pp.15–16.

10 Gaselee, pp.423–4.

11 MRJ to HJ, 28 February 1901, CUL.

12 WMF to Maisie Cropper, 24 November 1902, Hopkinson.

13 WMF to Maisie Cropper, 9 December 1902, Hopkinson.

14 MRJ to Leo Maxse, 14 September 1891, West Sussex; MRJ to HBS, 18 February 1903, Trinity.

15 Sibyl Cropper, 'Letters to a Child'.

16 WMF to Maisie Cropper, 2 March 1903, Hopkinson.

17 Maisie Cropper to Sibyl Cropper, n.d., Hopkinson.

18 Recipient unknown, n.d., CUL.

19 MRJ to HJ, 7 August 1903, CUL.

20 MRJ to Sibyl Cropper, 13 September 1903, Hopkinson.

21 ACB: Diary, October 1903.

22 Ibid., 26 February 1910.

23 Ibid., May 1904.

24 Ibid., 31 January 1905.

25 MRJ to Leo Maxse, 21 November 1902, West Sussex.

26 WMF to Maisie Cropper, 7/8 June 1904, Hopkinson.

27 HEL to MRJ, 11 June 1904, CUL.

28 ACB to MRJ, 15 June 1904, CUL.

29 ACB: Diary, 14 June 1904.

30 GMcB to MRJ, 13 December 1904, CUL.

31 Newsome, p.159.

12. *A PEEP INTO PANDEMONIUM. The Ghost Stories*

1 HEL to A. T. Loyd, 24 December 1903 (*Letters*, p.113).

2 HEL to A. T. Loyd, 24 December 1902 (*Letters*, p.110).

3 Richmond.

4 HEL to A. T. Loyd, 24 December 1903.

5 ACB: Diary, December 1903.

6 HEL to W. Stewart-Roberts, n.d. (Christmas 1913) (*Letters*, p.175).

7 Leo Maxse to MRJ, 8 January 1894, CUL.

8 Arthur Machen to MRJ, 15 March 1895, CUL.

9 JMcB to MRJ, 11 March 1904; L. F. Giblin to MRJ, 12 March 1904, CUL.

10 MRJ to JMcB, 13 March 1904, CUL.

11 JMcB to MRJ, 6 May 1904, CUL.

12 GMcB to MRJ, 13 December 1904, CUL.

13 GMcB to MRJ, 11 June 1904, CUL.

14 Edward Arnold to MRJ, 22 June 1904, KCC.

15 MRJ to Eric Millar, 5 February 1934, BL.

16 MRJ, 'Stories I Have Tried to Write', *CGS*.

17 S. M. Ellis to MRJ, 3 March 1905, CUL.

18 H. Ninash (?) to MRJ, 14 February 1905, CUL.

19 HEL to MRJ, 15 June 1914, CUL.

20 MRJ to A. F. Scholfield, 29 October 1925, CUL.

21 Florence Hardy to MRJ, '25 March', CUL.

22 MRJ to Eric Millar, 27 February 1923, BL.

23 24(1923–5), pp.79–80.

24 MRJ, 'Some Remarks on Ghost Stories', p.172.

25 Ibid., p.169.

26 Ibid., p.171.

27 Editorial preface to 'A Vignette'.

13. *THE LODGE. King's* 1905

1 ACB: Diary, 28 January 1905.

2 Ibid., 1 February 1905.

3 Ibid., 23 March 1905.

4 Walter Headlam to MRJ, 22 March 1905, KCC.

5 William Austen Leigh to MRJ, 24 March 1905, KCC.

6 ACB: Diary, 25 March 1905.

7 Wedd, p.35. The document MRJ circulated amongst the Fellows does not appear to have survived.

8 Malcolm Darling to MRJ, 2 May 1905, CUL.

9 ACB: Diary, 28 April 1905; Newsome, p.179.

10 ACB: Diary, 3 May 1905.

11 MRJ to HJ, 9 May 1905, CUL.

12 ACB: Diary, 6 May 1905.

13 Ibid., 11 June 1905.

14 MRJ to Sibyl Cropper, 18 May 1905, KCC.

15 ACB: Diary, 20 June 1905.

16 *Nobody's Business*, p.22.

17 Oscar Browning to C. R. Fay, 1912, CUL.

18 ACB: Diary, 10 October 1907.

19 Oscar Browning to C. R. Fay, 15 December 1920, CUL.

20 Wingfield-Stratford, *Before the Lamps Went Out*, p.167.

21 *E&K*, p.255.

22 ACB: Diary, 4 November 1906.

23 Ibid., 12 November 1905.

24 *Walter Durnford: Three Tributes.*

25 *Bright Countenance*, p.72.

26 MRJ to HBS, 18 February 1903, Trinity.

27 ACB: Diary, 2 February 1907.

28 Professor Charles Fletcher, personal communication.

29 MRJ to GMcB, 12 June 1906, KCC (*LTF*, p.30).

30 MRJ to GMcB, 30 June 1906, KCC.

31 *LTF*, Introduction, p.15.

32 Ibid., p.18. Punctuation amended.

33 *Eustace Talbot: Some Recollections.*

34 Eustace Talbot to MRJ, 21 December 1904, CUL.

14. *A PROVOST'S LIFE. King's* 1905–1914

1 Richmond. Keynes's thesis was on Probability.

2 C. R. Fay, 'King's College, Cambridge, 1902–6', *Dalhousie Review*, 30 (1950–1), p.334.

3 MRJ to GMcB, 14 April 1926, KCC (*LTF*, p.137).

4 Wilkinson, *A Century of King's*, pp.79–80.

5 *Walter Durnford: Three Tributes.*

6 *E&K*, p.179.

7 *Cam R*, 8 June 1927, pp.489–94.

8 ACB: Diary, 10 July 1908.

9 *E&K*, p.235.

10 ACB: Diary, 18 and 19 June 1905.

11 Ibid., 11 July 1905.

12 e.g. Wilkinson, *A Century of King's*, pp.49–50.

13 MRJ to GMcB, 15 November 1906, KCC (*LTF*, p.33).

14 Ibid. (*LTF*, p.32).

15 ACB: Diary, 29 April 1907.

16 Blunt, *Cockerell*, p.104.

17 MRJ to Sydney Cockerell, 31 May 1908, BL.

18 Blunt, *Cockerell*, p.135.

19 Ibid., p.136.

20 Francis Wormald and Phyllis M. Giles, *Illuminated Manuscripts in the Fitzwilliam Museum*, catalogue of an exhibition to commemorate the 150th anniversary of the death of the founder, the 7th Viscount Fitzwilliam of Merrion (1966), Introduction, p.3.

21 ACB: Diary, 16 December 1904.

22 Sydney Cockerell to MRJ, 9 February 1905, CUL.

23 MRJ to Walter Lamb, 16 and 18 November 1905, Trinity.

24 *Archaeologia*, LXII (1911).

25 Fletcher, *Edmond Warre*, pp.241–2.

26 MRJ to GMcB, 13 June 1909, KCC (*LTF*, p.35).

27 Nathaniel Wedd to MRJ, 19 June 1909, KCC.

28 ACB: Diary, 4 March 1910.

29 *Nobody's Business*, pp.96–7.

30 MRJ to Eric Millar, 18 February 1933, BL.

31 MRJ to GMcB, 19 October 1913, KCC (*LTF*, p.46).

15. *VALE. King's* 1914–1918

1 *CU Reporter*, 2 October 1914.

2 MRJ to GMcB, 7 October 1914, KCC (*LTF*, pp.50–1).

3 MRJ to GMcB, 17 February 1915, KCC (*LTF*, p.54); 16 March 1915, KCC.

4 *E&K*, p.263.

5 ACB: Diary, 26 February 1915.

6 Ibid., 1 October 1915.

7 GVC to Clive Carey, 15 November 1915, Carey.

8 *CU Reporter*, 2 October 1915.

9 Rupert Brooke to MRJ, 11 September 1914, CUL.

10 ACB: Diary, 12 December 1915.

11 Newsome, p.321.

12 MRJ to GVC, 28 January 1917; MRJ to Clive Carey, 9 September 1915, KCC; MRJ to Eric Millar, 9 October 1916 and 4 August 1917, BL.

13 *Nobody's Business*, p.172.

14 MRJ to GVC, 6 August 1915, KCC.

15 MRJ to GVC, 23 October 1916, KCC.

16 MRJ to Clive Carey, 14 June 1916, KCC.

17 MRJ, *The Wanderings and Homes of Manuscripts* (1928), p.12.

18 MRJ to Clive Carey, 14 November 1918, KCC.

19 ACB to MRJ, 3 February 1918, Eton.

20 MRJ to Clive Carey, 14 June 1916, KCC.

21 MRJ to GVC, 31 July 1917, KCC.

22 MRJ to GVC, 24 May 1918, KCC.

23 MRJ to GVC, Whitsunday 1918, KCC.

24 ACB: Diary, 21 April 1915.

25 Ibid., 1 July 1916.

26 HEL to G. H. Tristram, 15 May 1918 (*Letters*, p.234).

16. *OLD FRIENDS AND YOUNG CREATURES. Eton* 1918–1920

1 Fox, *Dean Inge*, p.139.

2 Ronald Norman to MRJ, 31 July 1918, CUL.

3 St John Parry, *Henry Jackson*, p.112.

4 Henry Jackson to MRJ, 30 July 1918; A. E. Housman to MRJ, 31 July 1918, CUL.

5 J. H. Clapham to MRJ, 31 July 1918, CUL.

6 Nathaniel Wedd to MRJ, 7 August 1918; G. L. Dickinson to MRJ, 10 August 1918, CUL.

7 E. G. Swain to MRJ, n.d. (July ? 1918), CUL.

8 MRJ to Henry Jackson, 31 July 1918, Trinity.

9 ACB: Diary, 7 July 1911 and 21 December 1914.

10 Clapham.

11 *Cam R*, November 1915.

12 MRJ to GVC, 30 September 1918, KCC.

13 MRJ to GVC, 27 January 1919, KCC.

14 MRJ to Clive Carey, 17 November 1918, KCC.

15 HEL to R.C.C.J. Binney, November 1918; HEL to R. D. Norton, December 1918 (*Letters*, pp.247, 248).

16 MRJ to Sydney Cockerell, 26 December 1918, BL.

17 Quoted by C. H. K. Marten, *ECC* obit.

18 *ECC* obit.

19 Oscar Browning to MRJ, 22 June 1919, CUL.

20 HEL to MRJ, '8 October', CUL.

21 Vincent Baddeley, *The Times*, 19 June 1936.

22 Richmond.

23 MRJ to GVC, 15 March 1920, KCC.

24 *The Times*, 21 June 1926, 4 July 1928.

25 Address given at the presentation of new buildings for the Department of Education, University of Liverpool, 23 April 1921, CUL.

26 Grimond, *Memoirs*, p.46.

27 Lehmann, *The Whispering Gallery*, p.100.

28 Connolly, *Enemies of Promise*, p.277.

29 MRJ to GVC, 26 November 1928, KCC.

30 *ECC* obit.

31 See A. J. Ayer, *Part of My Life* (1978), p.56.

32 *ECC* obit.

33 MRJ to A. F. Scholfield, 15 December 1927, CUL.

34 *ECC* obit.

17. *UNDISCOVERED ENDS. Eton* 1920–1936

1 Claude Elliott, *ECC* obit.

2 *ECC* obit.

3 Sermon, 7 December 1933, CUL.

4 Sermon, July 1935, CUL.

5 Maxwell Lyte, *History of Eton College*.

6 ACB: Diary, 12 December 1924.

7 HEL to C. A. Kirby, 11 December 1919 (*Letters*, p.268).

8 Oscar Browning to MRJ, 9 February 1920, KCC.

9 Alington, *Things Ancient and Modern*, p.185.

10 MRJ to GMcB, 7 April 1921, KCC.

11 Notebook, Fitzwilliam.

12 ACB: Diary, 15 July 1924.

13 Ibid., 12 December 1924.

14 Ibid., 30 October 1923, 23 January 1905.

15 HEL to A. A. Martineau, 23 October 1926 (*Letters*, p.359).

16 Michael Holroyd, *Lytton Strachey* (1971), p.920.

17 *E&K*, pp.97–8.

18 Nesbitt, *The Club of Nobody's Friends*, vol. III, p.2.

19 Pfaff, pp.389–90.

20 Barker, *Publications of the Roxburghe Club*, p.53.

21 MRJ to GMcB, 18 January 1934, KCC (*LTF*, p.199). Mrs McBryde omitted the word 'gutter' in her printed version of this letter.

22 MRJ to Eric Millar, 5 February 1934, BL.

23 Sermon, n.d., CUL.

24 J. M. Barrie to MRJ, 14 May 1925, CUL; Denis Mackail, *The Story of JMB* (1941), pp.594–5, 608.

25 Sir Robert Birley, *TLS*, 10 November 1972.

26 MRJ to Eric Millar, 22 December 1928, BL.

27 MRJ to GMcB, 27 October 1935, KCC (*LTF*, p.217).

28 MRJ to GMcB, 20 November 1935, KCC (*LTF*, p.221).

29 Fergusson, *Travel Warrant*, pp.66–7.

30 MRJ to GMcB, 25 September 1932, KCC (*LTF*, p.187).

31 GRJ to Eric Millar, 22 January 1936, BL.

32 GRJ to Eric Millar, 18 June 1936, BL.

SELECT BIBLIOGRAPHY

This bibliography is intended as an adjunct to the Notes, as a summary of the main published sources on which this book is based, and as a guide to further reading.

R. W. Pfaff (*Montague Rhodes James*, pp.427–38) has a complete chronological bibliography of MRJ's scholarly writings, which provides a useful résumé of his academic career. For MRJ's other writings, Scholfield's *Elenchus* (based on a list compiled by MRJ and reprinted, and corrected, at the back of Lubbock's *Memoir*) is adequate but not definitive.

1. *M. R. James: Published Biographical Material*

Clapham, J. H., obituary notice of MRJ, *Cambridge Review*, 9 October 1936 (reprinted in *Montague Rhodes James . . . Three Tributes*).

Cropper, Sibyl, 'Letters to a Child', *Cornhill Magazine*, 160(November 1939), pp.639–51.

Eton College Chronicle, 18 June 1936, obituary notices by C. H. K. Marten, D. P. Simpson, Bernard Fergusson ('a subaltern'), 'a young friend', C. A. Alington, S. G. Lubbock and Claude Elliott.

The Eton Register, Part IV 1871–1880 (1907), pp.105b, 125b.

Gaselee, Sir Stephen, 'Montague Rhodes James 1862–1936', *Proceedings of the British Academy*, 22(1936), pp.418–33.

James, M.R., *Eton and King's: Recollections, Mostly Trivial 1875–1925* (1926).

Leslie, Shane, 'Montague Rhodes James', *Quarterly Review*, 304 (1966), pp.45–56.

Lubbock, S. G., *A Memoir of Montague Rhodes James, with a list of his writings by A. F. Scholfield* (1939).

McBryde, Gwendolen (ed.), *Montague Rhodes James: Letters to a Friend* (1956).

Montague Rhodes James: Praepositus necnon amicus 1862–1936. Three Tributes (by J. H. Clapham, A. B. Ramsay and from *The Times*) (1936).

Pfaff, Richard William, *Montague Rhodes James* (1980).

Ramsay, A. B., obituary notice of MRJ, *Eton College Chronicle*, 25 June 1936 (reprinted in *Montague Rhodes James . . . Three Tributes*).

Scholfield, A. F., *Elenchus Scriptorum Montacutii Rhodes James quae typis impressa usque ad annum M.DCCCC.XXXV in lucem prodierunt* (1935).

——, article on MRJ, *Dictionary of National Biography* (1931–40), pp.471–3.

The Times, obituary notice (anon.) of MRJ, 13 June 1936 (reprinted in *Montague Rhodes James . . . Three Tributes*).

Venn, J. A., *Alumni Cantabrigiensis*, Part II 1752–1900, vol. III, pp.547–8.

Withers, J. J. *A Register of Admissions to King's College, Cambridge 1797–1925* (1903, 1929), pp.132–3.

2. *General Background*

Adelson, Roger, *Mark Sykes: Portrait of an Amateur* (1975).

Ainger, A. C., *Sixty Years at Eton* (1917).

Alington, C. A., *A Dean's Apology: A Semi-religious Autobiography* (1952).

——, *Edward Lyttelton: An Appreciation* (1943).

——, *Eton Faces, Old and Young* (1933).

——, *Lionel Ford* (1934).

——, *Things Ancient and Modern* (1936).

Austen Leigh, Augustus, *King's College* (1899).

Austen Leigh, R. A., *The Eton Guide* (1904, 1930).

Austen Leigh, William, *Augustus Austen Leigh: A Record of College Reform* (1906).

Baillie, Albert, *My First Eighty Years* (1951).

Balston, Thomas, *Dr Balston at Eton* (1952).

Barker, N.J., *The Publications of the Roxburghe Club 1814–1962* (1964).

Basileon, A Magazine of King's College, Cambridge 1900–1914, Introduction by Sir Charles Tennyson (1974).

Batchelor, Meston, *Cradle of Empire* (1981).

Benson, A. C., *From a College Window* (1906).

——, *Memories and Friends* (1924).

Benson, E. F., *The Babe, B.A.* (1897).

——, *David Blaize* (1916).

——, *David of King's* (1924).

——, *Our Family Affairs* (1920).

Birley, Sir Robert, *The History of Eton College Library* (Eton, 1970).

Blunt, Wilfrid, *Cockerell* (1964).

Browning, Oscar, *Memories of Later Years* (1923).

——, *Memories of Sixty Years* (1910).

Byrne, L. S. R., and Churchill, E.L., *Changing Eton. A Survey of Conditions Based on the History of Eton since the Royal Commission of 1862–4* (1937).

Carey, Hugh, *Duet for Two Voices: An Informal Biography of Edward Dent compiled from his letters to Clive Carey* (1979).

Chadwick, O., *The Victorian Church* (1970).

Coleridge, Gilbert, *Eton in the Seventies* (1912).

Compton Mackenzie, Faith, *William Cory* (1950).

Connolly, Cyril, *Enemies of Promise* (1938).

Cory, William, *Letters and Journals*, edited by F. Warre Cornish (1897).

Cust, Lionel, *A History of Eton College* (1899).

Dalton, Hugh, *Call Back Yesterday* (1953).

Dimont, C.T., *St Clair Donaldson* (1939).

Esher, Lord (Reginald Brett), *Cloud-capp'd Towers* (1927).

Eustace Talbot . . . Some Recollections (by Mrs Gwendolen Stephenson, W. M. Fletcher and MRJ) (1908).

Fay, C. R., *King's College, Cambridge* (1907).

Fergusson, Bernard (Lord Ballantrae), *Eton Portrait* (1937).

——, *Travel Warrant* (1979).

Fitzgerald, M. H., *A Memoir of Herbert Edward Ryle* (1928).

Fletcher, C. R. L., *Edmond Warre* (1922).

Fletcher, Maisie, *The Bright Countenance. A Personal Biography of Walter Morley Fletcher* (1957). Preface by MRJ.

Fletcher, Walter Morley, *The University Pitt Club 1835–1935* (1935). Preface by MRJ.

Forster, E. M., *Goldsworthy Lowes Dickinson* (1934).

Fox, Adam, *Dean Inge* (1960).

Fox, Sir John, *The Lady Ivie's Trial* (1929). Preface by MRJ.

Graves, C. L., *Hubert Parry: His Life and Works* (1926).

Graves, R. P., *A. E. Housman: The Scholar-Poet* (1979, 1981).

Green, V. H. H., *Religion at Oxford and Cambridge* (1964).

Grimond, Jo, *Memoirs* (1979).

Guthrie, Anstey, *A Long Retrospect* (1936).

Harrod, Roy, *Life of J. M. Keynes* (1951).

Hassall, Christopher, *Rupert Brooke* (1964).

Headlam, Cecil (ed.), *Walter Headlam: Letters and Poems* (1910).

Hill, B. J. W., *Eton Medley* (1948).

Hill, M. D., *Eton and Elsewhere* (1928).

Hogarth, D. G., *Accidents of an Antiquary's Life* (1910).

Hollis, Christopher, *Eton. A History* (1960).

Howarth, T. E. B., *Cambridge Between Two Wars* (1978).

Hussey, Christopher, *Eton College* (1922).

James, Sydney Rhodes, *Seventy Years: Random Reminiscences and Reflections* (1926).

Jones, L. E., *A Victorian Boyhood* (1956).

Keynes, Milo (ed.), *Essays on John Maynard Keynes* (1975).

King, Francis, *E. M. Forster and His World* (1978).

Lawrence, P. S. H., *An Eton Camera 1850–1919* (1980).

Lehmann, John, *The Whispering Gallery* (1955).

Leslie, Shane, *The Cantab* (1926).

——, *The End of a Chapter* (1917).

——, *The Film of Memory* (1938).

——, *Mark Sykes: Life and Letters* (1923).

——, *The Oppidan* (1922).

Lubbock, Alfred, *Memories of Eton and Etonians* (1899).

Lubbock, Percy (ed.), *The Diary of Arthur Christopher Benson* (1927).

Lyttelton, Edward, *Memories and Hopes* (1925).

McBryde, James, *The Story of a Troll-hunt* (1904). Preface by MRJ.

Macnaghten, Hugh, *Eton Letters 1915–1918* (1921).

——, *Fifty Years of Eton in Prose and Verse* (1924).

Malden, C. H., *Recollections of an Eton Colleger 1898–1902* (1905).

Maxwell Lyte, H. C., *A History of Eton College* (1911).

Nesbitt, R. C., *The Club of Nobody's Friends*, vol. III (privately printed, 1949).

Nevill, R. H., *Floreat Etona; Anecdotes and Memories of Eton College* (1911).

Newsome, David, *Godliness and Good Learning: Four Studies on a Victorian Ideal* (1961).

——, *On the Edge of Paradise: A. C. Benson the Diarist* (1980).

——, *Edwardian Excursions: from the Diaries of A. C. Benson 1898–1904* (1981).

'O.E.', *Eton Under Hornby* (1910).

Ollard, Richard, *An English Education: A Perspective of Eton* (1982).

Parker, Eric, *College at Eton* (1933).

——, *Eton in the Eighties* (1914).

——, *Playing Fields: School Days at Eton* (1922).

Prothero, G. W., *A Memoir of Henry Bradshaw* (1888).

Rice, F. A., *The Granta and its Contributors* (1924).

Roberts, S. C. (ed.), *The Cambridge Book of the Silver Jubilee of King George V 1910–1935* (1935).

——, *The Family: The History of a Dining Club* (1963).

Ryle, E. H. (ed.), *Arthur Christopher Benson, as seen by some friends* (1925).

St John Parry, R., *Henry Jackson, O. M. A Memoir* (1926).

Salt, Henry, *Memories of Bygone Eton* (1928).

Shipley, Arthur, *'J': A Memoir of J. W. Clark* (1913).

Stanford, C. V., *Pages from an Unwritten Diary* (1914).

Sterry, Wasey, *Annals of Eton College* (1898).

Stewart, H. F., *Francis Jenkinson* (1926).

Stone, C. R., *Eton Glossary* (1902).

Storrs, Ronald, *Orientations* (1937).

Tennyson, Charles, *Cambridge From Within* (1913).

——, *Stars and Markets* (1957).

Trevelyan, G. M., *Grey of Fallodon* (1937).

Vincent, J. E., *HRH Duke of Clarence and Avondale: A Memoir* (1893).

Walter Durnford 1847–1926. Three Tributes, printed for distribution to members of King's College, Cambridge (by J. H. Clapham, *The Times*, and MRJ) (1926).

Wayment, Hilary, *The Windows of King's College Chapel, Cambridge: A Description and Commentary* (1972).

Welldon, J. E. C., *Recollections and Reflections* (1915).

Williams, David, *Genesis and Exodus: A Portrait of the Benson Family* (1979).

Wingfield-Stratford, E., *Before the Lamps Went Out* (1945).

Winstanley, D. A., *Early Victorian Cambridge* (1940, 1955).

Wortham, H. E., *Oscar Browning* (1927), reprinted as *Victorian Eton and Cambridge* (1956).

3. Ghost Stories

Benson, A. C., *The Hill of Trouble* (1903).

Benson, E. F., *More Spook Stories* (1934).

——, *The Room in the Tower* (1912).

——, *Spook Stories* (1928).

Benson, R. H., *The Light Invisible* (1903).

——, *The Mirror of Shallott* (1907).

Blackwood, Algernon, *The Tales of Algernon Blackwood* (1938).

Briggs, Julia, *Night Visitors. The Rise and Fall of the English Ghost Story* (1977).

Browne, Nelson, *Sheridan Le Fanu* (New York, 1951).

Butts, Mary, 'The Art of M. R. James', *London Mercury*, 29(1934), pp.306–17.

Cox, J. R., 'Ghostly Antiquary: The Stories of M. R. James', *English Literature in Transition*, 12 (1969).

Crawford, F. Marion, *Wandering Ghosts* (1911).

Dare, M. P., *Unholy Relics and Other Uncanny Tales* (1947).

Ellis, S. M., *Wilkie Collins, Le Fanu and Others* (1931).

Fleming, Peter, 'The Stuff of Nightmares', *Spectator Literary Supplement*, 18 (April 1931), p.633.

Gray, Arthur, *Tedious Brief Tales of Granta and Gramarye* (1919).

Harvey, W. F., *Midnight House and Other Tales* (1910).

Hodgson, W. Hope, *Carnacki the Ghost Finder* (1913).

Holmes, Richard, 'Of Ghosts and King's', *The Times*, 23 November 1974.

Jackson, T. G., *Six Ghost Stories* (1919).

James, M. R., *The Collected Ghost Stories of M. R. James* (1931).

——, 'The Experiment: A New Year's Eve Ghost Story', *Morning Post*, 31 December 1931, p.8.

——, Introduction to V. H. Collins, *Ghosts and Marvels: A Selection of Uncanny Tales from Daniel Defoe to Algernon Blackwood* (1924).

——, *Ghost Stories of an Antiquary* (1904).

——, J. S. Le Fanu, *Madame Crowl's Ghost*, edited, with a bibliography of Le Fanu's novels and tales, by MRJ (1923).

——, 'The Malice of Inanimate Objects', *The Masquerade*, vol. I, 1 (June 1933), pp.29–32.

——, *More Ghost Stories of an Antiquary* (1911).

——, 'The Novels and Stories of J. Sheridan Le Fanu' (abstract of a lecture), *Proceedings of the Royal Institution*, 24(1923–5), pp.79–80.

——, 'Some Remarks on Ghost Stories', *The Bookman*, December 1929, pp.169–72.

——, *A Thin Ghost* (1919).

——, J. S. Le Fanu, *Uncle Silas*, introduction by MRJ (1926).

——, 'A Vignette', *London Mercury*, 35(1936), pp.18–22.

——, *Wailing Well* (1928). Limited edition by Robert Gathorne Hardy and Kyrle Leng at the Mill House Press, Stanford Dingley.

——, *A Warning to the Curious* (1925).

Lee, Vernon, *Hauntings* (1890).

Le Fanu, J. S., *Best Ghost Stories*, edited by E. F. Bleiler (New York, 1964).

Leslie, Shane, *Shane Leslie's Ghost Book* (1955).

Machen, Arthur, *Tales of Horror and the Supernatural* (1949).

Malden, R. H., *Nine Ghosts* (1943).

McCormack, W. J., *Sheridan Le Fanu and Victorian Ireland* (1980).

Munby, A. N. L., *The Alabaster Hand* (1949).

Penzoldt, Peter, *The Supernatural in Fiction* (1952).

Scarborough, Dorothy, *The Supernatural in Modern English Fiction* (1917).

Search, Pamela (ed.), *The Supernatural in the English Short Story* (1959).

Sullivan, Jack, *Elegant Nightmares: The English Ghost Story from Le Fanu to Blackwood* (1978).

Summers, Montague (ed.), *The Supernatural Omnibus* (1931).

——, *Victorian Ghost Stories* (1934).

Swain, E. G., *The Stoneground Ghost Tales* (1912).

Wakefield, H. Russell, *The Best Ghost Stories of H. Russell Wakefield*, selected and introduced by Richard Dalby (1978).

INDEX